'09/6

W9-AQF-754

Rrdel/5

8 12/7

High Noon
in Lincoln

HIGH NOON IN LINCOLN

Violence on the Western Frontier

Robert M. Utley

University of New Mexico Press
Albuquerque

Library of Congress Cataloging-in-Publication Data

Utley, Robert Marshall, 1929–
High noon in Lincoln.
Bibliography: p.
Includes index.
1. Lincoln County (N.M.)—History.   2. Violence—
New Mexico—Lincoln County—History—19th century.
I. Title.
F802.L7U86   1987   978.9'6404   87-10864
ISBN 0-8263-0981-X

Designed by Whitehead & Whitehead

978.9   1/7/99   14.95   GIFT
Utl

For Melody

Contents

Preface
A War
Without
Heroes

HIGH NOON evokes images of a classic western facedown and shootout. That is what happened in Lincoln County, New Mexico, in 1878 and 1879 as John Henry Tunstall and Alexander McSween engaged in a facedown and shootout with James J. Dolan and John H. Riley.

Unlike the *High Noon* in which Gary Cooper is the lone hero, the Lincoln County High Noon boasts not a single hero. Readers who must have a sympathetic character to identify with may put this book down now.

I did not set out to write a book without heroes. But historians must take history as they find it, and I found no heroes. I did not expect Billy the Kid to be a hero. Nor did Murphy, Dolan, and Riley seem likely candidates. I was surprised to find John Henry Tunstall and Alex and Sue McSween so lacking in appeal. But when I discovered that Lew Wallace, whatever his military and literary merits, made so few constructive contributions to resolving the troubles in Lincoln County, I knew that I would find no one to stir the sympathetic imagination of me or of my readers. Truly, the Lincoln County War was a war without heroes.

Yet it was a significant war. It captured the thought and behavior of a range of frontier personalities. It dramatized economic forces that underlay most frontier conflicts. It demonstrated the intensity and the varieties of frontier crime and violence. And it gave the world Billy the Kid, a figure of towering significance, not for the part he played in the war, but for the standing he achieved in American folklore.

Heroes are appealing, but they are not essential to historical consequence.

Acknowledgments

THIS BOOK owes a large debt to many people. Three friends and fellow historians, in particular, deserve the most generous thanks. All are first-rate authorities on the Lincoln County War.

Donald R. Lavash, recently retired as historian at the New Mexico State Records Center and Archives, pointed the way to key sources, loaned to me indispensable documents and microfilms from his personal collection (including the Lew Wallace Papers and the Dudley Court Record), and in long sessions over coffee and pastries at the Swiss Bakery shared his insights and helped me sharpen my own thinking. Don's researches have recently borne fruit in a biography of Sheriff William Brady.

Harwood P. Hinton, editor of *Arizona and the West* and biographer of John Chisum, played a role similar to Lavash. We spent much time together, both at the Haley History Center in Midland, Texas, and at the University of Arizona Library, gnawing at the imponderables of the Lincoln County War and, on the side, sampling the delights of the local Dairy Queens. Like Lavash, Hinton generously shared with me the results of his own research.

John P. Wilson, free-lance historian based in Las Cruces, New Mexico, also helped immensely in shaping my understanding of my subject. Jack was working on a history of Lincoln for the State Monuments Division of the Museum of New Mexico at the same time that I was writing this book. In long letters buttressed by notes and documents from his research, he guided me through the maze of public land law and procedure and the intracacies of frontier banking. We also swapped views on Lincoln County at various conventions where our paths crossed and even by remote hookup between two television studios.

Others who have contributed in more or less measure, and whose aid I acknowledge with gratitude, are: Beth Schneider, Mrs. Robin McWilliams, and Cindy Burleson at the J. Evetts Haley History Center in Midland, Texas, and of course Evetts Haley himself, both for establishing this fine research institution and for sharing with me his own deep knowledge of the subject; Michael Miller, formerly curator of the Southwest Collection at the New Mexico State Library, now New Mexico State Archivist; Edwin C. Bearss, chief historian of the National Park Service; David Laird, university librarian, and Louis Hieb, head of Special Collections, University of Arizona Library; Eileen Bolger at the Denver Federal Records Center; Rose Dias at the University of New Mexico Library; Thomas Caperton, director of New Mexico State Monuments; Arthur Olivas and Richard Rudisill at the Museum of New Mexico Library; Professor Richard Maxwell Brown of the University of Oregon; R. G. Miller, director of Lincoln Properties, and John Meigs, executive director, Lincoln County Heritage Trust; and Doyce B. Nunis, Jr., of the University of Southern California.

In addition to those named above, I appreciate the help of staff members at the New Mexico State Records Center and Archives, the New Mexico State Library, the Museum of New Mexico Library, the University of New Mexico Library, the University of Arizona Library, the Denver Federal Records Center, and the National Archives and Records Service in Washington, D.C.

Portions of this book first appeared in *Four Fighters of Lincoln County*, a volume containing four lectures that I delivered at the University of New Mexico in November 1985, which were published in 1986 by the University of New Mexico Press. Permission of the press to incorporate excerpts into this volume is acknowledged with thanks.

Also at the University of New Mexico, Professors Richard N. Ellis, Richard Etulain, and Paul Hutton, and University of

New Mexico Press editor David V. Holtby, contributed in various ways as this study progressed.

Finally, I give thanks to my hardest critic, my wife Melody Webb. Her piercing eye combed every word for clarity and definition and wrought many agonizing revisions.

1

The Englishman and the Scotsman

THE ENGLISHMAN met death in a remote New Mexico canyon, far from his London home, on February 18, 1878. In less than three weeks, he would have been twenty-five.

With several hands from his ranch on the Río Feliz, the Englishman was driving nine horses into the town of Lincoln when a galloping band of horsemen appeared in the rear. His companions scattered and reunited on a rocky hilltop, prepared to do battle. One of these men, skilled with Winchester carbine and Colt's .45, was a likable youth not yet nineteen. People called him Kid; one day they would know him as Billy the Kid. The assailants thought better of charging such well-posted gunmen. On the other side of the hill, however, three of them caught the Englishman alone. Perhaps he tried to surrender, or perhaps he tried to defend himself. A rifle bullet tore into his breast. Another smashed his skull and ripped through his brain.

He died instantly. Some people claimed he was murdered in cold blood; others insisted he had been shot down while resisting arrest by a lawfully commissioned deputy sheriff of Lincoln County.

The Scotsman, a man of peace, a man of books and words, died by equally violent means five months later, on the night of July 19, 1878. He died on his back doorstep, lighted by the flames of his burning home. The fire had eaten from room to room throughout the daylong battle, finally leaving the defenders with the choice of burning, surrendering, or making a break for it. From the kitchen door they dashed into the night. One was the same "Kid" who had ridden with the Englishman. Dodging bullets, the Kid made good his escape. The Scotsman did not. Five bullets riddled his frame, and he crumpled in a death as sudden as that of his English associate.

The Englishman's death touched off the Lincoln County War. The Scotsman's death should have ended it, for the rivals were either dead or ruined, and nothing remained to fight about. But the violence and lawlessness unleashed by the slaying of the Englishman tortured the land for months to come, and the Lincoln County War did not finally subside until nearly a year after the Scotsman's blazing end.

John Henry Tunstall first glimpsed the capital of the Territory of New Mexico from his painful perch on a "jerky," jolting down the final mile of the Santa Fe Trail behind four panting mules. The vehicle stirred clouds of dust, which turned to mud on sweating animals and passengers. Although nestled in the foothills of the Sangre de Cristo Mountains at an elevation of seven thousand feet, the town's flat-roofed mud buildings baked in late summer heat.

Tunstall's arrival in Santa Fe on August 15, 1876, climaxed an exhausting week's journey from San Francisco. He had ridden by rail to Cheyenne and Denver and thence to El Moro, Colorado, terminus of the Denver and Rio Grande Railroad. A stagecoach had taken him on to Trinidad, the Santa Fe Railroad's end of track. Here he had boarded the red-bodied jerky, whose springless undercarriage made an unrelieved agony of the run over the 220 miles of the Santa Fe Trail that had not been replaced by the advancing railroad. "I can assure you," he wrote to his father in London that night, "that one soon discovers why it is called a 'jerky.'" [1]

The jerky drew up at the Exchange Hotel, on the Santa Fe Plaza opposite the ramshackle "palace" of the governors, seat of New Mexico's government for more than two and one-half centuries. Tunstall did not check in at the Exchange, the town's best. Prompted by frugal habits and a dwindling reserve of cash, he walked down San Francisco Street to the west and, for a third less, took a room at Herlow's, a "very second class hotel." Herlow's table, however, fell short of the patrician Englishman's culinary standards, and he usually "picked his teeth" at the Exchange.

Tunstall found Santa Fe interesting but unappealing. He liked the cool nights, the pure, clear atmosphere, and the backdrop of pine-clad mountains. But the town itself, a jumble of run-down adobe buildings rising fortresslike from narrow, crooked streets, failed to impress one reared in the Victorian plushness of a fashionable London neighborhood. Daytime heat and the relentless diarrhea that greeted most newcomers did not improve his opinion.

Even less did he like the residents. "There are not many nice people here," he observed. The old Spanish families that might have appealed to his sense of class superiority clustered around Albuquerque, to the south, leaving Santa Fe to "greasers" of low repute and the roistering denizens of the saloons. Commerce rested firmly "in the hands of the jews who have their sons & brothers with them always." And everyone went about their business prepared for trouble. "All the men have a great 'six shooter' slung on their hip, & a knife on the other as a counter poise."

Tunstall carried his own six-shooter, a single-action Colt's .45, but he did not display it on his hip. Despite "a *needy ignorant* population" that made Santa Fe unsafe, he believed a man could usually avoid trouble by minding his own business, keeping out of politics, and staying away from the drinking establishments. If those precautions failed, he stood ready to defend himself. "I have contracted the habit of keeping my hands on my 'shooting iron,'" he wrote. "It carries a fearful ball & shoots quick, but I don't calculate to have to use it."

Santa Feans soon became aware of the foreigner in their midst. On the plaza, at Herlow's or the Exchange, people turned to look. Neat in tailored broadcloth or rough Harris tweeds, his tall, slender frame attracted curious glances. Sandy hair capped a smooth face decorated with thin mustache and side-whiskers, which failed to make him look any older than his twenty-three years. His speech, of suitably English accent and redolent of education and culture, amused and impressed listeners and stamped him as a young gentleman of merit and, they supposed, wealth.

3

More than his appearance, Tunstall's mission in Santa Fe gained him notice. Knowing how swiftly word would spread, he deliberately revealed his purpose. At once he sat down with "mine host," P. F. Herlow, and pumped him about cattle raising in New Mexico. The hotel proprietor had once been a stockman, and he poured forth a welter of facts, figures, and opinions about ranching economics, together with advice on where and how to obtain the best grasslands on which to launch the enterprise. Predictably, Santa Fe's army of land speculators caught the scent of English investment money, and they swarmed around the wily young entrepreneur.

Actually, Tunstall had no ready cash to invest, but he had ample prospects if only he could persuade his father to risk significant capital in the American West. John Partridge Tunstall had done extremely well in the mercantile business, and he had the capital to invest. But he did not share his son's explosive enthusiasm for every opportunity that came along. For the past year, the boy had dedicated himself single-mindedly to convincing the shrewd skeptic in London of the certainty of a rich harvest, if only he would provide the seeds.

John Partridge Tunstall expected to provide the seeds. He had said as much in 1872, when, at the age of nineteen, John Henry had embarked for America in quest of fortune. Since then, the road to riches had grown clear to the son, if not to the father. It did not lie in the mercantile world. Three miserable and penurious years of clerking in a branch of the family business in Vancouver, British Columbia, had produced that firm conviction. Increasingly, his dreams pictured an empire of sheep or cattle pastured on a great landed estate. In such a rugged outdoor life, he believed, watching his stock multiply and his bank account swell, "I shall be far happier than cuffed in white linen & coated in broadcloth, pedalling trifles to women with slim purses & slimmer education & refinement."[2]

Tunstall's appearance in Santa Fe was but the latest stage in the pursuit of his dream. In February 1876, he had quit his clerking job and headed for California. There, like a great sponge, he had soaked up information about sheep, cattle, and land. But California no longer offered opportunities for quick profits in

4

stock raising, and by summer he had turned his attention to New Mexico.

By the time Tunstall reached New Mexico, ambition had turned to obsession. He hungered for great wealth and thought of little else. He sought it not for personal luxury, but for the comfort and security of his family. All his affections centered on his family—his "Much Beloved Governor," his "dearest Mama," and his three sisters, especially the older one, Emily. On "Minnie," or "Min," he lavished a smothering love. "I feel quite sure that I am going to make money & *lots* of it," he wrote early in 1876, later explaining that "My desire is for wealth, that I may have the means of smoothing the path of life for Old Min & our two pets." He wanted the money for them, not for himself.[3]

Land preoccupied Tunstall in Santa Fe—land in great expanses, by whatever means it could be obtained. Few scruples limited the quest, which in general accorded with the nation's business ethic during the Gilded Age and assuredly mirrored the standards of frontier New Mexico. No religious teachings imposed ethical restraints. Always agnostically inclined, he grew increasingly contemptuous of organized religion as he entered manhood. "My religious principle is selfish & hard," he wrote to his mother a week after arriving in Santa Fe, "& is best expressed by Shakspere in the words 'To thine own self be true &c.'"[4] That Shakespearian creed, qualified always by his enormous love for his family, guided Tunstall's every thought and action in New Mexico.

"Land grabber," he explained, was the term applied by the envious to "men who have the foresight & price to buy up land, *in any way*, in large quantities, when it is cheap, in new countries." He planned to "grab" every bit of land he could, for as little as possible, and to make a living from it while it rose in value. "If I carry out my plans successfully I shall be called a 'Land Grabber.'"[5]

Tunstall came to New Mexico well posted on the opportunities presented by old Spanish and Mexican land grants. Much of the territory fell under such grants, some of which embraced millions of acres. In Santa Fe, a specialized legal profession had grown up around the manipulation of title to such grants.

One of Tunstall's most respected advisors in California had counseled him, not entirely in jest, to look less for land in New Mexico than for a woman with a Spanish grant. He would thereby gain two assets, for "some of those Spanish girls you know, by Jove! *are mighty nice looking girls, I tell yer.*" Tunstall had almost no interest in women and none at all in marriage; it would interfere with the program he had set for himself. Anyway, as a California matron convinced him, Spanish women, whatever their physical attractions, degraded "the proudest man that ever was, to the level of a brute." She believed that "a squaw would be infinitely preferable for a wife." Still, in picturing a great estate, the young man admitted "I don't know what I should say if I had the chance of getting 200,000 acres. I fancy I might say '*squaw or no squaw*, give me the acres.'"[6]

With practiced instinct, Tunstall quickly connected with the men most likely to aid him with specialized knowledge and advice. Torn between sheep and cattle, he inquired about both; but his central concern was land. He explored various possibilities in the tangled and risky world of Spanish land grants. He traveled north to Taos and east to the Pecos River to see the country in person. As a matter of business necessity, he taught himself the Spanish language, although he continued to look with condescension on the territory's Hispanic population. Of the cook on the journey to the Pecos, he wrote: "I would not have eaten what our Mexican had touched, if you had paid me a dollar a mouthful."

The relentless pursuit of information left Tunstall little leisure. The capital's señoritas did not interest him, nor did the "fandangos," or dances, at which they flourished. In earlier years, he had come to love long rides on horseback, accompanied only by his dog; but here he had no horse or dog, although he finally bought a mule for his travels. He liked to hunt and shoot. On one occasion, he joined with other youths to test his marksmanship in the hills outside of town. Tunstall matched his carbine against their more accurate rifles. Also, blind in the right eye, he had to sight and fire from the left shoulder. Even so, he gloated, he had outshot them all.

In Santa Fe, Tunstall made many acquaintances but almost no friends. Outside of his family, people existed simply to be manipulated and exploited for his own gain. One hot afternoon at Herlow's, however, Tunstall came upon a man destined to breach his armor. He was a "very common looking man," shoddily attired and, most offensively to a proper Englishman, sockless. Surprisingly, he proved himself "*very* highly educated" and spoke "with a flow of language & accuracy of information that very few possessed." His name was Robert A. Widenmann. A year older than Tunstall and a Georgian of German heritage, he had been educated in Germany, France, and England. "Rob" Widenmann became Tunstall's fast friend, perhaps the only true friend he had in the United States.

Toward the end of October 1876, Tunstall met another man with whom he would have an intimate relationship, though not one of friendship. Earlier, Tunstall had been urged to extend his investigations to Lincoln County, a sprawling, thinly populated jurisdiction in the southeastern corner of the territory. Much of this country remained unsurveyed, and none of it was encumbered with Spanish grants. If one lacked capital, a stock business could be launched on the public domain without any investment in land. Intrigued, Tunstall considered a trip to Lincoln County, and when a Lincoln resident checked in at Herlow's, he made haste to introduce himself.

The man turned out to be Lincoln's only lawyer. Tunstall thought him "a very nice young fellow" who had the "outward appearance of an honest man." The attorney described his home country in glowing terms and confirmed what Tunstall had already learned about ranching on public lands. That idea did not appeal to him so much as the other opportunities that Lincoln County appeared to offer. His informant, Tunstall wrote to the "beloved governor" in London on October 28, "has been trying to persuade me to go into stock & not buy land but I have seen too much of California to do so unless I am obliged. But I must say that his plan has a great deal to recommend it."[7]

Thus, almost casually, John Henry Tunstall met Alexander A. McSween.

Born of Scotch parentage on Canada's Prince Edward Island, Alex McSween was ten years Tunstall's senior. Supposedly, he had once been a Presbyterian clergyman but, in search of a better income, had studied law at Washington University in St. Louis. He had lived for a time in Kansas, where at Atchison, on August 13, 1873 he had wed Sue E. Homer.[8]

Mac and Sue McSween arrived in Lincoln, the adobe hamlet that served as the seat of Lincoln County, on March 3, 1875. They left a dim trail behind them, but not so dim as to discourage whispers about why they had left Kansas so abruptly, or how much formal education backed his legal credentials, or whether he had ever really occupied a Presbyterian pulpit. They came to Lincoln penniless, "hauled here in a farmer's wagon," as one observer remembered. "He announced his intention of making his El Dorado at Lincoln."[9]

However mysterious their antecedents, the McSweens found a modest El Dorado in Lincoln. He did well enough as a lawyer to afford a suitable wardrobe for both of them and to lay plans for a fine new home furnished in the elegant style of the time. In the dusty little village, they made a striking couple. Mac dressed in suit and tie, as befitted a frontier barrister. He was asthmatic and had a faintly glassy look in the eyes, but with his mop of curly hair and a mustache that swept like handlebars on each side of a long chin, he struck some as handsome.

Sue also attracted the attention, not always admiring, of Lincoln's predominantly Hispanic citizens. Piles of carefully curled hair topped a slightly puffy face and a figure a shade ample. Many thought her beautiful, although the impression sprang as much from her dazzling gowns and elaborate makeup as from physical features. "Mrs. McSween always looked like a big doll," recalled a resident, "she was the best dressed woman in Lincoln."[10]

So far as Tunstall could judge, or even much cared in October 1876, McSween was what he seemed to be. He was well informed about Lincoln County and appeared to be an able attorney, professionally industrious and ambitious. Personally, he projected an aura of pleasant, quiet, and unpretentious dignity, temperate habits, and peaceful inclinations. Like Tunstall, he preferred to avoid confrontation and abhorred violence. Unlike

Tunstall, he went about wholly unarmed, not even carrying a hidden weapon.

McSween and Tunstall parted in Santa Fe. McSween continued to New York City, in behalf of a client. Tunstall lost no time in heading south. The lawyer had excited his interest in Lincoln, and within a week he was on the road.

On this journey, Tunstall traveled with a prominent Lincolnite, Juan Patrón, who had driven McSween to Santa Fe and was now returning. A youth roughly Tunstall's age, Patrón had already attained distinction by teaching Lincoln's first school and serving as clerk of the probate court. He operated a small store that had fallen to him after the slaying of his father in 1873. He walked with a pronounced limp, the result of a bullet fired into his back a year earlier in a scrape with a hot-tempered Irishman, John H. Riley. An acquaintance recalled Patrón as a "man of genteel bearing, large stature, somewhat stout, imposing and quite fond of appearing in a dressy Prince Albert coat. He was much given to associating with americanos and was a glib sort of linguist between them and his people."[11]

Tunstall thought Patrón a "very good sort of fellow & the best educated Mexican I have met." But he turned out to be a wretched driver, which exasperated his passenger. Tunstall bore the ordeal silently, while inwardly "cursing the entire Mexican race from Patron upwards & downwards." In Lincoln, Tunstall lodged with Patrón while exploring the prospects.[12]

The day after his arrival, Tunstall sought out and introduced himself to another notable resident, Sue McSween. He "found her a very pleasant woman . . . she is the only white woman here & has a good many enemies in consequence of her husband's profession." Actually, her husband's profession had less to do with it than her own incompatibility with the Hispanic women. Tunstall left greatly impressed by Sue's command of the kind of information he sought. "She told me as much about the place as any man could have done," he marveled.[13]

Tunstall liked what he heard from Alexander and Sue McSween, and he liked what he saw around Lincoln. He did not return to Santa Fe.

2

Heritage
of
Violence

JOHN HENRY TUNSTALL had planted himself in a world scarcely less alien to his London home than the moon.

Lincoln County embraced nearly thirty thousand square miles of southeastern New Mexico Territory—about two-thirds the size of all England and roughly comparable to the state of South Carolina. Less than two thousand citizens peopled the entire county. Geographically, economically, and socially, it fell into two distinct worlds: the mountain world and the plains world. In the mountain world, native New Mexicans and Anglos farmed the fertile bottoms lining the streams that drained the forested high country of the Sierra Blanca and the Capitan Mountains, where the U.S. Army post of Fort Stanton and the Mescalero Apache Indian Agency offered markets for their crops. In the plains world to the east, Texas cattlemen pastured their herds on the rich grasses of the Pecos Plains and sold beef to the forts and Indian agencies of New Mexico and Arizona. Lincoln, formerly La Placita del Río Bonito, or simply La Placita, served as county seat.[1]

In 1876 Tunstall would have approached Lincoln from the west, down the Río Bonito from Fort Stanton. The military post perched on a low, level bench on the south bank of the Bonito, here a clear mountain stream lined with big cottonwood trees. To the south, a ridge spotted with piñon and juniper trees composed the foreground, while a jumble of pinecovered mountains traced the skyline. To the northeast, toward Lincoln, the valley widened to half a mile and more, opening a vista to the long flat hump of the Capitan Mountains. Aligned in military precision, officers' quarters, soldiers' barracks, offices, and storehouses formed a square enclosing a spacious parade ground. The national colors floated from the top of a tall white flagstaff. Blueclad soldiers busy at drill, fatigue labor, and ceremonial evolutions gave life to this outpost of national authority.

As a traveler approached Lincoln on the road from Fort Stanton, the valley narrowed. Steep ridges with rocky, yellowish outcrops and scattered clumps of piñon and juniper shouldered the valley on both sides and, on the north, occasionally hid the Capitans from the road. In twists and turns the tree-lined creek snaked eastward among the ridges and flowed among willows and cottonwoods edging Lincoln on the north.

The hamlet that John Henry Tunstall entered on that early winter day in 1876 strung for less than a mile along a single dirt street, alternately swirling in dust and deep in mud, compressed between the Bonito on the north and timbered mountains rising steeply on the south. It counted about five hundred residents, mostly Hispanic, and several dozen flat-roofed adobe dwellings strewn along both sides of the street. A haze of pungent piñon smoke hung over the town, fed by fires stoked in stoves and fireplaces for cooking and, in winter, warmth. Water came mainly from the Bonito and stood in barrels at kitchen doors. A few privies represented the state of sanitation. Dogs, horses, mules, pigs, chickens, and an occasional cow joined with villagers to give life to the community and to contribute to the mix of odors suffusing the atmosphere.

Among the nondescript adobes and pole jacales, Tunstall would have noted only three or four structures. On the west edge of town, south of the road, rose an imposing two-story adobe building, the new and commodious "big store" of Lawrence G. Murphy. Across the street stood the modest hotel where Sam Wortley served meals and provided sleeping rooms for transients. In the center of town, the community's landmark, now crumbling with neglect, competed with the Murphy store in height. This was the two-story "round tower," or *torreon*, erected of stone and adobe years earlier for defense against Indian attacks.

11

Although the county seat, Lincoln boasted no courthouse. When the itinerant district judge held court each spring and autumn, a large one-room adobe across from the *torreon* served the purpose. It belonged to "Squire" John B. Wilson, sometime justice of the peace, and when needed it also doubled as dance hall and public meeting house. Not until 1877 did the county have a jail, and then only a hole in the ground covered by a log guard room.

A heritage of violence burdened Tunstall's new home. He sensed it as soon as he arrived. It was "about the 'toughest' little spot in America," he wrote to his parents, "which means the most lawless; a man can commit murder here with impunity."[2]

A resident told him about one who had. His name was Alexander Hamilton Mills, a great strapping hulk who had once served as county sheriff. More than a year earlier, "Ham" Mills had shot and killed Gregorio Balensuela for calling him a "gringo." He had lit out for Texas, but in October 1876 had come back to stand trial. Convicted of manslaughter, he had drawn a one-year sentence in the county jail. That the county did not yet have a jail proved to be inconsequential, for a month after Tunstall wrote, on petition of 107 citizens, the territorial governor extended a full pardon to the popular Mills.[3]

Ham Mills seemed to be "rather bad medicine," Tunstall observed to his informant. "No! not a bit of it!" was the reply. "You never saw a better fellow than Ham anywhere; he gets mad quick, & shoots quick, but he's a good shot & never cripples; none of his men have ever known what hurt them & I really think he is sorry for it afterward when he cools off."[4]

The Mills episode was symptomatic of the chronic violence and lawlessness afflicting Lincoln County and the casual attitude with which people viewed it. Murder, assault, larceny, and lesser crimes regularly disturbed both the mountain and plains worlds.

In the mountain world, the violence contrasted with a pastoral simplicity. "This was a paradise when I came here," remembered an early resident.[5] The towering peaks of the Sierra Blanca and the flat-topped Capitans defined the world on the west and north, while the Sacramento and Guadalupe mountains tumbled southward to an abrupt termination in the sheer rampart of El Capitan, just across the Texas boundary. Most settlers lived along the streams flowing eastward to the Pecos, chiefly the Ruidoso and the Bonito, which joined to form the Hondo.

"Mexicans" and a few Anglos farmed the valleys. Although everyone called them Mexicans, they were really Hispanic native New Mexicans, many of whom had been in New Mexico for generations.[6] The first Hispanics had immigrated before the Civil War, with the founding of Fort Stanton. Others came after the war, together with the Anglos. Most of the latter were discharged soldiers, many veterans of the "California Column" who had rushed to defend New Mexico from Confederate invasion in 1862 and stayed to fight Indians. They took Hispanic wives—or mates, in the absence of resident clergy and the twenty-five-dollar marriage fee. "The Mexican women were fine cooks," a newcomer recalled, "could fry eggs and make coffee better than anyone. They made corn tortillas 8 inches in diameter, mixed red chile with beans, then scooped it up with tortillas cupped around their fingers."[7]

The farmers used methods handed down from past generations. "The Mexicans just squatted and went to farming with a wired fork out of a tree," said an observer. They grazed flocks of sheep in the canyons and on the mesas and also ran goats, which they used for both meat and milk. "The Mexicans are very slow," sniffed a clergyman newly arrived from the East. "They tramp out wheat with sheep or goats—fan it by the wind—blow with a stick—keep their guns tied to the plow beam—reap with a sycle. They take pride in doing as the ancients did."[8]

Typical was the life of Yginio Salazar, destined for a minor role in the Lincoln County War. Yginio came with his family to the Hondo as a boy in 1862. They farmed near Missouri Plaza until upstream diversion of water killed the little settlement. They raised corn, watermelons, oats, wheat, and barley. They sold some of the crops to the army at Fort Stanton, but most to cowboys trailing cattle herds up from Texas. At the plaza, the family joined with others in horse races, rooster fights, and fandangos enlivened by violin music. Yginio himself mastered the violin and once earned the princely sum of fifty dollars playing for a military hop at Fort Stanton.[9]

Besides Fort Stanton and Lincoln, few settlements disturbed

the rural character of the mountain world. On the Ruidoso, just above its union with the Bonito, some fifteen adobe buildings scattered along a single street made up San Patricio. A short distance down the Hondo stood Casey's Mill. Founded by Robert Casey, a stern veteran of several hitches in the regular army, it served as a social and economic center even after Casey was shot down in Lincoln in 1875, leaving the widow Casey to care for the mill and a brood of children.[10] Upstream, near the source of the Ruidoso, Dowlin's Mill played a similar role under the management of the brothers Paul and Will Dowlin. Beyond the Sierra Blanca summit, at the forks of the westward-flowing Río Tularosa, still another group of settlers took root near Blazer's Mills, a sawmill and a gristmill operated by a former Iowa dentist, Dr. Joseph H. Blazer.[11]

As John Henry Tunstall quickly learned, the mountain world's preeminent citizen was Lawrence G. Murphy, who headed the mercantile institution known simply as "The House."[12] An Irish immigrant in his middle forties, veteran of two enlistments in the regular army and commissioned service with the New Mexico volunteers, Major Murphy had come to Fort Stanton at the close of the Civil War. In partnership with another Civil War officer, Emil Fritz, he had set himself up as trader at the fort. Here and at a small branch store in La Placita, the partners had served both military and civilian customers.

From these modest beginnings, Murphy made himself the economic and political czar of Lincoln County. His success rested on government contracts for beef, flour, corn, and other staples at Fort Stanton and the Mescalero Apache Indian Agency. In turn, the contracts enabled him to dominate the civilian economy, for to fill them he stood ready to buy virtually the entire yield of the surrounding farmers. In fact, they had almost no other reliable market. The few other merchants offered no competition in buying and therefore, in a cashless economy, little in selling, for Murphy paid for agricultural produce at the store with credit rather than cash.[13]

Murphy's success also sprang from the cynical manipulation of people and institutions. Master of fraudulent practice, he regularly fattened his returns from government contracts by falsifying vouchers, overcounting Indians, inflating average beef weight, and other such crooked devices. From outlaw gangs he bought stolen cattle at cut rates and turned them in on his contracts at full price. For the area's farmers, he fixed the prices both of buying and selling. Not surprisingly, debits usually exceeded credits.[14]

Murphy's affable good nature and benign countenance masked unflinching ruthlessness. By fair means or foul, he intended to rule the kingdom he had staked out. He got ranchers into debt, then ran them off and resold their spreads to newcomers for exorbitant sums; since most of the county was public domain, such transactions rarely involved legal title. Farmers who objected to his accounting or resisted other demands usually went along after feeling his economic squeeze or, failing that, facing threats by hired gunmen. Men who stood up to Murphy, one citizen explained, "were either killed or run out of the County." "As a matter of business," charged another victim of The House, "they done as they pleased. They intimidated, oppressed and crushed people who were obliged to deal with them. They were a gigantic monopoly."[15]

Economic might laid the foundation for political might. As probate judge, Murphy held the most powerful position on the county level. He also controlled the Democratic Party in a staunchly Democratic county. He "dictated who should run for office and who should not," declared Juan Patrón.[16] Murphy boasted that he controlled the courts, and most people believed that he did, for court decisions usually went his way.[17]

When John Henry Tunstall arrived in Lincoln, Major Murphy commanded the fear and respect of everyone. In black suit and cravat and white shirt, he cut a conspicuous figure in town and at Fort Stanton. Always fastidiously groomed, with his carefully trimmed red beard and receding hairline framing a face marked by squinting eyes and pallid complexion, he played the part of benevolent despot, even though benevolence marked neither his purpose nor his methods. He was a bachelor, without visible interest in women; gossip connected him to his own gender.[18]

By 1877, the image of power was illusion. Although not widely perceived, Murphy's czardom rested on crumbling foundations. In 1873 the secretary of war had ordered him thrown out of Fort Stanton. He had moved his headquarters to Lincoln and erected a two-story "big store" on the western edge of town, but his fortunes had declined since then.[19] Economic dominance weakened under the assaults of rising competition and his own sloppy business practices. His political power eroded as lawyer McSween and other challengers strengthened the Republican Party. But the chief agent of Murphy's decline came in bottles. Increasingly, he fell victim to strong drink. As an acquaintance put it, "The old man Murphy was dissipated and got so he couldn't do business, just drunk whiskey."[20]

The House, however, was not to collapse in Murphy's whiskey vat, for the major had two young protégés who had learned well from their patron.

One was James J. Dolan, a New York Irishman who had come to Lincoln County as a soldier at Fort Stanton. Upon his discharge in 1869, he went to work for Murphy and Fritz as clerk and bookkeeper. Fiercely loyal, he rose rapidly in the chief's esteem and affection. Precocious, quick-witted, ambitious for power and wealth, and altogether without scruple, he brought the firm an aggressive drive and competence that offset Murphy's waning powers.

In some ways, Dolan resembled the other hot-tempered brawlers of Lincoln County. Like Murphy, he drank heavily and could carouse easily with them. He shared their contempt for human life and, as he demonstrated more than once, their readiness to shoot down anyone who crossed them.

But here the resemblance ended. He looked different. A mass of dark hair topped a dark-hued, beardless face of distinctly sinister aspect—beady eyes, small nose, and jaws that looked faintly swollen by a perpetual case of mumps. He indulged Murphy's fondness for a fine and varied wardrobe, and his slender, short frame draped with expensive clothes looked almost effeminate.

Also unlike his rowdy drinking friends, Dolan was shrewd, calculating, and smart. He could be ingratiating and profusely sincere, which made him a favorite of the Santa Fe business and political elite. He did not lack a sort of heedless courage, but, as one of the widow Casey's daughters noted, his greater strength lay in "practices that were dark and devious," in "concocting and carrying through crooked and underhanded deals, usually getting someone else to do the dirty work and take the consequences."[21]

The third leg of the House triangle was another Irishman in his middle twenties, John H. Riley. Riley dealt in beef cattle, in buying them one place and selling them another. This specialty made him useful to The House, and in 1876 he became a co-partner in The House.[22] A contemporary called Riley "a smart devil and a regular confidence man."[23] His record as representative of Santa Fe contractors, and as a House operative, fully supports his reputation for chicanery. Once, in upbraiding an Indian agent for lack of cooperation, Riley declared: "We have always made some money out of this agency until you came here. . . . The Department at Washington expects us to make money and it is expected that the Agent will aid us and we all make money including the Agent."[24] Although Riley bristled with noisy belligerence, he usually managed to be elsewhere when the shooting broke out.

Thus Murphy's legacy rested in the hands of men who were able and eager to carry on in his tradition.

As the figure of Lawrence G. Murphy towered over the high country, so the long shadow of John S. Chisum spread over the low country to the east. Newspapers called him "the cattle king of New Mexico," and by the middle 1870s he was already a legend. A "long rail" burned from shoulder to hip branded Chisum cows, and portions of their ears flopped about like long earrings. Eighty thousand of these Chisum "jinglebobs" grazed 150 miles of the Pecos Valley and as far on either side as they could range without water. Chisum line camps dotted the Pecos Plains from Bosque Grande almost to the Texas line. A hundred Chisum cowboys rode watch on the herds.

The Pecos Plains had first caught the attention of Chisum and other Texas cowmen at the close of the Civil War. The thousands of Navajo Indians imprisoned on the Bosque Redondo Reservation and their guardian soldiers at Fort Sumner offered a lucrative market for Texas beef. Charles Goodnight and Oliver Loving blazed the trail from Texas. The Fort Sumner market

pointed to other markets—Colorado to the north and other Indian agencies and forts to the west, in both New Mexico and
Arizona. In 1868, the Navajos returned to their traditional home-
land west of the Río Grande, but the markets held and the drives
continued. Despite heat, thirst, choking dust, and the ravages of
Comanche and Apache war parties, the great herds swung northward on the Goodnight–Loving Trail, fifty to a hundred thousand head a year.[25]

Not far behind Charles Goodnight rode "Uncle John"
Chisum. He brought his first herd up from Texas in 1867. Looking over the Pecos Plains, he saw advantages in New Mexico beyond simply markets for Texas beef. Mile upon mile of range land
stood unclaimed, except by roving bands of Apaches and Comanches. It was public domain, free to anyone who wanted to use
it. Grass richer than any in Texas beckoned. Nutritious black
grama, it carpeted the high rolling plains. "The grass is knee high
on every hill and mesa," marveled a traveler.[26]

Chisum stayed. At first, he made his headquarters at Bosque
Grande, on the Pecos River fifty miles below Fort Sumner. But in
1875 he moved down the valley to a beautiful oasis on South
Spring River, a clear, fish-laden artesian stream emptying into the
Pecos from the west. Nearby, on North Spring River, the fledg-
ling hamlet of Roswell took shape around a store and post office.[27]

Chisum was fifty-one and a confirmed bachelor when he
settled at South Spring Ranch. He looked plain and unpretentious—wearing rough-hewn clothes on a medium frame, with an
angular, leathery, heavily mustached face. Unlike his cowboys,
he never packed a pistol on his hip, although one always rested in
a holster strapped to his saddle horn. His cowboys accorded him
respect and loyalty and looked on him as an affable extrovert
with a keen sense of humor. A shrewd businessman, honest in
personal dealings but always alert for the main chance, Chisum
also knew cows as few Texans did. "He was a great trail man," said
Charles Goodnight. "No one had any advantage of him as an old-
fashioned cowman, and he was the best counter I ever saw. He
could count three grades of cattle at once, and count them thoroughly even if they were going in a trot."[28]

Chisum's sway over the Pecos Plains did not long go uncontested, especially after he moved to South Spring. Other Texans planted themselves along the southern margins of the Chisum ranges, making their headquarters at the village of Seven Rivers, sixty miles below Roswell. They started with small herds and, compared with Chisum, remained small-time operators. These people regarded Chisum as a domineering tyrant, intent on excluding all interlopers from the Pecos grasslands that, as public domain, belonged to all. "I don't think Chisum could be beat as a cow-man," recalled one of his neighbors. "But he seemed to want the Pecos river to himself."[29]

For his part, Chisum viewed the small ranchers not only as interlopers, but as thieving nuisances. They complained that their stock mingled with his and often went to market with his, which was true. But less accidentally, far more of his stock wound up in their herds. In fact, most of the herds in the Seven Rivers area owed their growth, if not their origins, to Chisum cows. Rustling or mavericking from his huge holdings became an accepted way of life for the little men. A few deft strokes of the branding iron readily changed the long rail into a pitchfork, a hatchet, or even a pigpen. "When they get to using my rail to build a pigpen," Chisum supposedly remarked, "it is time for me to squeal."[30]

The opposition to Chisum centered in old Hugh Beckwith of Seven Rivers. A British traveler described him as "a tall, lean, hard featured man with a curious tired expression in his eyes. He was tired, tired of being forever on his guard."[31]

Though not a Texan, Beckwith shared the instinct of his Texan neighbors for settling disputes personally and violently. He had come out of the Deep South before the Civil War, and during the war years he had rabidly promoted the Southern cause. He believed in direct action. So did his sons, John and Robert, who were both in their twenties. So did his son-in-law, William H. Johnson, whose service in the Union army made relations with volatile old Hugh always uncertain. And so did the Olinger brothers. Charles Robert Olinger, a huge bully, rode for Beckwith; and John Wallace Olinger ranched in partnership with Captain Johnson.

The Beckwith clan, the Olingers, Heiskell Jones and his throng of sons, Marion Turner, Milo Pearce, Joe Nash, Buck

Powell—these and others damned John Chisum's imperial preten-
sions, while building their herds at his expense.[32]

Chisum clearly saw the inevitable and took action. With
more and more newcomers stocking the open range, his troubles
could only grow worse. He decided, therefore, to scale back
drastically and either concentrate on upgraded stock or get out
altogether. Late in 1875, he sold the bulk of his cattle to the
St. Louis commission firm of Hunter, Evans and Company. He
agreed, however, to continue to manage these cattle until the
company, through normal sales, had disposed of them all, a
matter of several years. Thus, the transaction changed no one's
mind about John Chisum. To the Seven Rivers stockmen, he remained the enemy, and all the old causes of hostility continued to
fester.[33]

Hostility festered everywhere in Lincoln County, and it
regularly shattered the peace of both the mountain world and the
plains world. Law enforcement, which rested with the county
sheriff and precinct constables, was capricious, sporadic, uneven,
and virtually nonexistent beyond the neighborhood of the county
seat. The district court, based in Mesilla, 140 miles to the southwest, came to Lincoln only twice a year.

Violence occurred so frequently not only because of inade-
quate law enforcement. More important was the code of the West.
Fiction writers did not create the code. It actually governed men
throughout the frontier West. It may even have been stronger,
sharper, and more violent in Lincoln County because of the ties,
through the Texas cowboys, to the Texas feud country where it
flourished with special virulence. And it had more lethal consequences than at any other time in history because of the casual
attitude toward death and destruction spawned by the Civil War
and Reconstruction. Texans came into New Mexico with dark and
bitter memories of Reconstruction excesses at home.

The code demanded personal courage and pride, reckless
disregard of life, and instant redress of insult, real or fancied—all
traits with great appeal to the masculine young adventurers who
flocked to the frontier. Nearly everyone carried a Winchester
rifle or carbine and a Colt's six-shooter, and if someone wronged

you, no matter how trivially, you shot it out on the spot. It was "the rattlesnake's code," observed the contemporary writer Eugene Manlove Rhodes, "to warn before he strikes, no better; a queer, lopsided, topsy-turvy, jumbled and senseless code—but a code for all that."[34]

The code found steady inspiration in whiskey. Like firearms, whiskey was always within reach and more or less constantly imbibed. "Almost every person took a drink," recalled Lily Klasner. "Men who drank," she observed, "became quarrelsome, and were for settling their difficulties with some sort of fight, using fists, knives, or shooting irons."[35] The litany of shootings in Lincoln County during the early 1870s, as set down in the newspapers, betrays whiskey almost invariably as an ingredient. The code governed not only drunken riffraff. Time and again, prominent citizens shot it out as well.

The proclivity for violence intensified when the plains world rubbed against the mountain world. Although all the Anglos tended to look with condescension on the Hispanics, the Texans brought with them to New Mexico a well-developed sense of superiority and contempt. The Hispanics reciprocated. In addition to ethnic, cultural, and religious differences, mutual antipathy had roots in history. The Texas Revolution and the Mexican War had opened wounds not easily healed. New Mexicans of Spanish descent and Texans did not share Lincoln County comfortably.[36]

Twice the hostility between Anglos and Hispanics spilled over into violence approaching race war.

The planting season of May 1873 brought on the Tularosa Ditch War. Irrigating their crops from the waters of the Tularosa River, Anglo farmers around Blazer's Mills choked down the flow reaching the Hispanic town of Tularosa, on the flats where the stream issued from the mountains. Twice angry villagers destroyed the dams. Dr. Blazer, Lawrence Murphy, and others appealed to the commanding officer at Fort Stanton for military assistance.

In a move of dubious legality, Captain Chambers McKibben sent a lieutenant and five cavalrymen to the scene. They collided with an armed mob and in an exchange of gunfire one person was killed. Outnumbered, the troopers fell back to Blazer's Mills and,

joined by a dozen or more settlers, prepared to defend themselves. The Tularosa vigilantes attacked, but at this juncture Captain McKibben and a troop of cavalry charged to the rescue and
drove them off. McKibben then marched to Tularosa, unlimbered
a cannon, and threatened to blow the town down if the defenders
did not disperse to their homes. They obeyed.[37]

The smoldering racial animosity burst forth again in the
Horrell War of the winter of 1873–74. The five Horrell brothers
had brought their families to the lower Ruidoso after repeated
misdeeds had made their home country in Texas uncongenial. On
December 1, 1873, Ben Horrell and several companions went on
a spree in Lincoln and ran afoul the town constable and his deputies, all Hispanics. A shootout killed the constable and one of the
Anglos and wounded Ben and a friend, who surrendered only to
be shot down in cold blood.

"After the Mexicans killed Ben," a cowboy related, "the Horrells started in to clean up on the Mexicans and came damn near
doing it, too."[38] On the night of December 20, as a wedding
dance got under way in Squire Wilson's erstwhile courthouse, the
Horrells rode into town. "Come on," declared one, "we'll make
them dance to our music."[39] Creeping up on the dance hall, they
opened fire through the door and the windows. When the smoke
cleared, four men lay dead and three wounded. Among the dead
was Isidro Patrón, father of Juan Patrón.[40]

While federal authorities all the way up to the president debated whether the army should take a hand in the disorders, the
violence continued. Innocent people were shot down for no other
reason than their Hispanic blood. Even Anglos with Hispanic
wives found themselves targeted. Finally, the war petered out
simply because the Horrells decided to go back to Texas. As an
observer summed it up, "They fought and killed along until it got
so bad that the Horrells had to leave."[41]

The Tularosa Ditch War and the Horrell War created a cli-
mate of ethnic suspicion and tension that time failed to dispel.
The ready resort to violence and the polarization of Texans and
Hispanics forecast the dark times to come in 1878.

Not only Anglos and Hispanics contributed to Lincoln
County's heritage of violence. The Mescalero Apaches played

their part too. Killings and theft of stock occurred sporadically, and every now and then they stampeded to the mountains and had to be rounded up by the army.

Depredations fell with special ferocity on the horse herds of the Pecos stockmen. In the first half of 1873, John Chisum alone lost 175 horses to Indian raiders. "They seem to direct all their venom against Mr. Chisum," reported an army officer.[42] Finally, Chisum boiled over. "Bob, you know what I'm going to do?" he asked Robert Casey. "I'm going to steal these Indians out. By God, I'll show them I can steal some too."[43] And so he did. Chisum cowboys periodically made off with Indian stock, as did bands of professional horse thieves, both Anglo and Hispanic.[44]

Thus, John Chisum added his feud with the Indians to his feud with the small cowmen—and to all the other racial, personal, and criminal feuds that afflicted Lincoln County. In drunken disputes, in quarrels over "soiled doves" or wifely attentions, men shot one another down with rifle or pistol. Outlaws stole horses and cattle and killed or got killed in the process. Farmers and ranchers who toiled for a living indulged in occasional lawlessness, either against their neighbor's herds or their neighbor himself. Powerful men like Murphy and Chisum advanced or defended their interests with hired Winchesters. Indians slipped away from the agency to raid stock in the mountain valleys and on the Pecos Plains. Army patrols rode in pursuit and sometimes clashed with the raiders. Still more racial antipathy arose when elements of the Ninth Cavalry, black troopers under white officers, took station at Fort Stanton. Anglos, especially Texans, scorned the "nigger soldiers."

The Lincoln County in which John Henry Tunstall settled at the beginning of 1877 not only looked back on a history heavy with violence and lawlessness. Jostling together so many combustibles, it looked to a future heavy with the potential for more.

3

Rings within Rings

UNDER THE PRESIDENCY of Ulysses S. Grant, the word *ring* burst in bold letters over America's political landscape. As corruption seeped ever deeper into the Grant administration, the press ferreted out one ring after another. The Whiskey Ring, the Indian Ring, the Tweed Ring, and other sinister combinations of wicked men pursuing nefarious ends at the public expense set off scandal after scandal. Bombarded by exposés, Americans looked on public officials and corporate moguls with growing cynicism and blamed many of the country's ills on one shadowy ring or another.

Rings took different forms. Some operated in all the fullness of explicit conspiratorial organization. Some, called rings with doubtful accuracy, merely represented men of common purpose pursuing self-interest in similar ways that benefited all. Some existed mainly in the imaginations of sensation-seeking reporters and politicians in need of a club to wield against the opposition.

Although remote from the nation's political heartland, New Mexico Territory plunged enthusiastically into the ring mania. Among the many rings that New Mexicans perceived as riddling their governmental and other institutions, the Santa Fe Ring enjoyed uncontested supremacy. Just who belonged and how they were organized, if at all, remained vague; but their purposes did not: they sought power and wealth. Mainly, they concentrated on amassing huge landholdings through the manipulation of Spanish land grants and the laws regulating the public domain. But wher-

ever money was to be made, especially where facilitated by governmental action, people suspected ring involvement. Cattle,
railroads, mining, and army and Indian contracts all captured the
attention of the ring members.[1]

Identity of the ring's membership fueled endless speculation.
Popular belief focused on a handful of Santa Fe lawyers and merchants, some of the judges, the territorial governor, possibly the
United States marshal, and assorted other officials. Reflecting the
long Republican incumbency, most were Republicans. Each election featured a full-scale assault by the Democrats on the Santa Fe
Ring, and an equally vigorous defense ridiculing the notion that a
ring existed at all. The Republican label, however, did not bar
membership to like-minded Democrats.

However uncertain the other membership of the Santa Fe
Ring, no one doubted that Thomas Benton Catron reigned as
kingpin. An immigrant from Missouri at the close of the Civil
War, Catron had teamed up with Stephen B. Elkins—"Smooth
Steve"—in the law firm of Catron and Elkins. Nearly everyone
credited the two with founding the Santa Fe Ring. By 1876,
Elkins had put in two terms in the U.S. Congress as delegate from
New Mexico and was preparing to move his ambitions back to the
East. That left Catron, who enjoyed power and stature both as
United States district attorney for New Mexico and as an enormously successful lawyer specializing in land matters. Full of energy, domineering and abrasively partisan, and resolute and
ruthless in pursuing his aims, Catron fitted the stereotype of ring-
master. His portly frame and soft, fleshy face with bushy mustache dominated the New Mexico political scene for half a
century.[2]

In his travels around New Mexico, John Henry Tunstall had
watched rings insidiously working their way. In L. G. Murphy &
Co., Lincoln displayed almost a prototype of a small-scale ring.
The lesson did not escape the keen observation of the young
Englishman. "*Everything* in New Mexico, that pays *at all*," he wrote
to his parents in April 1877, "is worked by a 'ring,' there is the
'Indian ring,' the 'army ring,' 'the political ring,' the 'legal ring,'
the 'Roman Catholic ring,' the 'cattle ring,' the 'horsethieves ring,'
the 'land ring' and half a dozen other rings; now to make things

stick 'to do any good,' it is necessary to either get into a ring or to make one for yourself."

He made one for himself. "My ring is forming itself as fast & faster than I had ever hoped," he told his family, "& in such a way that I will get the finest plum of the lot."[3]

By April 1877, he counted three members besides himself. First in importance, of course, was Alexander McSween. By February, the Englishman and the Scotsman had entered into an intimate, almost daily collaboration. The lawyer gave legal and business advice, acquainted Tunstall with conditions and personalities in Lincoln County, served as a conduit between him and the local community, and finally, once the money starting flowing from London, used his Santa Fe bank account to receive and disburse funds.[4]

Richard M. Brewer ranked after McSween in point of usefulness. Dick Brewer was remembered by one who rode with him as "a great big, fine looking fellow, a cowboy farmer."[5] He was twenty-six, an immigrant from Wisconsin, and farmed and ran cows on the old Horrell place on the lower Ruidoso, which he rented from Lawrence Murphy even though Murphy had no legal title to it. By 1877, The House had Brewer so deeply in its debt that he despaired of ever breaking free. As a strong and vigorous cowboy, a good horseman and good hand with rifle and pistol, Brewer entered critically into Tunstall's plans for a cattle ranch. "I esteem him highly," Tunstall wrote, "as he is a very fine specimen of humanity both physically & morally."[6]

The other member of the ring was Robert A. Widenmann, the young German Tunstall had met at Herlow's Hotel in Santa Fe and so warmly, and uncharacteristically, embraced as a friend. Tall and heavy, with a receding chin and filmy mustache, Rob Widenmann showed up in Lincoln in February 1877. He came at Tunstall's written invitation and functioned as a sort of all-purpose gadfly. Tunstall gave him a few dollars whenever he needed money, and he did whatever needed doing, even serving as a valet. Most acquaintances thought him a noisy braggart, but Tunstall had nothing but praise. "He is one of the very few men of my own age that I ever cared a 'red' cent about," he wrote. The two bunked together, and Tunstall's expressions of affection grew so profuse as to suggest an extraordinary intimacy.[7]

First, the ring concentrated on realizing Tunstall's ranching dreams. With Brewer's help, the Englishman found a suitable spread on the Feliz and Peñasco rivers, about thirty miles south of Lincoln. As a British subject, however, he could not obtain direct title to federal lands. Therefore, McSween rounded up six dummy entrants, including himself and Brewer, to file on 640-acre parcels of the ranch under the newly enacted Desert Land Act, an ingenious piece of special-interest legislation promoted by cattlemen to allow the assembly of large holdings under the guise of watering desert lands. Tunstall put down a filing fee of twenty-five cents an acre on between three and four thousand acres.[8]

Next, Tunstall turned to stocking his range. In May 1877, to satisfy a court judgment, the sheriff seized some of the widow Ellen Casey's cattle and offered them at public auction. McSween, acting for Tunstall, bought 209 for bargain prices of less than five dollars a head. Tunstall assembled the herd on Brewer's Ruidoso range and, with Widenmann and a helper, branded the animals and drove them to the Peñasco and Feliz. Brewer, with a few hands, served as ranch foreman while continuing to work his own spread.[9]

For more than a year, all of Tunstall's thought and energy had been devoted to his ranching project. Nothing else had attracted his interest, least of all a mercantile enterprise. Yet the accumulation of wealth remained his obsession, and Murphy's example pointed the way to greater and more immediate profits than ranching. By the spring of 1877, Tunstall's feverish mind had mapped out a many-faceted operation designed to challenge and ultimately displace The House as Lincoln County's reigning monopoly. His goal now, he boasted to his family, was no less than "to get the half of every dollar that is made in the county *by anyone*."[10]

First, Tunstall would open a store to compete with Murphy's. By issuing "grain notes" against the future harvest of crops, he would lure farmers away from Murphy and attach them by debt to his own business. This would enable him to corner the entire

27

local crop of corn and wheat, thus displacing The House as the source of produce for government contracts at Fort Stanton and the Indian agency. Like Murphy, he wanted to get into land—buying ranches for a pittance or to satisfy debt and selling them to newcomers at great profit. And like Murphy, he fixed an acquisitive eye on the post tradership at Fort Stanton and explored the lucrative possibilities of the Indian agency.[11]

Tunstall's new strategy brought a new member to the robust ring, none other than John Chisum. McSween, Chisum's attorney, introduced the two, and the cowman agreed to lend his name to another of Tunstall's projects—the Lincoln County Bank. Conceived as part of the store, the Lincoln County Bank consisted mainly of a letterhead unsupported by significant assets. But it served as a vehicle for Tunstall's credit transactions, and the letterhead bore the name of John S. Chisum as president.

Not once in his letters home did Tunstall name Murphy, Dolan, or Riley, although he sometimes alluded to them in vague terms, such as "some men who need killing very badly."[12] But he surely knew that they would not stand idly by while he displaced them on every front.

And now Tunstall faced a more formidable opponent even than Murphy, for in March 1877 the major sold out. L. G. Murphy & Co. became Jas. J. Dolan & Co., a partnership between Jimmy Dolan and Johnny Riley backed by the financial strength of the reputed head of the Santa Fe Ring, Thomas B. Catron. Murphy's name still commanded fear and respect in Lincoln County, but in truth he had lost his grip, and power had passed to Dolan. He stood ready to apply it brutally, without even the genial facade that cloaked Murphy's brand of coercion. In Jimmy Dolan, the Tunstall ring contended with an adversary immensely more cunning and merciless than Lawrence Murphy.[13]

John Chisum's alliance with Tunstall added still another ingredient to the mix, for Dolan maintained a cow camp near Seven Rivers, on the southern edge of Chisum's range. In the spring of 1877, Dolan moved some two thousand cattle there from Murphy's Fairview Ranch and placed them in charge of Fairview's foreman, William B. "Billy" Morton. The plan was to augment this herd with Chisum stock. "Morton laughed and told me he could steal from Chisum," recalled Sue McSween. "He said he could change the rail into a hatchet."[14]

Dolan's operation on the Pecos forged links with the Seven Rivers stockmen, mortal enemies of John Chisum. In fact, Dolan ventured to the Pecos at the very time that the rancor between Chisum and his neighbors exploded in the Pecos War of April 1877. Not much blood flowed, but several shooting affrays ended in a siege of Hugh Beckwith's ranch by Chisum cowboys. They cut off the water, but then balked at an assault that might get them killed. Chisum escaped arrest only by coming down with small-pox—one of many, including Tunstall, Brewer, and Widenmann, who almost died in an epidemic that killed scores of people throughout 1877.[15] In the Seven Rivers cowmen, Dolan cultivated a band of allies whose hatred of Chisum might be put to good purpose in the conflict shaping up with Chisum's Lincoln friends.

In addition to these potential warriors, Dolan and Riley counted other weapons. For one, they had their own gang of outlaws, known as "The Boys," a band of some thirty or forty horse and cattle thieves headed by Lincoln County's most accomplished cutthroat, Jesse Evans. "Captain" Evans, about twenty-five years old in 1877, had come up from Texas in 1872 and had served as one of Chisum's horse thieves for several years before putting together his own gang. Of medium stature, with gray eyes and light hair and complexion, he pursued his profession with relaxed impudence. Evans never acted in anyone's interest but his own. Increasingly, however, his interests coincided with those of Dolan and Riley. The Boys furnished them with stolen beef and did other chores to which they preferred to have no visible link.[16]

Another House advantage lay in the courts. If not actually controlled by The House, as Murphy boasted, they at least favored The House. Judge Warren Bristol presided over the Third Judicial District Court in Mesilla, which tried both territorial and federal cases. A meek little man with bald head, untidy beard, and a frightened look in his eyes, Bristol tried to be fair and impartial. But sometimes he had a hard time of it, especially when dealing with the likes of Dolan and Riley on their home

29

turf, where he held court twice a year. Not even pretending impartiality, District Attorney William L. Rynerson, a great hairy
giant with a fiery temper, shamelessly favored his friend Dolan.[17]

Closer to home, Sheriff William Brady had ties to The
House that predisposed him to Dolan and Riley. He had a commitment to the public welfare that set him apart from most of his
associates, and since his election as sheriff in November 1876 he
had shown himself to be an able lawman. But he and Murphy had
been friends for years, since serving together in the war. They
had come to Lincoln County at war's end and had collaborated in
various ways ever since. A respected citizen, Major Brady had
served in several public posts, including U.S. commissioner and
legislator from Lincoln County. He farmed a homestead east of
Lincoln, where he lived with a Hispanic wife and a growing family. For years he had been in debt to The House. Although he did
not take orders from Murphy, he could usually be counted on to
do what Murphy wanted. Brady made the fourth of a band of
fraternal Irish Catholics, three of them ex-soldiers, all hard
drinkers, and none, given their sense of the afflictions of Ireland,
with any great affection for Protestant Englishmen or Scotsmen.[18]

Dolan's coalition hung together with more solidarity than
Tunstall's, which endured some internal stresses. Tunstall and his
associates all liked Brewer, and Chisum remained a remote figure-
head. McSween liked and admired Tunstall. But McSween did not
like Widenmann. He had a habit, McSween thought, of "poking
his nose in where it does not belong," and suffered besides from
"laziness, youthful pomposity, [and] lack of discretion."[19]

For his part, Tunstall shared his inner self with no one but
Widenmann. Although McSween believed the Englishman to be
a friend, he was not. He looked on McSween impersonally,
simply as an instrument to aid in accomplishing his ends. "I have
worked his affairs & mine in such a shape that they spur him just
the way I want him to go," he wrote in April 1877. And a week
later: "I believe I have him in such a shape that he can't slide back a
single point; anyhow, he can't make anything by so doing."[20]

Sue McSween had doubts about the course on which her
husband had embarked. She was a sharp, perceptive woman, ner-

vous but even more unswervingly ambitious than Mac and with none of his ambivalence of character. She clearly foresaw that Dolan would fight back. "I told Tunstall and Mr. McSween they would be murdered if they went into the store business," she later declared. "I did my best to keep McSween from entering the business, but he went in against my will. Tunstall was the cause of his getting into it."[21]

Despite his wife's fears, McSween lent himself enthusiastically to Tunstall's designs. English money in large sums offered the means of achieving his El Dorado in Lincoln. After the gold drafts from London began to swell his modest bank account, he saw his dream coming true. From Murphy, in February, he bought a lot containing Murphy's old branch store, now replaced by the big store on the western edge of town. During the spring, carpenters and masons worked to enlarge and modernize the building for a dwelling, and ornate Victorian furniture arrived to lend it elegance and comfort. Sue, an accomplished musician, acquired both a piano and an organ. In the summer, the Tunstall store began to rise next door to the east, on the same lot, and McSween looked forward to moving his law office from Squire Wilson's dance hall and sometime courthouse to more fitting quarters in the store and bank. Anticipating a prospering practice, he invited his brother-in-law, lawyer David P. Shield, to bring Sue's sister and their young daughters to Lincoln and join him in a partnership. In September, McSween bought more property from Dolan, which extended his holdings farther east and provided room for the school and Presbyterian Church that he hoped to build. He petitioned the Santa Fe Presbytery to obtain a minister for Lincoln.[22]

The lawyer did not picture himself as part of a ring, nor as the author of devious or dishonorable practices, and still less as a tool of Tunstall. But as he became more and more entangled in the Englishman's schemes, and as his visions materialized in home, store, office, bank, and partnership, his ambition seduced him into self-deception. Both he and his friends and admirers saw only an upstanding community leader, a model of pious rectitude. His growing band of enemies saw a crooked, conscienceless shyster determined to make money at any cost. That both assessments contained a measure of truth defined the depth of Alex McSween's weakness of character.

Tunstall, in contrast to McSween, won the approval of most Lincolnites. His open ways and genial disposition beguiled people, even while his English mannerisms and peculiar dress drew snickers. *El Inglés*, the Hispanics called him. "That brown-coated, steak-eating Englishman," the cowboys called him. One cowboy, at least, remembered him as "just a damn crazy Englishman."[23] Those not especially attracted to Tunstall's personality welcomed his money, and many looked on him as a liberator, come to free them from the tyranny of The House. That Tunstall sought to liberate the people only to substitute his own brand of tyranny, possibly less brutal but no less absolute, would have been plain to anyone who read his letters home. The people figured in his schemes only as a source of dollars. In fact, one person *was* reading Tunstall's mail, Postmaster Jimmy Dolan, and he shared none of the common illusions about his adversary.[24]

Dolan hardly needed Tunstall's letters to alert him to a formidable threat. The adobe walls rising from the vacant space next to McSween's home served as a daily reminder during the summer months. Early in July, Tunstall left for St. Louis to buy stock for his store, but McSween remained to further the ring's design in the chief's absence. Tension mounted as The House confronted not only the specter of ruinous competition but of its own plunge into ruinous debt. In addition to ten thousand dollars in notes to Murphy for his share of the firm, Dolan and Riley had signed other notes adding up to more than twelve thousand dollars that would fall due in November, and even without Tunstall's competition they had little hope of paying off.[25]

Signs of their growing desperation multiplied. Riley warned McSween that Tunstall would be stolen poor—not by himself but by others. Rumors flew that McSween and Tunstall had been marked for assassination. Both Juan Patrón and James Farmer declared that Murphy had told them that Tunstall and McSween would have to be killed.[26]

The "others," everyone knew, were Jesse Evans and The Boys. Already that summer of 1877, the arrogant larceny of The

Boys had risen to a tempo that troubled citizens and formed a menacing backdrop to the escalating commercial dissension. In late August, however, The Boys shifted their operations farther west, to the vicinity of Mesilla and Silver City.

During this period, The Boys took on a recruit destined to make a name for himself in Lincoln County and ultimately attain towering stature in American folklore. Barely eighteen, he looked his youth—spare, 140 pounds, of medium stature, with brown hair, light complexion, and a smooth face betraying the downy beginnings of a beard and mustache. He rode well and shot well and practiced all the time. With winning ways, he made friends easily. He was a scrappy tough, seasoned by the raw life of the Silver City mining camp. He had killed at least one man, a bully at Fort Grant, Arizona. Like many another drifter, he gave a false name, William H. Bonney; but he also took his stepfather's surname and answered to Henry Antrim, Kid Antrim, or just Kid.[27]

At last, as long expected, The Boys made their move against Tunstall. He had not returned from St. Louis, and in fact lay ill with smallpox in a Las Vegas hotel room. But he had stock at Brewer's ranch on the Ruidoso. At midday on September 18, Evans and a few of his men invaded the ranch and, before Brewer's very eyes, brazenly appropriated two of his horses and two especially fine horses and a pair of mules belonging to Tunstall. With some neighbors, Brewer gave chase, but after a long pursuit they had to return empty handed.[28]

Tunstall had learned of the theft of his animals while still sick in Las Vegas, and at once he set forth for Lincoln. He arrived on October 16 to find that his foreman had not given up the effort to get back the animals.

Indeed, unknown to Tunstall, Brewer already had them. Fortified by indictments of Evans and his sidekick Tom Hill returned at the October term of court, Brewer had assembled a fifteen-man posse, armed it with Winchesters from the Tunstall store, and persuaded Sheriff Brady to lead it down to the Pecos in search of Evans. At Hugh Beckwith's ranch, the posse cornered four of the gang—Evans, Frank Baker, Tom Hill, and George Davis—and after a lively exchange of gunfire, forced them to surrender. With a herd of stolen horses, including one of Tunstall's, Brady and his deputies shepherded the outlaws back to Lincoln and locked them in the county's newly completed cellar jail.

The capture of the outlaws presented enticing new challenges for Tunstall's agile mind. Even before they reached Lincoln, he had a chance to meet them. On October 20, while taking a wagon load of merchandise down to Chisum's ranch, he came across the captors and their prisoners on the Hondo. Amid general rejoicing, Tunstall and the outlaws began to banter one another. Tom Hill wisecracked: "Well, have you got any whiskey, Englishman?" "Merely a dram," answered Tunstall. He did not need it to keep his blood warm, he said, but in Lincoln "I would soak you if you wished." "Well, we'll be in the jug then," replied Hill, "you get back & you can soak us there if you like." "All right," agreed Tunstall.[29]

Tunstall's return to Lincoln plunged him into matters more weighty than whiskey for The Boys. The widow Casey, from whom he had acquired most of his cattle, had decided to return to Texas. Before leaving, she had rounded up his cattle and run them into her herd. Although worn out by the pursuit of Evans, Brewer had enlisted six men and, with legal papers drawn up by McSween, set forth to head off the widow.

Again Brewer triumphed. Ten miles short of the Texas line, the pursuers came up with the herd, faced down the Casey cowboys, and returned with all the stolen stock.[30]

With his cattle safely back on the range, Tunstall turned again to The Boys. He paid them a frolicsome visit in the Lincoln jail, where "they found that I could joke as well as they could & we laughed a good deal." Later, Tunstall sent them the promised bottle of whiskey and again, this time with Brewer, visited them while they were outside exercising. "We laughed and joked a good deal more." When Sheriff Brady ordered the prisoners below, Evans asked Tunstall to come with them "to talk over matters & things." Brady would not consent; "he is an Irishman," Tunstall explained, "a slave of whiskey & a man I think very little of, he is a tool."[31]

No one expected the Lincoln jail to hold Evans and his henchmen for long. The break finally came before daylight on November 17. Brady had withdrawn the six-man guard, leaving a lone attendant. About thirty of The Boys, including Billy Bonney alias Kid, rode into town, put a pistol to the jailer's head, and knocked down the door of the prison room with big rocks that had been helpfully assembled in advance. From Lincoln the outlaws made their way to Brewer's ranch. Brewer was not home, but several of his hands cooked breakfast for them, then watched as they saddled eight of Tunstall's horses in Brewer's corral and rode off. With Brewer's hands they left apologies for Tunstall and a promise never again to steal anything from him. And true to their promise, they sent back all but one of his animals.

Each camp loudly accused the other of helping The Boys to escape. Tunstall and McSween charged Dolan with furnishing the tools and Brady with failing to retrieve them as well as ensuring that no deputies interfered on the appointed night. Dolan's friends replied that Brewer had served as a messenger between the prisoners and their accomplices on the Ruidoso, letting them know on which night the jail would be unguarded, coming to town on the night of the escape, and remaining conveniently absent from his ranch when The Boys appeared there for breakfast and mounts.[32]

The charges defy proof, but the evidence, mostly circumstantial, suggests an abundance of dirty hands in both camps. The tools almost certainly came from the Dolan store, smuggled in by a House employee. Brady likewise helped, either actively on behalf of The House or passively, from a sense of resigned inevitability. Tunstall probably played a part too. Besides the whiskey and the jollification and Brewer's alleged contribution, he appears to have bought two of the prisoners new suits.[33] Tunstall wanted his animals back, and he may also have hoped to counter the reported attempt of The Boys to assassinate him and McSween. He got his animals back, but if he thought he could attach Evans to his own cause, he badly underestimated the cost.

The furor over the antics of the Jesse Evans gang tended to obscure the worsening conflict between Dolan and Tunstall. By November the Tunstall store had become, for the first time, more than a future threat to Dolan. The building had been completed in August, and since spring Tunstall and McSween had been industriously collecting "grain notes," and thus customers. But only in November, when the goods purchased in St. Louis at last filled the shelves, and clerk Sam Corbet manned the store each day, did the new competition take tangible and alarming form.

This occurred just as The House's debts fell due in Santa Fe. After defaulting on one note, Dolan sent Riley hurrying to the capital to take action. Riley succeeded in having all the notes consolidated and refinanced, with a partial guarantee from Tom Catron. That astute money-maker probably sized up the partners as bad risks, but he also surely knew the value of their property. Predictably, the loans turned out to be a stopgap measure. Six weeks later, Dolan and Riley made a final desperate attempt to stave off disaster. On January 19, 1878, they mortgaged to Catron all their holdings in Lincoln County—real estate and improvements, merchandise, accounts receivable, fifteen hundred head of cattle, thirty-five horses, and twelve mules. In return, Catron lent the partners twenty-five thousand dollars. If they defaulted, he would own all the mortgaged property. Suddenly, Tom Catron acquired more than a distant interest in Lincoln County.[34]

Nor was the competition all that prosperous. Tunstall had invested thousands of dollars in his many schemes for replacing The House as the economic overlord of Lincoln County, but the profits he anticipated existed only in his dreams, and profits of any magnitude remained in the future. With his father's fortune behind him, Tunstall hardly faced lean times. Strangely, however, his collaborator did. McSween had spent a great deal of money on Tunstall's enterprises and his own, and in fact the affairs of the two had become so entangled as to defy separation. But his bank account had not received sufficient infusions of Tunstall money to offset the outward flow. By the end of November, the balance stood at $65.32, and early in December he received the first of a series of increasingly threatening overdraft notices. No less than Jimmy Dolan, Alex McSween teetered on the edge of bankruptcy.[35]

Thus financial stress afflicted both antagonists and drove them to a desperation that contributed in large measure to the violence soon to erupt.

McSween had two immediate prospects for avoiding insolvency. One was his connection with Chisum, and through him with Hunter and Evans, the St. Louis firm that had bought all of Chisum's cattle in 1875. McSween handled the legal business between the two, and in their service he planned to accompany Chisum back to St. Louis in late December.

The other was an insurance policy, part of an estate that he had been engaged to settle. That insurance policy turned out to be the explosive charge that set off the Lincoln County War.

4

The Opening Round

TUNSTALL AND MCSWEEN had taken on a cunning opponent who would not hesitate to use any weapon at his command to defend his turf. That reality, they should have known, demanded the most alert attention to their own defenses. If they dropped their guard even momentarily, Jimmy Dolan would be sure to thrust into the opening. In his handling of a routine legal matter, McSween made the tactical missteps that gave Dolan his opening.

Shortly after arriving in Lincoln, and while still friendly with Murphy, McSween had been engaged to help in settling the estate of Emil Fritz. Murphy's partner had died in June 1874, during a visit to his home in Germany. McSween's first task was to collect debts owed to The House at the time of Fritz's death. Later, he took on the added assignment of pressing the receivers of a bankrupt New York insurance company to make good on a ten-thousand-dollar policy on Fritz's life. The lawyer's fee would be 10 per cent of whatever sums he collected.[1]

McSween succeeded admirably. By the autumn of 1876, he had collected more than thirty thousand dollars in debts to The House. Then, his New York trip in October 1876 (during which he met Tunstall in Santa Fe and pointed him toward Lincoln) led finally to payment of the insurance money—reduced, however, by more than three thousand dollars in fees to New York lawyers and bankers.

And here, McSween made his first mistake. By the time the insurance money materialized in August 1877, the Fritz estate had become a pawn in the desperate attempt of Dolan and Riley to stave off financial collapse. The insurance money offered almost the only tangible asset that could be reached in an estate so muddled by the financial chaos of Dolan & Co. as to defy adjudication. Before relinquishing the money, McSween wanted his fee and expenses, almost four thousand dollars. Rather than having it deposited in Santa Fe, therefore, he had it sent to his East St. Louis bank.

Another reason for holding the money sprang from the character of the administrators of the estate: Charles Fritz, Emil's brother, and Emilie Scholand, a sister. Mrs. Scholand, a divorcée who lived in Las Cruces, spoke little English and was rarely in Lincoln when needed. Charles was weak, besotted, and dominated by Murphy, Dolan, and Riley, who held him in debt and threatened to run him out of the country without even a shirt on his back if he failed to do their bidding.[2] McSween feared that the money, when paid to the administrators, would find its way at once into Dolan's pocket. Even so, he repeatedly promised to relinquish it if formally released from all responsibility for the estate.

McSween should have had the insurance payment deposited in a Santa Fe bank, subject to the order of the probate court. Murphy no longer presided over this court, and the new judge, Florencio Gonzales, was able, honest, and no friend to The House. More than once he had been victimized by Murphy, and in the factional contest brewing in Lincoln his sympathies lay with Tunstall and McSween. The lawyer's interests could better have been entrusted to Gonzales.

Next, McSween made another bad mistake. On December 18, 1877, with the dispute still stalemated, he and Sue left Lincoln, intending to meet John Chisum at Anton Chico and proceed to St. Louis. McSween had made no secret of the trip, and in fact he had specifically alerted several people in Lincoln and Mesilla to his plans. He left David Shield, his partner, with full power to take all action needed, including payment of the insurance money by check if the probate court made a final ruling.

McSween's departure threw him into the clutches of the wily Dolan. Already, Dolan had convinced himself that McSween meant to keep all the insurance money, and Dolan had hastened to Mesilla to hire an attorney. No sooner had McSween and Sue put Lincoln behind them than a Dolan associate rushed word to Mesilla. The news only confirmed Dolan's suspicions. The McSweens had left, he later said, "as everyone believed never to come back." Dolan hurried from Mesilla to nearby Las Cruces, corraled Emilie Scholand, and ushered her before Judge Bristol to swear an affidavit charging McSween with embezzlement. Under Dolan's prodding, the judge lost no time in issuing a warrant for McSween's arrest. The newly strung telegraph wires sped word of the action northward. In Santa Fe, U.S. District Attorney Catron bestirred himself to aid in the cause, and on Christmas Eve both John Chisum and Alex McSween found themselves clapped in the Las Vegas jail.[3]

McSween languished behind bars for almost two weeks. Chisum, whose troubles sprang from an unrelated legal and financial fight with Santa Fe contractors, remained even longer. Finally, McSween managed to free himself from the Las Vegas authorities. Sending Sue on to the East, he turned toward Lincoln and ultimately Mesilla, where he would appear before Judge Bristol to answer the charge.

With the judge absent from Mesilla, McSween lingered at home for more than two weeks. During this time, Tunstall gave Dolan fresh cause for wrath. On January 26, 1878, the *Mesilla Independent* published a letter from the Englishman, noting that Governor Samuel B. Axtell had declared Lincoln County in default on 1877 tax receipts. Citing a canceled check of the previous summer from McSween to Sheriff Brady, endorsed by Riley, Tunstall charged that Brady, as tax collector, had allowed The House to steal money belonging to the territory. In fact, Brady had just deposited the entire amount due with the territorial treasurer in Santa Fe, and the county no longer stood in default. He had been delayed by family illness in taking the money to Santa Fe. Dolan rushed into print with a rebuttal, but the episode left him with renewed determination to use every means at his command to smash his tormentors.[4]

The embezzlement charge against McSween offered the best means, and Dolan, with Charles Fritz in tow, rushed to Mesilla for McSween's hearing before Judge Bristol. McSween traveled in company with Tunstall, Shield, Justice of the Peace Wilson, and a Las Vegas deputy sheriff, Adolph P. Barrier, who had been assigned to guard him.

If the lawyer thought that a simple legal explanation would clear up the matter, he was badly mistaken. When he appeared before Judge Bristol on the second of February, and again on the fourth, prosecution and defense agreed that, as additional witnesses and documents were needed, the case should be put off until the April term of district court in Lincoln. Bristol set bail at eight thousand dollars, to be approved by District Attorney Rynerson, and instructed Deputy Barrier to take McSween back to Lincoln and turn him over to Sheriff Brady, to be held until bail could be posted.[5]

As the McSween party began the return journey on February 6, Dolan remained in Mesilla, busily spinning new strands of the web that already ensnared his enemy. All day he worked, with Fritz, Mrs. Scholand's attorney, and even his friend District Attorney Rynerson, who probably had never heard of conflict of interest. By evening, they had prepared papers for Fritz and Scholand to bring civil suit against McSween for ten thousand dollars. As security, they asked the court to attach McSween's property in that amount. In this measure—the ordinarily routine formality of attachment—rather than in the criminal charge of embezzlement or the civil suit for recovery of the insurance money, lay the origins of the catastrophe soon to befall Tunstall and McSween.

After leaving the writ of attachment to be filed for Judge Bristol's approval the next day, Dolan promptly took the road to the east. He left so hastily, at nightfall, because he had an appointment at Shedd's Ranch, at the western portal of the pass through the Organ Mountains east of town. There, about midnight, he met Jesse Evans and several of his gunmen, fresh from a horse-stealing foray in which Evans had picked up a bullet in his groin.

Also camping at Shedd's were McSween and his companions. Dolan still seethed over Tunstall's newspaper attack on The House. At breakfast the next morning, with Jesse Evans looking on in amusement, he angrily stomped over to the enemy's cook

41

fire and tried to provoke a duel. Three times he drew down his Winchester on Tunstall and dared him to shoot it out on the spot. But the Englishman refused to go for his own weapon, and Dolan finally gave up in disgust. During the day's journey, the Dolan party overtook the McSween party. In Dolan's buggy rode Evans, hurting from his wound.[6]

Dolan's angry attempt to bait Tunstall into a fight, and his flaunted association with Jesse Evans, forecast stormy times. The writ of attachment, already in the pocket of a courier galloping to overtake Dolan, could provoke a confrontation in which Evans's special brand of dirty work would prove useful. To have him poised nearby for action made sense. If Tunstall ever aspired to win Evans over to his cause, the sight of the bandit captain speeding along the road to Lincoln in Dolan's carriage should have disabused him. Banter, whiskey, and new suits had gained the return of his stolen stock, but they were unlikely to drive a wedge between him and Jimmy Dolan.

McSween and Tunstall reached Lincoln on February 10, two days after Dolan, to confront the consequences of Dolan's plotting. Sheriff Brady and a posse had invaded McSween's home and office and inventoried all his possessions under the writ of attachment. They had even occupied the Tunstall store and, over Widenmann's vehement protests, recorded the entire stock of merchandise. Brady based this action on the assumption that Tunstall and McSween were partners and that McSween's share was legally attachable. Technically they were not, although articles of partnership were to be signed in May. In fact, their affairs had become so intertwined that no one, least of all Sheriff Brady, could be blamed for believing that they were already partners. In addition, in the hearing on February 4, they had left Judge Bristol with this impression.[7]

Besides the attachment, McSween found Dolan, Riley, and Brady jubilantly looking forward to dropping McSween into Lincoln's cellar jail. Brady made great fun of the prospect, and Riley even swept out the cell in anticipation of its distinguished resident. The revelry, on top of the threatening events of the journey back from Mesilla, convinced Deputy Barrier that to turn McSween over to the sheriff would be to sentence him to execution by The House. Barrier stalled.[8]

Bested in his own province of legal infighting, McSween still remained steadfast in his well-known aversion to violence. Not so Tunstall, whose disposition to meet violence with violence had been growing ever since October, when he returned from St. Louis to find his horses and cattle run off.

The measure of Tunstall's new pugnacity lay in the skills of the men on his payroll. Ostensibly they were ranch hands, hired to tend his cattle on the Feliz. A few were what they seemed— Godfrey Gauss, for example, the fatherly cook, and "Dutch Martin" Martz, who had charge of branding the three hundred cows that now made up the herd.

But others handled Winchesters better than steers and seldom appeared on the Feliz. Dick Brewer, a stalwart fighter in his own right, began recruiting in October 1877. The first was John Middleton, a sturdy, tenacious drifter with a huge mustache and a proficiency with guns. Another was young Billy Bonney, the Kid, who also knew how to shoot fast and accurately. He signed on shortly after helping to break Jesse Evans out of the Lincoln jail. Frederick T. Waite and Henry C. Brown handled firearms dexterously. Six years older than the Kid, and a Choctaw from the Indian Territory, Fred Waite became his inseparable companion.

Under Brewer's leadership, these men made a formidable force if Tunstall wanted to use them as warriors. And so he regarded them, as he betrayed in a complaint to his family about the expense of his business. "It has cost a lot of money," he wrote, "for men expect to be well-paid for going on the war path."[9]

The seizure of Tunstall's store brought his gathering truculence to the surface. Whatever sympathy he felt for McSween's plight drowned in outrage over Sheriff Brady and his possemen occupying his store day and night and methodically inventorying the merchandise purchased in St. Louis as if it belonged to McSween. The day after reaching Lincoln, February 11, Tunstall and Widenmann stormed into the store and began berating the sheriff for his actions. With pistols conspicuously displayed, they warned that everyone in the store would suffer and that they had better look out. Bonney and Waite stood outside the door, brandishing their Winchesters. Brady relented so far as to release six horses and two mules that he had included on the inventory. Tunstall sent Widenmann and the other employees to drive them to safety on the Feliz.[10]

The Feliz afforded scarcely more safety than Lincoln, for Brady, doubtless egged on by Dolan, had already laid plans to attach Tunstall's stock. Again, Brady rationalized—throughout, the intent was not justice but legal rationale—that what belonged to Tunstall also belonged to McSween and could be attached. And technically, though Brady probably did not know it, the cattle McSween bought at the sheriff's auction still belonged to him. Tunstall had not reimbursed him. That would likely have been part of a general settlement agreed to when the two signed the planned articles of partnership in May.[11]

Brady entrusted the mission to a man of less sense and fortitude than he, Jacob B. "Billy" Mathews, a silent partner in The House and staunch ally of Dolan. En route, his four-man posse, all House employees, picked up some uninvited companions—Jesse Evans, Frank Baker, and two other of The Boys. They said they wanted to get back a horse they had loaned to Billy Bonney.

Widenmann and the Tunstall hands confronted this threat shortly after daybreak on February 13. While breakfasting in the two-room adobe that served as ranch headquarters, they looked out to see the nine horsemen approaching. Widenmann and Brewer stepped out and halted the party fifty yards from the cabin. Middleton, Bonney, Waite, and the others stood by to back them up.

Riding forward, Mathews explained that he had been deputized by the sheriff to attach McSween's cattle. Assured that McSween had no cattle on the Feliz, he grew confused. Brewer offered to surrender the few cattle he grazed on the Feliz and let the court decide who owned them, but Widenmann stoutly refused to give up any of Tunstall's stock without a fight. Mathews decided he would have to go back to Lincoln for new instructions.[12]

For Widenmann, the appearance of Evans and his thugs presented a dilemma. The Boys had been indicted not only for the territorial offense of stealing Tunstall's horses, but for the federal offense of stealing stock from the Indian reservation. Ever the posturing busybody, Widenmann had persuaded U.S. Marshal John Sherman to commission him as a deputy and entrust him with federal warrants for the arrest of Evans and others. Earlier in the month, Widenmann and a detachment of soldiers from Fort Stanton had tracked the fugitives to Murphy's ranch and, while they watched merrily from the hills, accepted Murphy's bland assurance that his property harbored no outlaws.[13]

Now, Widenmann had his chance to show his mettle. He asked Brewer, Middleton, Bonney, and the others to help him serve his warrants. All flatly refused, explaining that any such attempt would get them all killed, now or later. Relishing Widenmann's predicament, the outlaws advanced on him, with Evans swinging his Winchester on the lever and catching it at full cock aimed at the "marshal." Evans asked if Widenmann had a warrant for him. That was his business, Widenmann bravely replied. Evans said that if Widenmann ever came to serve a warrant, he would be the first to be gunned down. Widenmann replied that two could play that game. Meanwhile, Frank Baker methodically spun his pistol on his trigger finger, stopping it at full cock aimed at Widenmann.

Breakfast calmed tensions somewhat, but Widenmann doubtless welcomed the chance to join Mathews's party in the journey back to Lincoln. Bonney and Waite went along too. Evans and his men remained at the ranch.

In Lincoln that night, Brady gave Mathews unequivocal new instructions: raise a large force, return to the Feliz, and attach all the stock. While Mathews recruited men in Lincoln, a messenger rode down to the Pecos with orders for Billy Morton, boss of Dolan's cow camp, to round up some of the Seven Rivers stockmen. Morton engaged Bob Beckwith, Wallace Olinger, and seven others, and rode up the Peñasco. By the evening of February 17, Mathews had a combined force of twenty-three men camped at Paul's ranch on the Peñasco, eight miles south of the Tunstall cabin. Among them was Jimmy Dolan.

Also in camp, not surprisingly, were Jesse Evans and his lieutenants, who still had not recovered their horse from Billy Bon-

45

ney. Mathews went to great lengths to stress that they did not belong to his posse, and several times he perfunctorily ordered them away. He acted in response to a letter from Sheriff Brady, written the day after the new posse's departure from Lincoln, and almost certainly brought to the Peñasco by Dolan, who did not accompany Mathews but took a direct route. The letter commanded: "You must not by any means call on or allow to travel with your posse any person or persons who are known to be outlaws." Why the sheriff found it necessary to instruct his deputy not to admit outlaws to his posse, neither Brady nor Mathews ever clearly explained—perhaps because Dolan drafted the letter. With curious logic, Brady later cited this letter as proof that the posse included no outlaws.[14]

Back in Lincoln, Tunstall, McSween, and Widenmann plotted strategy. Early on February 14, Widenmann, Bonney, and Waite headed back to the Feliz to prepare the defenses. As the posse assembled eight miles to the south, the men at the ranch cut firing ports in the walls of the ranch house and barricaded doorways with grain sacks filled with earth.

Already, however, Tunstall had begun to have second thoughts. Alarming reports reached him that the enlarged posse intended to seize the cattle by force and kill all the ranch hands. Prudently, he decided not to risk his warriors in a stand on the Feliz.

The decision did not necessarily signal a new faith in the courts. Tunstall's militance subsided not at all. As late as February 16, he returned to his rooms in the store from a daylong absence to berate James Longwill, Brady's deputy in charge of the store, as a "damned thief," to threaten him with a pistol, and to score the courts as "the worst God Damned outfit of them all." Longwill thought that Tunstall had been riding the valleys to mobilize fighters who would stand with him against The House.

First, however, the Englishman had to head off a battle at his ranch. Late at night on the sixteenth, after the encounter with Longwill, he rode out of town. The next evening, he arrived on the Feliz and informed his men that they would not resist, but would return to Lincoln the next morning. He sent one of them,

William McCloskey, to the Peñasco to let Mathews know that he could impound the herd.[15]

Early on February 18, wary of treachery and primed for a fight, Mathews's posse crept up on the Tunstall ranch from front and rear. They found only Godfrey Gauss, the cook, and "Dutch Martin" Martz, assigned by Tunstall to round up and count the herd for Mathews. From Gauss, Mathews learned that Tunstall and the others had left at daybreak for Lincoln. They drove nine horses. Six were those that Brady had released on February 11, and the other three belonged to Brewer and Bonney (or Evans).

At once, however, Dolan and Mathews decided that these animals had to be attached along with the cattle. Together, the two named fourteen men to form a subposse and give chase. Mathews deputized Billy Morton, Dolan's man from the Pecos, to lead them. Jesse Evans, Frank Baker, and Tom Hill, supposedly still seeking the horse they had loaned to Bonney, also made ready to go. Mathews objected, but one of them replied that they had a right to go after their property. "Hurry up boys," Morton exclaimed impatiently, "my knife is sharp and I feel like scalping someone."[16]

By 5:00 P.M., with daylight fading, Tunstall and his men had ridden about thirty miles. Tunstall, Brewer, and Widenmann drove the horses, while Middleton and Bonney lagged some five hundred yards in the rear. They rode single file, on a trail that wound its way down a narrow, steep-sloped canyon opening on the Ruidoso. Fred Waite had been sent with a buckboard on the road, which followed a less difficult but longer route.

The Tunstall trio had just topped a crest at the head of the canyon and started down when a flock of wild turkeys rose from the grass beside the trail. Widenmann offered his rifle to Tunstall, who insisted that his friend could shoot more accurately and should go after the birds. Widenmann and Brewer gave chase, leaving Tunstall alone on the trail with the horses.

To the rear, Middleton and Bonney had crossed the divide and, hearing a commotion in the rear, turned to see horsemen galloping over the brow of the hill at full speed. Instantly, the two spurred their mounts to overtake the rest of their party. They split, with Bonney veering to the left to join Brewer and Widenmann, and Middleton making for Tunstall. By now, Brewer and Widenmann had spotted the threat. "Look there, Dick," said Widenmann as a bullet cracked between them and a fusillade sent them scampering for cover on a rocky hilltop.

Middleton reached Tunstall just as the firing erupted. He was in front of the horses and on a hillside above the trail. Calling to the Englishman to follow him, Middleton reined about and hastened up the slope to join the rest of the party. Tunstall "appeared to be very much excited and confused," Middleton stated later. "I kept calling out to him for God's sake to follow me. His last word was 'What John! What John!'"

On the reverse slope, out of sight of Tunstall, Middleton came up with his companions. Bonney had already overtaken Brewer and Widenmann, and the four urged their mounts to the top of a hill covered with trees and boulders, where they dismounted to make a stand. From the canyon came the sound of another burst of gunfire. "They've killed Tunstall," Middleton remarked.[17]

Like the Tunstall party, the subposse had strung out on the narrow trail. Some, with tired horses, lagged in the rear. Evans, Baker, and Hill had kept their distance even farther in the rear until the last ten miles, and then had pushed forward. With his horse giving out, Baker hung back, but Evans and Hill hurried to the head of the column, where Morton rode.

"Here they are," shouted someone in front as the subposse surmounted the divide at the head of the canyon. Down the trail stormed the possemen, some angling to the left and opening fire at Widenmann and Brewer, and others pushing on to round up the horses. In advance of these latter, Morton, Evans, and Hill turned from the trail and, about one hundred yards up the slope, rode into a thicket of scrub oaks that masked them from view below. A rattle of gunfire followed.

Morton came out of the thicket and explained what had happened. With Evans and Hill, he said, he had overtaken Tunstall on the hillside and, commanding him to surrender, begun reading the writ of attachment. At the same time, Evans had shouted for Tunstall to throw down his arms and he would not be harmed.

Instead, Tunstall had drawn his revolver and fired two shots, one whizzing over the neck of Morton's horse. Thereupon, all three had opened fire with their Winchesters. Morton's shot hit Tunstall in the breast, and as he turned to fall another bullet, either from Hill or Evans, smashed into the back of his head, tore up his brain, and emerged over the left eye. The horse dropped too, struck by one of the bullets. All who heard Morton agreed on what he said, although none had actually seen the shooting.

A few of the possemen went to look at the corpse. The horse still struggled in his death throes, and Tom Hill shot him again with his carbine. The men spread Tunstall's blankets beside the dead horse, dragged his body from where it had fallen, and laid it out on the blankets. Tom Hill picked up the Englishman's revolver—he carried no rifle—and passed it along to Sam Perry, who placed it beside the body. Several of the subposse remembered hearing two or three shots fired about this time, but they could not recall whether it was before or after Hill had handed them the pistol. Those who examined it before laying it beside Tunstall noted that two rounds had been fired.

With the impounded horses, the subposse made its way back to the Tunstall ranch, where they reported to Dolan and Mathews. A few men, such as Sam Perry, felt sadness over the outcome of the expedition. Others betrayed no emotion. Jesse Evans, or one of his companions, was heard to quip that Tunstall's death was small loss, that he deserved to be killed.[18]

According to the official version, Tunstall died while resisting arrest. No one on the other side believed the official version, but no credible witness stepped forward to dispute it. Of those who actually participated, only Jesse Evans later gave testimony, and he denied even being there.[19] Those certain that Tunstall had been murdered in cold blood seized on the testimony of one Albert Howe, who declared that posseman George Kitt had told him that "the boys" had told him that Morton and Hill had gunned down Tunstall after persuading him to give up, and then had fired two shots from his revolver to support their story.[20] (Whether "the boys" was meant to refer to Evans, Baker, and Hill or merely to "the boys" in the posse cannot be known.) The McSween faction fervently embraced this interpretation, even though Howe's indirect evidence, twice removed from the source, stands up in neither judicial nor historical inquiry.

Even if Tunstall drew his pistol, his death still must be seen as murder. The only uncertainty is whether it was premeditated or simply a response to opportunity. The subposse pressed its mission with a zeal that went beyond the mere legal attachment of nine horses. As soon as they spotted the quarry, Morton's men opened fire. And Morton, Evans, and Hill rode past the horses that were supposedly the object of the expedition in order to get at Tunstall, then pursued him one hundred yards off the trail. In view of this aggressive assault, Tunstall could hardly be faulted for instinctively trying to defend himself. If he did, he afforded his executioners a pretext for doing either what they had planned all along or simply what, presented with the opportunity, they knew would not displease Jimmy Dolan.

In most interpretations, Tunstall is pictured as an honorable man of business, come to free Lincoln's citizens of the yoke of The House and to sell them merchandise and buy their produce at fair prices. He is honest, open, trustworthy, public-spirited, a courageous battler against injustice, yet withal a man of peace. Opposed to violence, and trusting the courts to uphold his rights, he dies the innocent victim of greedy, wicked, and murderous men.

Greedy, wicked, and murderous they were, but Tunstall had chosen to meet them on their own terms. His motives were no less greedy, his intended exploitation of the citizens no less complete, and his style of combat only a little less violent. James Longwill was probably correct in supposing that Tunstall spent February 16 in recruiting men to strike back at The House with methods no different from those of the Mathews posse. Even as he died, men gathered at the McSween house in Lincoln. Death prevented him from taking command.

John Henry Tunstall and Jimmy Dolan had gambled in the same game. Dolan had assembled the higher hand and played it more astutely. Tunstall had lost. But Dolan had not yet won, for the lethal bullets fired on the canyon slope above the Ruidoso plunged him into a shooting war that was destined to rank as one of the most memorable conflicts in the history of the American frontier.

Maps
and
Illustrations

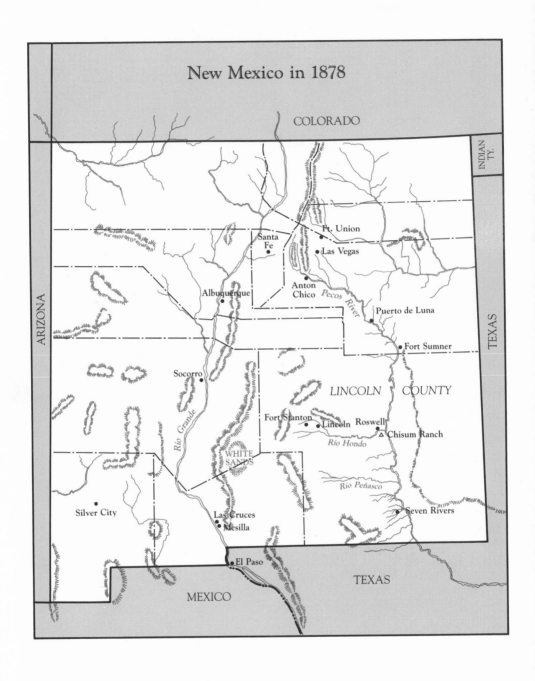

New Mexico in 1878

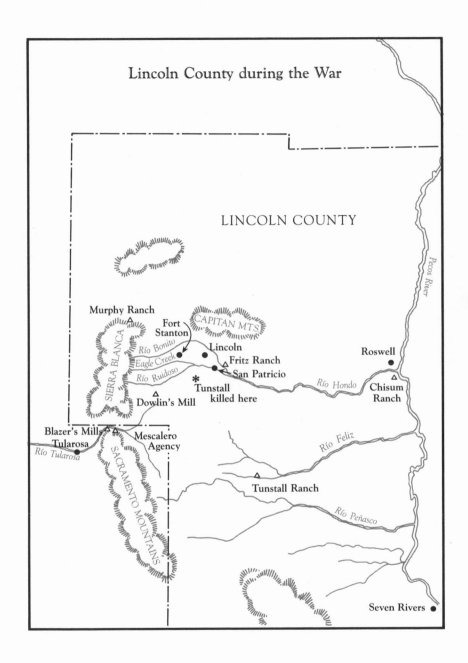

Lincoln County during the War

LINCOLN COUNTY

Pecos River

Murphy Ranch

CAPITAN MTS.

Fort
Stanton

Río Bonito

Lincoln

Roswell

Eagle Creek

Fritz Ranch

SIERRA BLANCA

Río Ruidoso

San Patricio

Río Hondo

Chisum
Ranch

Tunstall
killed here

Dowlin's Mill

Blazer's Mills

Mescalero
Agency

Río Feliz

Tularosa

Río Tularosa

SACRAMENTO MOUNTAINS

Tunstall Ranch

Río Peñasco

Seven Rivers

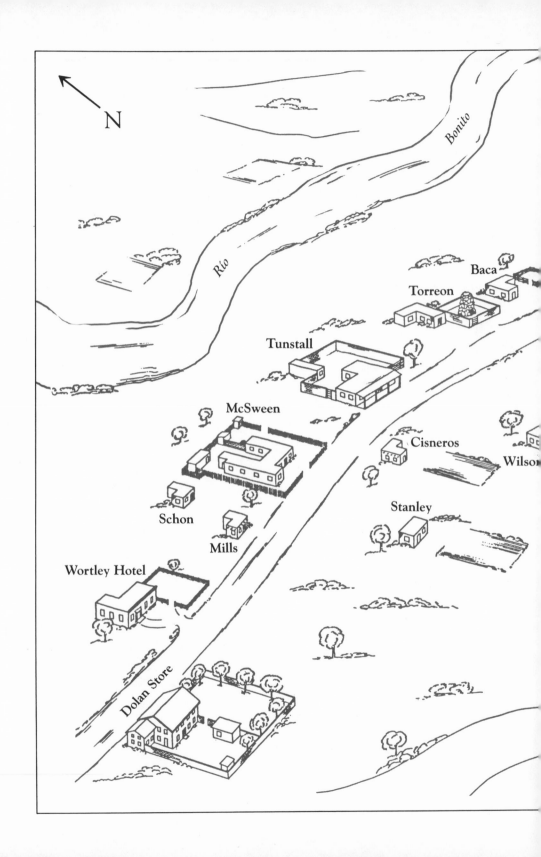

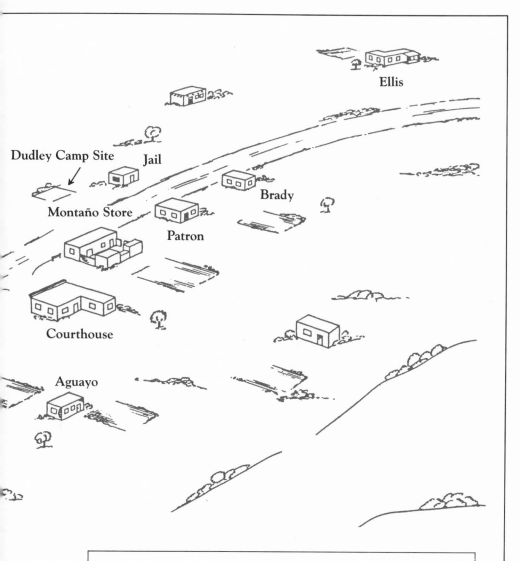

Ellis

Dudley Camp Site   Jail

Montaño Store

Patron

Brady

Courthouse

Aguayo

Lincoln in 1878

As reconstructed by Robert N. Mullin, Mullin Collection, Haley History Center, Midland, Texas. Adapted from the original in the Haley History Center.

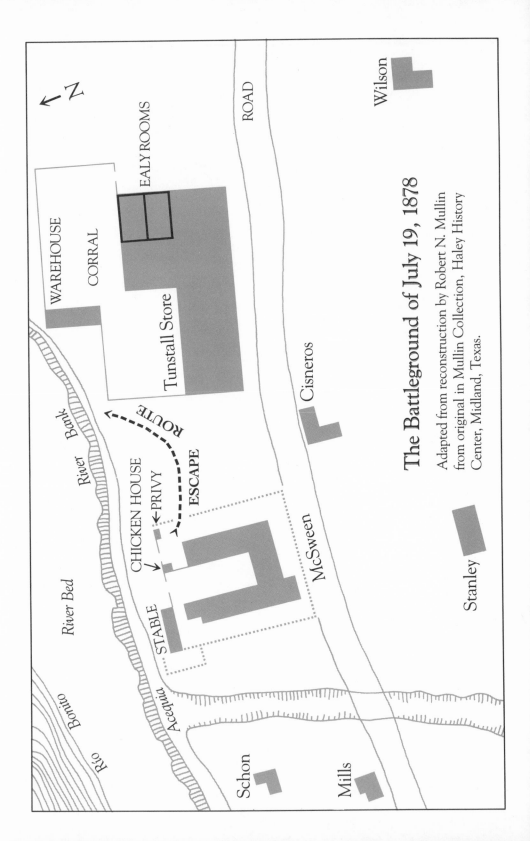

The Battleground of July 19, 1878

Adapted from reconstruction by Robert N. Mullin from original in Mullin Collection, Haley History Center, Midland, Texas.

John Henry Tunstall, the young Englishman of ample means whose
ambitions led to the Lincoln County War. With lawyer McSween, he
challenged the Murphy-Dolan-Riley combine's economic stranglehold
on Lincoln County, and the attempt cost him his life. Tunstall has
often been portrayed as a high-minded, philanthropic fellow determined to free the people from the tyranny of The House. Actually, he
intended to exploit the people in the same fashion as his opponents.
(*Special Collections, University of Arizona Library.*)

Alexander A. McSween. A lawyer of obscure credentials, a Presbyterian divine of even more obscure credentials, Mac McSween sought a personal El Dorado in Lincoln County. Ambition (and possibly an ambitious wife) drove him into schemes of dubious ethics in the effort to overturn the commercial monopoly of The House. Like his associate Tunstall, he paid with his life. (*Special Collections, University of Arizona Library.*)

Sue E. McSween. Cast of sterner material than her husband, Sue pursued an ambition even more powerful. She was more ready than Mac to use guns and gunmen to win the war, and she probably supplied the stiffening that kept his resolve from collapsing. (*Special Collections, University of Arizona Library.*)

This view of The House leadership dates from the prosperous times of the early 1870s, before Murphy was thrown out of Fort Stanton, Fritz succumbed to dropsy, and Dolan tried unsuccessfully to save the firm from bankruptcy. Left to right: James J. Dolan, Emil W. Fritz, W. J. Martin, and Lawrence G. Murphy. (*Special Collections, University of Arizona Library.*)

Post Trader's Store at Fort Stanton. (*above*) This was the center of Lawrence Murphy's commercial empire until 1873, when the War Department expelled him from the military reservation and he moved his headquarters to Lincoln. There he built the "big store" that figured in the Lincoln County War. During the war, the store at Fort Stanton, operated by Will Dowlin, provided room and board for transients. (*Special Collections, University of Arizona Library.*)

John Chisum. (*left*) Based at South Spring Ranch, near Roswell, the "cattle king of New Mexico" lent his name to the McSween faction in the Lincoln County War, but took no direct part in the fighting. The struggle between Chisum and his neighbors for Pecos grasslands was a sideshow of the war, but it lined up the small cowmen of Seven Rivers on Dolan's side against Chisum's Lincoln friends. (*Special Collections, University of Arizona Library.*)

Lincoln. A photographer named James H. Tomlinson took pictures in and around Lincoln and Fort Stanton in the late 1870s, but none has surfaced, and the earliest pictures date from the 1880s. Although taken in the 1920s (note the electrical poles and the auto garage), this picture gives an accurate over-all view of the town. The old courthouse and Murphy-Dolan store is in the foreground. (*Special Collections, University of Arizona Library.*)

The Lincoln County Courthouse, formerly the Murphy-Dolan store. This is the earliest known photograph of the "big store," later the scene of Billy the Kid's spectacular breakout. It dates from about 1883, and the men are Lincoln's lawmen of that time. (*Museum of New Mexico,* Neg. 54418.)

Fort Stanton. The military post on the Bonito nine miles above Lincoln played a crucial role in the Lincoln County War. Government contracts here and at the Indian agency afforded the only market in the area and thus the foundation of The House's monopoly. After the shooting started, the Stanton troops shifted the balance of power back and forth between the contenders according to which side controlled the sheriff. This and the following picture date from the 1880s. (*National Archives.*)

Fort Stanton.

William Brady. Prominent and respected citizen, honored war veteran, Major Brady wore the sheriff's badge in Lincoln County. As sheriffs went in that remote and violent realm, he was a good sheriff, although his longtime friendship with Lawrence Murphy subverted his impartiality in The House's struggle against Tunstall and McSween. Brady died in the middle of Lincoln's single street, riddled with bullets fired by Billy the Kid and other Regulators. (*Special Collections, University of Arizona Library.*)

Samuel Beach Axtell. A generally
able governor, Axtell was vain and
easily flattered. He uncritically
accepted the Dolan version of
events in Lincoln County and by
his blatant partisanship wrote a
record that led to his downfall.
(*National Archives.*)

Carl Schurz. Able, honest, and energetic, the German emigré served as President Hayes's relentlessly reformist Secretary of the Interior. He was the Washington official to whom both Governor Axtell and Governor Wallace reported and the intermediary between them and the President. (*National Archives.*)

Thomas Benton Catron. If there was a Santa Fe Ring, Tom Catron headed it. U.S. district attorney for New Mexico and also a shrewd, wily, and ambitious lawyer specializing in Spanish land grants, he became the most powerful man in the territory. As Jimmy Dolan's financial backer and later mortgager, he had a monetary stake in Lincoln County's troubles, but played only an indirect role in the war. (*Museum of New Mexico*, Neg. 56041.)

Judge Warren Bristol presided over the Third Judicial District Court. A timid, easily frightened man, he shrank from forceful treatment of Lincoln County's ruffians. (*Museum of New Mexico*, Neg. 8815.)

Soldiers of the Lincoln County War. Experts debate who these men were. Two are said to have been Buck Powell and Marion Turner. Another identification is Bob Speakes and John Jones (sitting) and Jim Jones and Billy the Kid (standing). Whatever their names, they graphically personify the kind of men who fought on both sides in the Lincoln County War. (*Mullin Collection, Haley History Center.*)

Charles Bowdre and wife. A farmer from the Ruidoso, Bowdre fought with the Regulators throughout the Lincoln County War. At Blazer's Mills, he shot and killed Buckshot Roberts. After McSween's death, he rode with Billy the Kid and was killed in December 1880 by Pat Garrett's posse. (*Museum of New Mexico*, Neg. 105048.)

A. M. "Gus" Gildea, a fair specimen of the Lincoln County warrior of the late 1870s. When not gunslinging, Gus punched cows or carried the mail. In 1878, the year of this picture, he rode with John Selman and the Wrestlers. (*Special Collections, University of Arizona Library.*)

William H. Bonney. People knew him as Billy Bonney, Kid Antrim, or just Kid, but not until after the Lincoln County War as Billy the Kid. He fought for McSween in every engagement of the Lincoln County War and plunged out of the lawyer's burning house with guns blazing to become a celebrity, a famous outlaw, and ultimately a demigod in the folklore of the nation. This is one of two almost identical tintypes of the Kid taken at the same time in Fort Sumner. The original of the first disappeared years ago, and most reproductions are indistinct. This is taken from the original of the second, which came to light only in 1986. Since tintypes are reversed images, this picture led to the myth of the left-handed gun. (*Museum of New Mexico, with special permission of the Lincoln County Heritage Trust.*)

Robert G. Widenmann. A German with family ties to Interior Secretary Carl Schurz, Rob Widenmann became Tunstall's closest friend in America. Others thought him an untrustworthy blowhard. When the McSween cause began to collapse in June 1878, Widenmann went to Mesilla and never returned. (*Special Collections, University of Arizona Library.*)

Richard Brewer. Tunstall's foreman and McSween's friend and ally, Dick Brewer was a good farmer, a good cowman, and a good shot with a Winchester. Most Lincolnites liked and respected him. Yet he seems to have had some part in the conspiracy to break Jesse Evans out of the Lincoln jail, and he may have been involved in stealing cattle, or buying stolen cattle, for J. H. Tunstall and Co. His part in the Lincoln County War ended abruptly with a bullet in the brain at the Blazer's Mills fight. (*Special Collections, University of Arizona Library.*)

John H. Riley (sitting) and Jacob B. Mathews. With Jimmy Dolan, Johnny Riley formed the partnership that took over L. G. Murphy & Co. in 1877. They were terrible businessmen and were tumbling into bankruptcy even as the Lincoln County War began. Riley blustered a lot, but never seemed to be around when the shooting started. Billy Mathews served as Sheriff Brady's deputy in the attempt to attach the Tunstall cattle and thoughout the conflict loyally hewed the Dolan line. (*Mullin Collection, Haley History Center.*)

Fred Waite and Henry Brown. Prominent among the Regulators, these two bravos fought in most of the skirmishes of the Lincoln County War. Waite was a close friend of Billy the Kid. The two had planned to farm together until diverted to other concerns by the war. (*Mullin Collection, Haley History Center.*)

Saturnino Baca. A leader of Lincoln's Hispanic community and respected war veteran, Captain Baca tried to stay neutral but wound up
at enmity with the McSweens. Baca's appeal for military intervention
in the Five-Day Battle proved critical in Colonel Dudley's decision to
march to Lincoln. (*Mullin Collection, Haley History Center.*)

Sam Corbet clerked for Tunstall in the Tunstall store in Lincoln. He poses here with three of Saturnino Baca's daughters. (*Mullin Collection, Haley History Center.*)

Fatherly Godfrey Gauss was chuck wrangler at the Tunstall ranch when the Mathews posse arrived to attach Tunstall's cattle. Later, as courthouse custodian in Lincoln, he witnessed the escape of Billy the Kid and even helped him try to pry off his shackles. (*Mullin Collection, Haley History Center.*)

Blazer's Mills. Scene of the classic Old West shootout that took the lives of Buckshot Roberts and Dick Brewer. The house in the right center, shared by Dr. Blazer and Indian Agent Godfroy, was the focus of the battle. This picture was taken in 1884. (*Special Collections, University of Arizona Library.*)

Nathan Augustus Monroe Dudley, lieutenant colonel of the Ninth Cavalry and post commander at Fort Stanton in 1878–79. Vain, bombastic, temperamental, muddle-minded, and bibulous, Colonel Dudley played a key role in the Five-Day Battle that ended in McSween's death. (*Collections of the Massachusetts Commandery, Military Order of the Loyal Legion, U.S. Army Military History Institute, Carlisle, Pa.*)

Edward Hatch, colonel of the Ninth Cavalry and commander of the U.S. Army's District of New Mexico. Quiet and soft-spoken, respected and well liked, Colonel Hatch willingly followed the lead of Governor Wallace in efforts to end the troubles in Lincoln County. Hatch and Dudley detested each other. (*Collections of the Massachusetts Commandery, Military Order of the Loyal Legion, U.S. Army Military History Institute, Carlisle, Pa.*)

Dr. Daniel P. Appel, post surgeon at Fort Stanton during the Lincoln County War. Although partial to the Dolan cause, Appel possessed better judgment and intellect than the other officers at the fort, and Colonel Dudley relied on him for assignments beyond the purely medical. (*Fort Davis National Historic Site, Texas.*)

Seven Rivers Warriors: Robert and John Beckwith, John Jones, Charles Robert Olinger. All four fought with Peppin's posse in the Five-Day Battle. On the final night, Bob Beckwith walked into McSween's back yard to accept the lawyer's surrender. A bullet in the left eye killed him instantly and set off the wild melee of shooting that cut down McSween and his associates. John Beckwith and John Jones were ranching (and probably rustling) partners. In 1879 Jones shot and killed Beckwith, only to be shot and killed himself by Bob Olinger, who in turn was shot and killed by Billy the Kid in his breakout from the Lincoln County courthouse in 1881. (*Mullin Collection, Haley History Center.*)

Emilie Scholand. As one of the heirs of Emil Fritz, Mrs. Scholand was
a key to Jimmy Dolan's scheme to entangle McSween in a web of legal
technicalities. Her embezzlement charge against McSween led to his
arrest, and her civil suit for recovery of damages led to the attachment
of Tunstall's cattle and his slaying. (*Special Collections, University of Arizona
Library.*)

David F. and Elizabeth Shield. Sue
McSween's sister and her husband
moved in with the McSweens in
the summer of 1877. David and
Mac formed a law partnership, but
it collapsed in the rubble of war.
David went to Las Vegas to establish a new practice, while Elizabeth
remained in Lincoln. She was with
Sue in the McSween house when
the Peppin posse set it afire. (*Special
Collections, University of Arizona
Library.*)

Reverend Taylor F. Ealy. A "medical missionary" dispatched by the Presbyterians at McSween's behest, Dr. Ealy patched up the casualties of the Lincoln County War while decrying the iniquitous ways and Catholic leanings of the citizenry. (*Special Collections, University of Arizona Library.*)

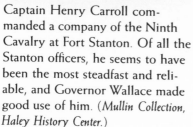

Captain Henry Carroll commanded a company of the Ninth
Cavalry at Fort Stanton. Of all the
Stanton officers, he seems to have
been the most steadfast and reliable, and Governor Wallace made
good use of him. (*Mullin Collection,
Haley History Center.*)

Lew Wallace. Soldier, lawyer, politician, and literary light, Lew Wallace was appointed New Mexico's
governor after Frank Angel's investigation discredited Governor Axtell. Wallace was supposed to clean
up Lincoln County, but he became
so engrossed in writing *Ben-Hur*
that he slighted this mission for five
months and then made only modest contributions to its fulfillment.
(*Museum of New Mexico,* Neg. 13123.)

Tomas O'Folliard. A late-comer to the Regulators, young O'Folliard was in the McSween house on July 19, 1878, and escaped with Billy the Kid and others. He worshiped the Kid and rode with his gang until shot down by Garrett's posse in December 1880. (*Museum of New Mexico,* Neg. 10472.)

5

The
Regulators

SHORTLY BEFORE NOON on February 19, 1878, the new preacher arrived in town. Acting on McSween's request of the previous autumn, the Presbyterian Board of Home Missions had assigned a "medical missionary" to Lincoln. The Reverend Dr. Taylor F. Ealy, a dour zealot from Pennsylvania, would find this tough and distant corner of the frontier almost equally divided in its spiritual allegiance between the pope in Rome and the devil in hell. Followers of both would pose severe challenges to his talents.

The clergyman and his party—his wife and two little girls and a young lady, Susan Gates, recruited as a mission assistant—drove their buckboard into the middle of the Lincoln County War. Dolan gunmen draped with cartridge belts stopped them on the edge of town and searched their wagon. At the McSween house, Mac walked out to welcome them. It was a bad time to start a church, he remarked, but invited them to come in. The Ealys carried in their belongings and set up housekeeping temporarily with the Shields, who lived in the east wing of the big U-shaped adobe.[1]

Ealy's medical skills were called upon immediately. After dark on February 19, John Newcomb, Brewer's neighbor on the Ruidoso, drove into town with the slain John Henry Tunstall in the back of his wagon. With the body laid out on a table in the Tunstall store, Dr. Ealy joined with Dr. Daniel Appel, the post surgeon at Fort Stanton, to perform an autopsy. A coroner's jury gathered to hear the testimony of Ealy and others. Next day, with the aid of rancher Frank Coe, the two doctors embalmed the body, for McSween supposed that ultimately the family would want it shipped back to London. Coe recalled that Billy Bonney walked in, gazed for a time at the body, and then declared solemnly: "I'll get some of them before I die."[2]

The slaying also called on Dr. Ealy's spiritual services, for McSween asked him to officiate at the funeral. Sebrian Bates, the McSweens' black servant, dug a grave just east of the Tunstall store, and on the afternoon of February 21 many of the townspeople gathered to hear the new preacher's funeral oration. Sue's organ was carried to the graveside, and in her absence in the East Mary Ealy played hymns while Juan Patrón and a few of the men sang. Then, with Squire Wilson translating for the Hispanics, Ealy held forth on "If a man die, shall he live again?"

For himself, Ealy thought so. In "Our Father's House," he ruminated, there were many mansions, and in one, someday, the dead man's "dear parents" would surely be reunited with their son.

Three days later, on a Sunday, twenty people gathered in the McSween parlor for what Ealy termed "the first Sabbath School ever held in Lincoln." Mary played hymns on Sue's piano, and Ealy preached. He felt very encouraged, he wrote optimistically, "because there is such a vast field for usefulness, if the enemies to Christianity only allow us to live."[3]

More than spiritual matters occupied Lincolnites in the hectic days following the death of Tunstall. In a tumble of bewildering moves fraught with the potential for bloodshed, the rival factions maneuvered for advantage.

On the night of February 18, forty to fifty armed men crowded McSween's big house in Lincoln. They did not come in response to word of Tunstall's death, for Brewer, Widenmann, Middleton, Bonney, and Waite did not arrive with that news until around midnight, hours after the men had assembled. Almost certainly, they came instead at Tunstall's invitation two days earlier.[4]

These fighters had diverse motives for embracing Tunstall's cause. For one thing, he had offered them wages of up to four dollars a day; as he had observed to his parents, men expected to

be well paid for going on the warpath.[5] Some had personal grievances against The House. Others resented The House's control
over their lives and saw in Tunstall's challenge a hope of throwing
off the economic yoke. Most disliked the corrupt and brutal practices of The House. About half were Anglo and half Hispanic.

The events of February 18 further braced these men to their
mission. Tunstall's death came as a shock, and they vowed to
avenge what everyone present regarded as premeditated murder,
perpetrated by men deputized by Brady but paid by Dolan. Incit-
ing the people in the McSween house even more, damning evidence of the evil ways of The House fell almost providentially
into their midst. A very drunk Johnny Riley intruded into the
McSween parlor and, in a maudlin demonstration that he came
unarmed, emptied his pockets. Left behind among the papers
were a notebook with cryptic entries that suggested all manner of
dirty work by The House and a letter from Rynerson to "Friends
Dolan and Riley" that clearly arrayed the district attorney on
their side. "Shake that McSween outfit up until it shells out and
squares up," he had written in reference to the insurance money,
"and then shake it out of Lincoln. . . . Be assured I shall help you
all I can, for I believe there never was found a more scoundrelly
set than that outfit."[6]

Alexander McSween had no aptitude for the kind of fight
Tunstall had probably intended. He excelled at manipulating
legal, commercial, and financial systems, but he had no experience in fighting a war with guns. Almost alone of Lincolnites, he
carried neither rifle nor pistol, and by temperament he shrank
from physical combat. Words, not bullets, were his weapons. Already demoralized by the maneuvers that had placed him outside
of the law, he now instinctively groped for legal rather than violent solutions.

Clearly, McSween could expect no acceptable legal solution
from the district court—Judge Bristol and District Attorney
Rynerson had amply demonstrated where their sentiments lay—
and certainly not from Sheriff Brady and his posse manned by
Dolan employees. The only other lawful authority rested in the
justice of the peace and constable of Precinct No. 1. McSween's
strategy, therefore, centered on Squire Wilson. Dull witted and

barely literate, the bumbling old man could be persuaded to almost any course of action, however senseless, by almost anyone.
Like Judge Bristol, he could issue arrest warrants. And like Sheriff
Brady, Constable Atanacio Martínez could assemble a lawful
posse—the men gathered in the McSween house—to serve
them. Thus, the gathering conflict pitted a faction claiming the
lawful sanction of the district court and the county sheriff against
a faction claiming the lawful sanction of the justice of the peace
and the precinct constable.

McSween went into action the very next day, February 19,
even before John Newcomb brought in the body of Tunstall.
Brewer, Middleton, and Bonney swore affidavits before Justice
Wilson charging eighteen members of Mathews's posse, including
Dolan, with the murder of Tunstall. Based on the affidavits,
Wilson wrote out warrants for the arrest of these men.

At the same time, McSween went before Wilson to accuse
Sheriff Brady of larceny. The day before, apparently alarmed by
the ominous activity at the McSween house, Brady had called on
Captain George A. Purington to send some soldiers from Fort
Stanton to protect him from harm, and then had thoughtlessly
authorized the deputies in the Tunstall store to provide a small
amount of hay for the detachment's horses. The hay belonged to
the Tunstall estate, not the county, and McSween lost no time in
invoking the law. Dutifully, Justice Wilson issued warrants for the
arrest of Sheriff Brady and his men in the Tunstall store for larceny.[7]

Constable Martínez viewed his part in McSween's strategy
with understandable trepidation. Sheriff Brady and his deputies
could not be expected to submit tamely to arrest, and to call on
the formidable shooters in the McSween house to aid in serving
Wilson's warrants made a bloody gun battle almost inevitable.
When the constable balked at the role assigned him, however,
Billy Bonney stepped forward with a blunt threat to do as he was
told or be killed.[8]

Before Martínez had to act, help came from an unexpected
source: Rob Widenmann and the U.S. Army. While McSween
worked on Justice Wilson on February 19, Widenmann rode to
Fort Stanton with news of Tunstall's death. During the night a
courier brought word from Lincoln that Jesse Evans was in town.

Still a deputy U.S. marshal and still carrying the warrants for Evans's arrest, Widenmann asked Captain Purington once again to furnish him with a military posse to help in serving the warrants.[9]

Widenmann's soldiers provided a perfect screen for Martínez's operation. Neither Brady nor his deputies would dare resist if they endangered U.S. soldiers. Before daybreak on the twentieth, therefore, Widenmann and his twenty-five black cavalrymen, accompanied by Martínez and his posse of about a dozen men, searched the Dolan store. They found no one for whom either had warrants. Afterward, they proceeded to the Tunstall store. There they failed again to find Evans, but they did find Brady, Longwill, and the other men who had held the store since February 9 and who now stood charged with theft of Tunstall's hay. With soldiers present, Brady and his deputies choked back their impulse to resist and peacefully surrendered to Martínez and his men, who hauled them before Justice Wilson for arraignment. Wilson released the deputies, but made Brady post a two-hundred-dollar bond for his appearance at the spring term of district court. Later, in retaliation, Brady had Martínez and all of his possemen charged with riot and resisting a sheriff, but he made no attempt to recapture the store.

Martínez still had murder warrants against members of the Mathews posse, who were now in part gathered at the Dolan store. Later on February 20, after the arraignment of Brady before Justice Wilson, the constable deputized Billy Bonney and Fred Waite and went to the store to serve the warrants. Brady had taken about all he could for one day, and he and his deputies met the trio with drawn guns, disarmed them, and placed them under arrest for resisting a sheriff. Later that day, they allowed Martínez to leave, but they held Bonney and Waite until the next night. Only the presence of soldiers prevented the rising tension from erupting in a gun fight between the two forces, and even so a stray bullet killed a trooper's horse.[10]

McSween's maneuvers had gained him the Tunstall store, but little else. He remained a fugitive, free of Brady's jail only because Deputy Barrier refused to turn him over to the sheriff. He had attempted to post bond for his appearance at court in April, but the bond came back from Mesilla disapproved by Rynerson on the spurious grounds that the sureties, some of the most prosperous men in the county, could not make good their pledges. The truth dawned that Rynerson would not approve any bond and that McSween would have to spend six weeks in jail awaiting the opening of district court. Barrier would have none of it; he decided to stick with McSween.[11]

Dolan counterattacked. On February 21, he left for Mesilla to get new warrants from Judge Bristol for the arrest of McSween and Barrier. According to a report that reached McSween on February 24, Dolan had sent a message telling Riley to alert the military at Fort Stanton to aid Brady in serving the warrant once it had been obtained, and to have Jesse Evans ready "to do his part" as soon as the soldiers had withdrawn. Picturing himself murdered by Evans in Brady's jail, McSween decided that he had to flee. With Tunstall properly buried, he made out his will and, accompanied by the faithful Barrier, headed for the mountains.[12]

McSween thus forfeited control of his little army. Martínez had scant stomach for the role, and probably lacked leadership qualities as well. With the lawyer's flight, command devolved on Dick Brewer.

The Martínez posse gave birth to the fighting force that styled itself the "Regulators." Although they professed to be above the partisanship of McSween and Dolan, for the next five months they fought McSween's battle. Like Dolan's warriors, they rode under color of law, for Brewer bore a commission as special constable from Justice Wilson and carried the warrant issued from his court for the arrest of Tunstall's killers.

About a dozen men, all Anglo, formed the core group of the Regulators and figured in almost all their operations from the maneuvers of late February to the shootout at McSween's home in July. Other men, both Anglo and Hispanic, on occasion swelled the ranks to twenty and even thirty. In the final battle for Lincoln, they numbered as many as sixty.[13]

These men were not mere hired guns. Enemies accused McSween of paying each Regulator four dollars a day. Tunstall had probably promised such wages, but McSween had no money.

While holding forth the prospect of reward from the purse of the elder Tunstall in London, he managed to furnish them with only food and ammunition. The Regulators fought, therefore, in the hope of ultimate gain and because they wanted to break the grip of The House on their daily lives. They were as lawless and violent as Dolan's fighters, as given to settling disputes with Winchester and Colt, and as prone to supplementing their income with occasional larceny. But like them, also, they were farmers, stockmen, or laborers who worked at honest toil. Paradoxically, although they resorted to the same lawless tactics as their enemies, they genuinely saw themselves as fighting for restoration of law that had been corrupted by those entrusted with its integrity, and they went about their bloody task with the same lofty sense of purpose that characterized vigilante movements elsewhere on the American frontier.[14]

Yet McSween's Regulators were not typical vigilantes, although *regulators*, as a noted authority has pointed out, is the good old American term for vigilantes—men assembled to "regulate," or to set right, an intolerable situation.[15] That, of course, is how McSween and his followers saw their purpose, and that was the image that they wanted to project. McSween probably coined the term; he was the only one widely enough read to know the century-old history of vigilantes who called themselves "regulators."

The Lincoln County Regulators, however, differed in several important ways from the usual vigilantes. True vigilantes formed in the absence or breakdown of the regular law enforcement and judicial machinery. In Lincoln County, the machinery had not broken down; it had simply been captured by the other side. The McSween Regulators, moreover, presented themselves as agents of the law—the justice of the peace court—rather than as extralegal friends of the law. Unlike vigilantes elsewhere, they were not defending an established order, they adopted no written compact or rules of organization and procedure, and they held no formal trials of offenders. They could try no one without belying their posture as officers of the justice of the peace's constabulary, so they simply executed their victims on one pretext or another.

57

Although displaying some characteristics of typical vigilantes, the Lincoln County Regulators did not ride in the mainstream of the American vigilante tradition.[16]

While McSween and Barrier hid first at one mountain farmhouse, and then at another, Brewer led the Regulators down to the Pecos to search for Billy Morton, boss of Dolan's cow camp near Seven Rivers. As head of the subposse that had cut down Tunstall, he was the most wanted man named on Justice Wilson's warrant.

Near Seven Rivers on March 6, the Regulators flushed Morton and Evans's henchman Frank Baker. After a galloping chase of five miles, during which almost a hundred bullets failed to drop the fugitives, their horses gave out and they holed up in a dugout. Cornered and outnumbered, they gave up. One of the Regulators wanted to dispatch them without further ceremony, but Brewer objected. Even so, he was sorry they had surrendered, Brewer told Morton and Baker, for he had not wanted to take them alive. In Roswell, Morton posted a letter to a friend in Virginia that predicted his and Baker's death before they could reach Lincoln.[17]

En route to Roswell, William McCloskey had attached himself to the party. Formerly an employee of Tunstall, he had also been friendly with many of the Mathews possemen, including Morton. Brewer distrusted him. Although destined for Chisum's ranch, McCloskey sensed homicide in the offing and decided to stay with Morton.

Morton's fears proved to be well founded. On March 9, in the Capitan foothills, he paid with his life for his part in the Tunstall killing. Brewer's story of what happened paralleled, in some ways, Morton's story of Tunstall's death. According to Brewer's version, while riding beside McCloskey, Morton snatched his pistol and shot and killed him. Morton and Baker then broke for the hills, only to be gunned down by the Regulators. The other version, however, had the Regulators agreeing to kill their prisoners and McCloskey objecting. One of the Regulators, possibly Jim French, solved that problem by shooting McCloskey, which signaled the break of Morton and Baker. The bodies of each, by no coincidence, contained eleven bullets, one for each Regulator.[18]

Hardly anyone believed Brewer's story. Yet no participant ever admitted to any other, and it stood as the official version. If Morton actually tried so foolhardy a move, however, he was desperate to the point of irrationality and also willing to kill the only friend he had in the group. More plausibly, the slaying of Morton and Baker was as surely an act of murder as the slaying of Tunstall, and perhaps more so.

While the Regulators pursued their brand of justice, Dolan continued to mobilize new and more powerful forces, as McSween discovered when he and Barrier returned to Lincoln on March 9. Only hours earlier, New Mexico Governor Samuel B. Axtell had visited Lincoln. His presence testified to the Santa Fe connections of Dolan and Riley, now strengthened immensely by the direct interest of the most powerful man in the territory. Thomas B. Catron held the mortgage on their property, and naturally he did not want to see it endangered.

Chiefly through Catron, with an assist from Rynerson, Dolan had captured Governor Axtell. Able but vain and impulsive, quick to form judgments and slow to surrender them, the governor surely never thought to doubt the Catron–Rynerson version of events in Lincoln County. On March 4, he telegraphed President Rutherford B. Hayes, urging him to order federal troops to take a hand in the conflict. In due course, orders reached Fort Stanton for the garrison to assist the territorial civil officers— that is, Bristol, Rynerson, and Brady—in enforcing the law.[19]

The governor's three-hour visit to Lincoln on March 9 left the McSween cause in wreckage. He refused to listen to anyone partial to McSween. Worse, he issued a proclamation declaring Squire Wilson to be occupying the office of justice of the peace illegally, and naming Judge Bristol as the only proper source of legal processes and Sheriff Brady as the only proper authority to execute them. Thereby, in one stroke, Axtell demolished McSween's legal edifice, invalidating Dick Brewer's commission as special constable as well as the warrant he carried, and dissolving the color of law under which the Regulators operated.[20]

Brewer reported to McSween the next day, March 10, and learned that he and the Regulators had been outlawed. To avoid arrest for the killing of Morton, Baker, and McCloskey, they took to the mountains.

McSween, of course, still remained outside the law. Again he fled, with the loyal Barrier still at his side. This time, he took refuge at John Chisum's ranch on the Pecos, and here Sue, returning from the East, joined him.

For the balance of March, while awaiting the opening of district court, both sides marked time. For one thing, fifty miles distant from Lincoln, McSween exerted little influence on the activities of the Regulators. For another, Dolan did not feel up to pushing the fight very aggressively either, for on March 11, in Lincoln, he dismounted before his horse had come to a stop and wound up with a broken leg.[21] McSween agonized over what to do. District court offered his only hope of clearing himself of the crime of embezzlement. But he had to get before the court without first falling into the custody of Sheriff Brady, for McSween and all his friends firmly believed that the arrest warrant that the sheriff carried would, if served, turn out to be a death warrant, and he would never get his day in court.

Near the end of March, a party of the Regulators met with McSween at Chisum's. What passed between them is recorded mainly in the recollections of an octogenarian with a sharp memory for events but almost none for chronology. Francisco Trujillo, one of the group, heard McSween say that he was going into Lincoln on the next Monday for the opening of court, and add: "As soon as I arrive, Brady is going to try and arrest me and you should not let him get away with it. If I am arrested I shall surely be hung and I don't want to die, while if you kill Brady you shall earn a reward." Whether at McSween's urging or through their own unprompted agreement, the Regulators headed for Lincoln resolved to kill Sheriff Brady.[22]

If McSween urged Brady's assassination, he stepped out of character. By the end of March, however, he was a truly desperate man, faced with personal and financial ruin and possibly even murder. Moreover, Sue must have had her say. Made of tougher fiber than her mate, she was even more obsessively ambitious for wealth and more ruthless in its quest. As the war grew hotter, she showed herself just as ready as the Regulators to fight back with violence and even homicide. To have urged Brady's slaying would have been less out of character for her than for her husband.[23]

On the night of March 31, six men slipped into the corral behind the Tunstall store. An adobe wall with a gate projected eastward from the rear of the building, hiding the corral from the street. The executioners were Frank McNab, John Middleton, Billy Bonney, "Big Jim" French, Fred Waite, and Henry Brown. Shortly before the fatal moment, Rob Widenmann came out—to feed Tunstall's dog, he explained later. Most people believed that he was part of the group, too, and anti-McSween newspapers later contemptuously labeled him "the dog-feeder."

About nine o'clock on the morning of April 1, Sheriff Brady walked down the street from the west, accompanied by deputies Billy Mathews, George Hindman (a member of the Morton sub-posse), George Peppin, and John Long. They were on the way to the courthouse to post notice that court would not meet this day, as had been erroneously advertised, but on the second Monday of April.

As the officers passed the wall, the men behind it rose, leveled their Winchesters, and let loose a fusillade of deadly fire. Brady fell, riddled by a dozen bullets. Another bullet hit Hindman, and still another went wild and pierced both thighs of Justice of the Peace Wilson, who was hoeing onions at his home across the street. Hindman, moaning for water, tried to rise. Ike Stockton, who kept a saloon nearby, dashed out to help, but another shot finished the deputy. The other deputies ran to the safety of a house across the street.

One reason for killing Brady was to obtain the warrant for McSween's arrest. Bonney and French sprinted from the corral into the street and stooped over Brady to rifle his pockets. From their refuge, Mathews and his companions opened fire. The Kid picked up Brady's Winchester, but was struck in the thigh by a slug, which went through him and hit French in the thigh too. Billy dropped the rifle, and the two limped back to safety.[24]

Bonney's wound did not disable him, but French could not ride. While Bonney and the other Regulators lost themselves in the timber along the Bonito behind the Tunstall store, French hobbled to the back door of the McSween house, where Rever-

61

end Ealy and his family were living in McSween's absence. The doctor ran a silk handkerchief through the wound and turned French over to Sam Corbet, Tunstall's former clerk. Corbet hid French somewhere—under the floor, with two pistols clutched in his hands, according to Ealy. The surviving deputies quickly tracked the blood to the back door and searched the house three times without finding French. That night, the Kid stole back to town and rescued his friend.[25]

The slaying of Brady threw Lincoln into an uproar, and the appearance, later in the day, of Alex and Sue McSween and John Chisum added to the confusion. Deputy George Peppin, assuming Brady's mantle with questionable legality, arrested almost everyone he found at the McSween house and the Tunstall store— Widenmann, Shield, and the two blacks, George Washington and George Robinson. He also resolved to arrest McSween on the warrant retrieved from Brady's body.

The lawyer had gone to the home of Isaac Ellis. Recent arrivals from Colfax County, the Ellis family operated a store on the east edge of Lincoln and had risen to prominence in community affairs. A staunch ally of McSween, Isaac also served as administrator of the Tunstall estate.

For the task of seizing McSween, Peppin went backed by soldiers. Earlier in the day, he had sent word to Fort Stanton of Brady's murder, and Captain Purington had hurried to town with a troop of black cavalrymen. While Peppin remained outside the Ellis store, Lieutenant George W. Smith played the part of mediator. McSween refused to surrender to Peppin, contending that Brady's death cancelled his status as deputy. He agreed to give up to Smith, however, on condition that he be taken to Fort Stanton and held there until court opened a week later. The lieutenant accepted the terms.[26]

Peppin did too, though reluctantly and only after a loud argument with McSween in front of his house. Captain Purington had his cavalry drawn up there, and Peppin's possemen were once more searching the house for Brady's assassins. McSween vehemently protested against any search without a legal warrant. Peppin replied that he did it on Purington's authority. Purington denied giving Peppin permission for any action, but refused to interfere.

As the argument grew more and more heated, a stranger in town dove into the fray. Montague R. Leverson was a high-strung Englishman seeking suitable fields to colonize immigrants. He had ridden up from the Pecos with the McSween party in Chisum's buckboard. A verbosely emotional meddler, he lectured Purington on the constitutional prohibition against unlawful search, even warning his soldiers of dire consequences if they did not stop it. Exasperated, Purington exploded: "Damn the constitution and you for a fool." The shouting ended when the captain simply started back to Fort Stanton, and the McSween party hurried to catch up rather than fall into the clutches of Peppin and his deputies.[27]

Whether at McSween's instigation or not, the killing of Brady badly harmed the McSween cause. Cutting down a lawman from ambush, without warning, violated the code to which most people subscribed. Besides, Brady enjoyed wide respect, even from McSween supporters, and many of them began to doubt that the Regulators were any better than the Dolan warriors who rode in Brady's posse. Then, only three days after Brady's death, the Regulators once more offended public opinion.

On April 4, fourteen Regulators appeared at South Fork, the location of Blazer's Mills and the Mescalero Apache Indian Agency. Dick Brewer led, and Billy Bonney and Jim French were there, seemingly no worse for the bullet that had drilled them both in the Brady shooting. As they ate lunch at the Blazer residence, Andrew L. "Buckshot" Roberts rode up on his mule. A small-time stockman from the Ruidoso, he had formerly worked at Dolan's South Fork store and had friends in the tiny community. He had also ridden with the Mathews posse that killed Tunstall, and Brewer had his name on the warrant from Justice Wilson, although that document, of course, had been invalidated by Governor Axtell.

Roberts was a tough scrapper, not easily intimidated. Before the others came out of the house, Frank Coe took him around to a side porch and tried to persuade him to surrender. He refused.

Some of Brewer's men came around the corner of the building intent on making the arrest. At once, firing erupted. Charlie Bowdre put a bullet into Roberts's groin. Crumpling to the porch, the game little fighter, despite a bad arm, worked his Winchester carbine with accurate effect. One bullet tore off Bowdre's gun belt, another hit John Middleton in the chest, and still another smashed the stock of George Coe's rifle and mangled his trigger finger. As the Regulators backed off, Roberts struggled through a doorway, dragged a mattress from a bed, and barricaded himself for defense.

Billy Bonney had remained in the front of the house. Now, according to Frank Coe, "the Kid slipped in between the wall and a wagon. Roberts took a shot at him, just shaved his arm. Kid backed out as it was too hot there for him."[28]

Dick Brewer thought he saw a way to fire at Roberts without exposing himself. Circling through a corral and down the creek, he posted himself behind a stack of logs about one hundred yards from the doorway. Roberts glimpsed the puff of smoke from Brewer's first shot and took careful aim. When he rose for a second shot, Roberts fired. The bullet hit Brewer in the forehead and sliced neatly through his brain.

That cooled the ardor of the Regulators. They pulled out, leaving Roberts to linger painfully through the night before dying. In Lincoln, Middleton and Coe sought treatment from Dr. Ealy. Of Coe, Ealy remembered, "I took off a thumb and finger for him after that fight."[29]

Blazer's Mills cost McSween further public sympathy. Even the death of the well-liked Brewer did not offset the feeling that Roberts had fallen before an overwhelming and somehow unfair onslaught. His courageous defense, moreover, earned the admiration of people who set high store on skilled gunfighting. To make matters worse for McSween, rumors circulated that the Regulators had been at Blazer's Mills as part of a plot to ambush Judge Bristol and District Attorney Rynerson, traveling from Mesilla to hold the April term of court in Lincoln.[30]

At last, after six weeks of evading the arrest warrant issued by Judge Bristol, McSween would have his day in court.

For the Reverend Dr. Ealy, those had been six trying weeks. He had launched his Sabbath school, with ten to twenty communicants showing up at the McSween parlor each Sunday evening. But nothing in his theological training had prepared him for his other experiences. One such was an encounter with Peppin deputy Jack Long. On March 12, in his fairly common state of inebriation, Long accosted Ealy as he made his way down the street to the Ellis store. Leaning on Ealy's arm, Long informed him in slurred speech that he had helped hang a preacher over in Arizona and, while Ealy need not expect the same fate, a whore would be more welcome in Lincoln than the Pennsylvania missionary. Leaving his errand incomplete, Ealy scurried back to the safety of home.[31]

The clergyman tried to be objective, but he quickly embraced the McSween cause. For his Scotch host, he had nothing but praise. "He is a noble man," he informed the head of Presbyterian missionary work in the West, "and would have done well to have belonged to the Covenanters" (an allusion to Scotch Presbyterian history). As for the opposition, "they are a dirty set of Irish cut throats, and you know what their religion is. They drink whiskey, gamble, and nothing is too bad for them."[32]

In one of his rare attempts at humor, Ealy summed up the state of affairs in Lincoln: "They say it is very healthy here. None, scarcely, die a natural death. Because they do not get an opportunity. There is too much lead in the air."[33]

Less elegantly, a cowboy down on the Pecos pronounced the same verdict: "They all wanted to kill somebody. Every son-of-a-bitch over there wanted to kill somebody."[34]

6

Judicial
Interlude

LIEUTENANT COLONEL NATHAN A. M. DUDLEY, Ninth
U.S. Cavalry, assumed command of Fort Stanton at noon on
April 4, 1878.

The new commanding officer looked every inch the veteran
of twenty-three years of service in the United States Army—his
large, erect frame surmounted by a finely shaped head; his sweeping dragoon mustache, graying hair, and brushy eyebrows shad-
ing piercing eyes; his prominent forehead and assertive nose; and
with even a monocle suspended from a chain around his neck.

Behind the imposing facade, however, lurked a man whose
genuine professional dedication consistently fell victim to a small
intellect and a huge vanity. He suffered from muddled thought
and bad judgment, the result of mediocre endowments impaired
by years of dissipation. He got drunk often, and whiskey more or
less influenced most of his actions. He compensated for his deficiencies with pomposity, bellicosity, petty despotism, and an extraordinary aptitude for contention. Quick to resent a slight,
whether real or imagined, and quick to criticize, whether justly
or not, Dudley rocked from one controversy to another, and
from one court-martial to another, throughout his career.[1]

Dudley came to Fort Stanton simply because he had to be
sent somewhere. A bruising court-martial at Fort Union had un-
fitted him for continued command of that post, and Fort Stanton
offered the only opening in New Mexico suited to his rank. He
arrived ignorant of the issues and personalities that had plunged

the area into factional warfare, and just as it exploded in new crises. Four days earlier, Brady and Hindman had been gunned down in Lincoln, and at almost the exact moment that Dudley assumed command the shootout at Blazer's Mills erupted.[3]

Despite his deficiencies, Dudley promised some improvement over his predecessor. A plodding mediocrity, Captain Purington did not think too clearly or too quickly. Orders from Washington had plunged him into a civil conflict calling for the most delicate balancing of the military role, and he lacked the subtlety to cope with it. His responses to the killing of Tunstall in February and the assassination of Brady and Hindman in April had been clumsy and inappropriate and reflected his open partiality for Jimmy Dolan. Dudley would do better, though not much.

Indians, not feuding citizens, were the main concern of the fort's garrison. The Mescaleros had a history of unpredictability, occasional thefts, and periodic outbreaks. The post mustered roughly a hundred men, black troopers of the Ninth Cavalry and white footmen of the Fifteenth Infantry. They were too few for their Indian mission, much less for civil duty in addition.

But Governor Axtell had induced the president to send in the troops with orders to assist the territorial officials in upholding the law. Which territorial officials, Purington asked—Sheriff Brady, Deputy U.S. Marshal Widenmann, Justice Wilson? The district commander, Colonel Edward Hatch, ruled in Brady's favor, and thus unknowingly allied the federal soldiers with The House.[2]

Colonel Dudley quickly perceived something awry. Without a shred of legal documentation, he found himself officially responsible for five civil prisoners, one of whom held appointment as a deputy U.S. marshal. These were McSween, Widenmann, Shield, and the two blacks, Washington and Robinson, whom Captain Purington had accepted from Deputy Peppin on April 1, after Brady's slaying. Dudley promptly released these men, but allowed them to remain at the fort under military protection.

Dudley understood what Purington's slower mind did not: the detention of Widenmann placed the army in the awkward position of interfering with a federal law officer.[3] This had more than remote significance, for one of the men for whom Widen-

67

mann carried an arrest warrant had been at Fort Stanton for several weeks. On March 9, Jesse Evans and Tom Hill had tried to rob the camp of a sheep drover near Tularosa. In an exchange of gunfire with a camp attendant, Hill had been killed and Evans so severely wounded in the wrist that he had come to Fort Stanton for medical treatment.[4]

Judge Bristol and other officers of the district court reached Fort Stanton on the afternoon on April 7, accompanied by the cavalry escort Dudley had sent to meet them after learning of the threat from the Regulators. A flurry of arrests followed. U.S. Marshal John Sherman joined with Widenmann to arrest Jesse Evans on the federal charge, pending since November, of stealing stock on the Indian reservation. Judge Bristol issued warrants for the arrest of McSween for embezzlement and Shield, Widenmann, Washington, and Robinson as suspects in the Brady murder. He then appointed John Copeland, the post butcher at Fort Stanton, as a special deputy sheriff to serve the warrants. All six wound up in military custody, and Dudley had the documentation he needed to hold them until court convened.[5]

The term of court proved to be chaotic. Almost a week elapsed before juries could be assembled and empaneled. Soldiers escorted the judge and attorneys to Lincoln for each day's session and stood guard to ensure order. Passions flared in and out of court. Almost everyone in the county had chosen sides, and in neither witnesses nor jurors could objectivity prevail over partisanship, or public duty over fear instilled by the atmosphere of intimidation.

In his opening charge to the grand jury, Judge Bristol himself set the partisan tone. Affecting a great show of impartiality, he threw off all judicial detachment and treated the grand jury to a detailed statement of the case against McSween for embezzlement. No prosecutor could have presented a more accusatory bill of particulars, nor painted in darker colors McSween's culpability in the troubles besetting the county.

The grand jurors were unreceptive. Most favored the McSween cause and looked upon Bristol as a servant of The House. Juan Patrón, for example, openly supported McSween, and the other eight Hispanics doubtless followed his lead, for he now sat in the territorial legislature and had been elected speaker of the lower house. The foreman, Dr. Blazer of Blazer's Mills, came as close to being uncommitted as any of the twelve.

The grand jury went about its task in the most disorderly fashion imaginable, and the results defied logic. The jurors heard many witnesses, few of whom could have offered any but hearsay evidence, and they ended by returning indictments that fell almost indiscriminately on those implicated while omitting men everyone knew to be guilty.

In the Tunstall killing, both Billy Morton and Tom Hill had by now met violent death, but murder indictments were returned against Jesse Evans and three of his gang who were not even at the scene of the killing. At the same time, Dolan and Mathews, who had remained at the Tunstall ranch that day, were indicted as accessories to Tunstall's murder. Murder indictments named John Middleton, Henry Brown, and Billy Bonney in the Brady killing and Fred Waite in the death of Hindman, but the others in the Tunstall corral drew no mention. Alone among the Regulators at Blazer's Mills, Charles Bowdre stood charged with the murder of Buckshot Roberts. And the killing of Morton, Baker, and McCloskey escaped the official notice of the grand jury altogether.

Other actions more clearly favored the McSween cause. The jurors threw out the frivolous charges against Shield, Widenmann, Robinson, and Washington in the Brady murder, and they steadfastly defied Judge Bristol's disingenuous invitation to indict McSween for embezzlement. "We fully exonerate him of the charge," they reported, "and, regret that a spirit of persecution has been shown in this matter."

No criminal cases came up for trial. All those resulting from the grand jury's indictments were continued to a later term of court, some with changes of venue to other counties. Even cases growing out of earlier indictments were put off. Such was the disposition of the charge against Jesse Evans and the dead Tom Hill for stealing Tunstall's stock the previous September, as well as the charges that Brady had brought against Widenmann and the Martínez posse for riot and resisting a sheriff when they recaptured the Tunstall store in February.

Although freed of the criminal charge, McSween still faced

the civil suit brought by Fritz and Scholand. From this suit, rather than from the embezzlement charge, had grown the attachment process that led to Tunstall's death and the outbreak of violence. As a parting shot at McSween, on the final day of court Judge Bristol noted that the attachment had been only partly executed and directed that another writ be issued with instructions to the sheriff to take possession of all the property covered in the original writ.[6]

Court adjourned on April 24, with McSween the apparent victor. In a burst of good feeling, Lincoln's citizens—or at least those partial to McSween—assembled that evening at the courthouse and adopted resolutions expressing confidence that the county verged on a new era of peace and prosperity. The old feuds would now cease, they predicted, "since the cause has been removed."

From their viewpoint, so it seemed. Threatened with death by the Regulators, Lawrence Murphy had fled to Fort Stanton and placed himself under Colonel Dudley's protection in preparation for moving to Santa Fe. Also, seemingly in surrender, Dolan and Riley had closed their store and soon turned over their mortgaged property to Thomas B. Catron.[7]

Despite the rout of the enemy and the fine words of the resolutions, McSween had not won, and peace had not returned. Many people, even McSween supporters, judged the court term a failure, both in the inability of jurors and witnesses to act responsibly and in the haphazard distribution of indictments among those suspected of crime. The Pecos stockmen had not brought down John Chisum, and Dolan and his friends had fresh cause for hostility in the financial collapse of The House and the indictment of Dolan as an accessory to Tunstall's murder. "All agree that a collision is imminent," the *Independent* editorialized, "and that it will end in bloodshed."[8]

The predicted collision grew out of the advent of a new sheriff. On April 10, with district court in progress and a sheriff badly needed, the county commission had appointed John Copeland, the butcher whom Judge Bristol had temporarily commissioned two days earlier to arrest McSween and his friends at Fort

Stanton.[9] A hulking man of thirty-seven, he moved and thought slowly, and he could be easily influenced by nearly anyone of stronger will. One such was McSween, and the new sheriff quickly fell under his domination.

Copeland carried a pocket full of arrest warrants originating in the murder indictments recently returned by the grand jury. Among the fugitives were at least five of the Regulators—Middleton, Brown, Bonney, Waite, and Bowdre. They and the other Regulators made their headquarters at the home of McSween, who was now free of the embezzlement charge and no longer on the run. There, Copeland caroused with them daily, without making the slightest attempt to serve his warrants.[10]

Now and then, the men in the McSween house asked Mary Ealy to play Sue's piano while they sang—"and how they did sing," she remembered. "They stood behind me with their guns and belts full of cartridges; I suppose I was off the tune as often as on it as I felt very nervous, though they were very nice and polite."[11]

Despite the murder indictments, the Regulators remained an organized body. They had a new leader, Frank McNab. A former "cattle detective" who had hunted rustlers for big cowmen like Chisum, he had been a member of the Regulator party that gunned down Sheriff Brady from ambush. Now, to preserve the Regulators' facade of legality, he obtained a commission as deputy constable from the justice of the peace of Precinct No. 2 at San Patricio.[12]

Dolan and his friends bridled at the turn of events that had lost them the allegiance of the county sheriff. Copeland's open partisanship, and his refusal to serve arrest warrants on any of the Regulators, infuriated them. They concluded that he needed help in recognizing where his duty lay. And so Billy Mathews and George Peppin, still claiming status as deputy sheriffs by appointment of the dead Brady, rode down to the Pecos to recruit a posse. They had no trouble in signing up about twenty of the Seven Rivers stockmen, most of whom had been with Mathews at the Tunstall ranch in February. Frank McNab's association with John Chisum gave them heightened incentive to support Jimmy Dolan.

Including the Beckwith and Olinger brothers, the group rode under the captaincy of William H. Johnson, Hugh Beckwith's son-in-law.[13]

On the afternoon of April 29, Johnson's self-proclaimed possemen paused at the Fritz ranch, nine miles down the Bonito from Lincoln. From Mrs. Fritz they learned that Regulator Frank Coe had been there that morning on the way from his ranch to Lincoln. He would be returning in the afternoon with his brother-in-law, Ab Saunders, and Frank McNab. The Pecos gunmen posted themselves in ambush.

Too late Coe spotted the posse's horses. Riding about a hundred yards in advance of his companions, he had passed the ranch when the concealed men opened fire on the two following in the rear. Their horses both fell, dumping them on the road. McNab sprinted up a ravine, but was followed and killed. Saunders, hit in the foot, rolled behind a knoll, but took another bullet in his hip. A shot from the house dropped Coe's horse. He ran up a gully, as pursuers gave chase and at length cornered him. After an exchange of gunfire, the brothers Wallace and Bob Olinger talked him into giving up. Leaving the wounded Saunders to be brought in next day, the Johnson band, with Coe a prisoner, headed for Lincoln.[14]

Early the next morning, April 30, Johnson's party approached Lincoln. A few men circled the town and took station in the Dolan store, now closed in bankruptcy and in charge of Edgar Walz, Tom Catron's young brother-in-law. The rest spread out in the timber along the river opposite the Ellis store, on the eastern edge of town. They sent word to Sheriff Copeland in the McSween house that they had come to help him arrest Middleton, Bowdre, the Kid, and the other Regulators for whom he had warrants. The Regulators answered with gunfire.

The Battle of Lincoln opened as George Coe fired from the roof of the Ellis store and shattered the ankles of "Dutch Charlie" Kruling, sitting on a cow skull several hundred yards distant.[15] The men in the Dolan store rushed out and, leaving Frank Coe free to walk away, headed down the street toward Ellis's. But McSween's fighters had posted themselves on other rooftops and behind walls and laid down a hot fire. The attackers veered off to the north, crossed the river, and united with their confederates downstream. For four hours, the two sides banged away at each other without scoring any hits.

Meanwhile, Copeland had sent to Fort Stanton for military aid. At about 3:30 in the afternoon Lieutenant George W. Smith and twenty cavalrymen galloped into town. Gesturing wildly with a pistol, Copeland led the troopers to the lower end of town. Smith rode between the battle lines and waved his uniform cap. Several of Johnson's men came forward. Which men did he want arrested? Smith asked the sheriff. "I want the whole damn business," he replied. Fearful of assassination if they trusted themselves to Copeland, the Seven Rivers men all surrendered to the lieutenant. Smith sent them around town on the north side of the river in order to avoid more shooting, and then conducted the "whole damn business" to Fort Stanton, where he turned them over to Colonel Dudley.[16]

The affair now took on comic-opera overtones. McSween wrote out a warrant for the arrest of eighteen of the Pecos men for the murder of McNab, hastened to San Patricio, and had it signed by Gregorio Trujillo, the compliant justice of the peace of Precinct No. 2. Copeland then took it to Fort Stanton and asked Dudley to hold the men named.

Meanwhile, these men fired their own legal salvo. Three of them swore an affidavit charging the Regulators with riot. Colonel Dudley sent it by courier to Blazer's Mills, where the justice of the peace of Precinct No. 3, David Easton, issued a warrant for the arrest of McSween and some twenty of his men.

Back at the fort, Dudley lectured Copeland on his duty to enforce the law impartially, handed him the warrant, and sent him off with a detachment of cavalry to round up McSween and his followers. The posse arrested some in Lincoln, but could not find McSween, who had gone to San Patricio. There, on the evening of May 2, the military posse scooped up McSween, although Copeland served the warrant only under the prodding of the detachment commander. They had just missed Middleton, Bonney, Bowdre, and others, who had left for the mountains an hour or so earlier.[17]

With nearly thirty men now in military custody and the

number rising, Copeland stampeded. On May 4, mindful of the legal prohibition against holding prisoners without formal examination, he requested Dudley to release them to his custody. When the colonel complied, Copeland discovered that he alone could not handle them. Confused, he simply turned everyone loose with the injunction to go home and quit feuding. "Both parties seem to have had a scare," Dudley observed dryly.[18]

And well they might. The battle of April 30, even though bloodless, marked the opening of a new and more dangerous phase of the Lincoln County War. For the first time, the fighting forces of the two factions had squared off against each other in pitched battle on roughly even terms. From scattered killings and shootouts, the conflict had escalated into open warfare.

By this time, moreover, with the bravos of both sides dashing about the country looking for a fight, neither Dolan nor McSween had much influence on events. Possibly goaded by Sue, McSween tried to overcome his instincts and go along with the activities of his rowdies. Widenmann, ever the blusterer, gloried in the role of swaggering gunslinger. Colonel Dudley observed him and young Ben Ellis strutting around Fort Stanton like "walking Gatling guns," and a farmer told how Widenmann had so often threatened him with death unless he joined the McSween forces that he finally abandoned his farm and fled the country.[19]

For his part, Dolan appeared to have left the field altogether. Early in May, he helped Lawrence Murphy move to Santa Fe and remained there for a month. While there, he used his time to good advantage, for Santa Fe contained powerful men whose sympathies lay with him.

However hostile the Santa Fe establishment, McSween had his own connections to high places, and he and his associates had not hesitated to exploit them. Rob Widenmann had ties to Interior Secretary Carl Schurz. Reverend Ealy wrote letters to an uncle, Rush Clark of Pennsylvania, who sat in the U.S. House of Representatives. Montague Leverson, the emotional Englishman who had tangled with Captain Purington on the day of Brady's murder, turned out to be a friend of President Hayes. Leverson bombarded both Hayes and Schurz with lurid accounts of fraud, corruption, and murder involving virtually the entire federal and territorial officialdom of New Mexico. But the most insistent pressures on Washington authorities came from Sir Edward Thornton, British minister to the United States, who made known the distress with which the Foreign Office viewed the killing of one of Her Majesty's subjects with, so it was alleged, the complicity of United States officers.[20]

All this fuss produced results. The administration designated Frank Warner Angel as "special agent of the Departments of Justice and the Interior." His mission was to investigate the death of Tunstall and the Lincoln County War, the similar strife that had broken out in Colfax County, and the allegations of corruption against Governor Axtell, U.S. District Attorney Catron, and other federal appointees. Newspapers dignified the government agent as "Judge" Angel. In fact, he was a thirty-three-year-old New York lawyer who had worked for the Hayes candidacy and now wanted a federal appointment in the West. He turned out to be a young man of moderate ability, persistent though somewhat careless and imprecise in gathering evidence, and susceptible to occasional lapses of the judicial detachment implied by his honorific title.[21]

Frank Angel reached Santa Fe on May 4, 1878, and put up at the Exchange. For a week he conferred with Axtell, Catron, and others. On May 10, he set out for Lincoln County. His advent a few days later coincided with a new offensive by the McSween forces.

With McNab dead, the Regulators elected their third captain, Josiah G. "Doc" Scurlock. A stockman from the Ruidoso, Doc was a devoted family man and a sensitive intellectual with some medical training in his background. He was also a ruthless killer, faithful to the Regulator aims.[22] He called together Middleton, Bonney, and about ten of the usual crowd and, bolstered by an equal number of Hispanics under Josefita Chavez, headed for the Pecos. He carried the warrant, by now well worn, issued by Justice Wilson in February for the arrest of Tunstall's killers.

On May 14, the Regulator force fell on the Dolan cow camp near Seven Rivers. They drove off the herders, scattered the herd, and seized twenty-five horses and two mules. They also captured the cook, known simply as "Indian." He had been in the posse that killed Tunstall and had also figured in the slaying of McNab. Under the usual cloak of attempted escape, the Regulators killed him, with the Kid and Chavez acting as executioners.[23]

While Scurlock's men crashed through the Dolan cow camp, John H. Riley and Captain Johnson's band of Seven Rivers warriors hesitated at the Johnson ranch only a mile away. Riley had come down from Lincoln to round up a herd to drive to the Indian agency for the biweekly beef issue. Reluctant to get caught up in a gun battle, he contented himself with sending an appeal to Colonel Dudley for military aid. Unless troops intervened, he implied, the Apaches would go hungry and possibly cause trouble.[24]

Dudley sent no troops after the stolen stock. "The finest or largest body of cavalry," he said, "in my judgment could not have overtaken them, if I had felt disposed to have attempted their recovery." He did not feel so disposed. For one thing, he did not know to whom the cattle truly belonged. For another, Riley had all of Johnson's men at his command, which seemed ample to retake the animals. And finally, stockmen closer to home stood ready to help Riley in meeting his contract deadline.[25]

There was another reason, too—the guidelines under which Dudley operated in civil matters. For the nation, this had been a murky legal area since the Judiciary Act of 1789, which empowered U.S. marshals to requisition citizens as a *posse comitatus* when extraordinary measures were necessary to enforce the decrees of the federal courts. Under this law, when disorders prevented citizens from serving, the army could be called upon, but only after the president had proclaimed a state of insurrection and commanded the dissidents to disband. In 1854, however, an attorney general's ruling had relaxed this requirement and allowed any individual or "organized body" to be deputized, and ever since marshals had turned to the army for a military *posse comitatus* without the formality of a presidential proclamation.[26]

This ruling, lacking the force of law or judicial decision, had recently come under heavy political attack. The Republican administration's use of federal troops at Southern polling places in the bitter presidential election of 1876, followed by their heavy-handed employment in the railroad strikes of the summer of

1877, had aroused the antagonism of congressional Democrats, now in control of the House of Representatives. They struck back with a variety of legislative proposals to cripple the army, and they especially took aim at the *posse comitatus* authority that allowed troops to be employed in civil disorders.

For the army, therefore, the Lincoln County War could not have come at a worse time. Almost any action locally was bound to anger one side or the other and produce political fallout in Washington. President Hayes had ordered the army to take a hand, but from the top down the chain of command approached the mission gingerly and embraced the narrowest possible interpretation of the presidential directive. That meant furnishing military posses to the sheriff, on written request, for the purpose of aiding in the service of arrest warrants. It did not include any other initiative in behalf of law and order, and certainly not in helping Johnny Riley run down cattle scattered by the Regulators. But like Purington before him, Dudley had trouble operating within such narrow limits when only the army stood between Lincoln County and anarchy.[27]

The Fort Stanton personnel approached their civil mission with mixed feelings. On the one hand, they felt that the task had to be done. They looked on themselves as the only effective check on plunder, destruction, and the killing of innocent people, the only force that could ensure the impartial enforcement of the law. As Dudley observed, "Nothing but the strong arm of the military in my judgement will put a stop to the constant shedding of blood."[28]

On the other hand, the soldiers found the duty itself utterly repugnant. It wore them out in trying to keep an eye on the Indians while also chasing around the country in usually futile attempts to serve warrants. Also, besides the potential for grievous political damage to the army as a whole, it earned them the ill will of the surrounding community. It was, concluded one of Dudley's officers, "the most disagreeable duty that can be assigned either officer or soldier."[29]

And it confronted officers with a baffling dilemma, for their orders had an unintended effect in allying the army with whichever side at the moment claimed the allegiance of the sheriff.

Military posses could ride only in the service of the sheriff. Thus, through Sheriff Brady the Dolanites had enjoyed military aid against the Regulators. Then, through Sheriff Copeland the Regulators enjoyed military aid against the Dolan faction, most notably in the Battle of Lincoln on April 30. Dudley's preferences ran to the Dolan side, however, and he proved far less supportive of Copeland than Captain Purington had been of Sheriff Brady. Even so, the partisanship of sheriffs prevented the army from steering the neutral course that the officers preferred and the mission demanded.

And at the end of May, Dudley confronted still another abrupt shift in allegiances, when Jimmy Dolan recaptured the sheriff's badge.

7
Dad
Peppin

JIMMY DOLAN spent part of May and June 1878 in Santa Fe. Aided by James Longwill, he accompanied Lawrence Murphy to the capital and helped him to get settled in a new home. Besides nursing his broken leg and writing self-serving letters to the *New Mexican*, what else he did can only be surmised. But with such friends and sympathizers as Governor Axtell and U.S. District Attorney Catron, Dolan found Santa Fe a battleground plainly superior to Lincoln for contending against McSween and his captive sheriff, John Copeland.

Axtell's move against Copeland, like his earlier move against Justice of the Peace Wilson, suggests the dexterous hand of Jimmy Dolan. The law required a new sheriff to post bond as tax collector within thirty days of taking office. Because the tax lists needed to fix the amount of the bond had not been compiled, Copeland missed the deadline. There is no evidence that Dolan pointed out these facts to Axtell. But it is unlikely that the governor thought of them alone, and Dolan's presence in Santa Fe makes him a logical informant.

On May 28, two weeks after Dolan's appearance in Santa Fe, Axtell issued a proclamation removing Copeland as sheriff because of his failure to post bond within the prescribed time. As the new sheriff, the proclamation named George W. Peppin, a deputy under Brady. Axtell later said that Peppin had been chosen on the recommendation of District Attorney Rynerson, Dolan's friend and ally.

The proclamation also commanded all armed men to disband, return to their homes, and not act as possemen so long as U.S. soldiers could be summoned. In other words, only soldiers could serve in posses, and then only under control of the new sheriff.[1]

Two days after Axtell's proclamation, another development revealed the depth of Dolan's support in Santa Fe. Tom Catron received a letter from Lincoln telling of Doc Scurlock's raid on the Dolan cow camp near Seven Rivers. If Colonel Dudley felt uncertainty over who owned the cattle that the Regulators had scattered, Catron did not. They were listed on the mortgage he had foreclosed on the property of Dolan and Riley, and they now belonged to him.

When he learned the fate of his stock on May 30, Catron promptly went to Axtell. The governor, in turn, requested Colonel Edward Hatch, military commander in New Mexico, to send troops to the Pecos to protect Catron's interests and disarm all groups ranging that area. Hatch helpfully complied, but his superiors told him that he had overstepped his authority, and he called off the operation.[2]

Although it came to nothing, the episode, especially in conjunction with the dismissal of Copeland, had ominous overtones for the McSween faction. The most powerful man in New Mexico, politically and economically, now had large property holdings in Lincoln County that gave him a vested interest in the fortunes of Jimmy Dolan. The territorial governor stood ready to aid both Dolan and Catron in any way he could, and the commander of the District of New Mexico was, at the least, thoughtlessly or ignorantly predisposed to support them militarily. In attacking the Dolan cow camp, the Regulators had blundered badly.

"Dad" Peppin qualified for his appointment as sheriff in Mesilla in mid-June. A thirty-nine-year-old Frenchman and Union veteran, he had settled in Lincoln County after the Civil War, reared a family, and made his living as a stonemason. The cellar jail and the McSween home were monuments to his craftsmanship. Although he had served Brady faithfully as a deputy, he was no better equipped to be sheriff than Copeland. In fact, except in his dislike of the McSween faction, he was almost another John Copeland: amiable, well intentioned, weak of intellect, and easily dominated. He promised to serve Jimmy Dolan's interest as loyally as Copeland had served McSween's interest.

Shortly before daybreak on June 19, Peppin arrived in Lincoln. Besides his commissions as sheriff and deputy U.S. marshal, he brought United States warrants for the arrest of ten Regulators involved in the killing of Buckshot Roberts. The rationale for federal warrants was that Blazer's Mills lay within the Indian reservation and thus came under federal jurisdiction. The warrants made these Regulators federal fugitives, a more serious matter than if they were territorial fugitives.[3]

The new sheriff also brought with him a formidable army to help in serving the warrants. In violation of the governor's ban on citizen posses, he not only had the usual collection of Dolan henchmen and Pecos warriors, but a gang of eleven outlaws headed by John Kinney, a ruffian and stock thief from the Río Grande even more notorious than Jesse Evans. To back them up, the sheriff obtained a detachment of soldiers from Colonel Dudley at Fort Stanton. And finally, accompanying Peppin, Jimmy Dolan came home.[4]

Dolan's homecoming ended a calm that had settled over Lincoln in his absence. While he politicked in Santa Fe, the Regulators had passed several quiet weeks in helping investigator Frank Angel gather evidence for his report. Even Billy Bonney gave testimony. His deposition, in Rob Widenmann's handwriting, bore such a resemblance to Widenmann's own deposition as to suggest that the Kid's principal contribution was his signature. Of Angel, Widenmann quipped: "May he prove an angel to us not only in name but also in deed."[5] Then, on June 12, Widenmann left for Mesilla to testify before Judge Bristol in the Tunstall murder case. He would never return.

The approach of Peppin and Dolan triggered an abrupt shift in the fortunes of war from the McSween to the Dolan camp. Unwilling to face the combination of possemen, outlaws, and soldiers, the Regulators hastily abandoned Lincoln. They took refuge in the mountains around San Patricio, the tiny adobe village on the Ruidoso just above its junction with the Bonito; and they often came into town. It was a congenial place, whose almost completely Hispanic population favored the McSween cause and contributed about a dozen gunmen to the Regulator ranks.

Although no warrant stood against him, McSween took the field with his men. He made his way to San Patricio on foot, reported the ubiquitous black handyman George Washington, who went along as cook, "clean shaved and with a very large hat."[6] The lawyer's talents did not run to field-soldiering. He may have departed from habit to shoulder a rifle, but he did not command. That role continued to fall to Doc Scurlock, McNab's successor and the captain who had led the raid on the Dolan cow camp.

The Dolanites exulted in their new might. They had the enemy on the run and clearly outside the law, both territorial and federal. They had a compliant sheriff and Dolan himself, his broken leg now much improved, to give energy and direction to the counteroffensive. They had "Colonel" Kinney and his gang, drawn by visions of Tunstall's cattle and other plunder, to stiffen the regular posse. And they had the army's backing; however reluctantly, Colonel Dudley could hardly withhold troops if needed by a deputy U.S. marshal carrying federal warrants.

Reflecting their new certainty, these champions of justice anointed themselves the "law and order party" and assigned a term to the enemy less dignified than Regulator. One of the Seven Rivers cowboys had fought in the Modoc Indian War of 1873 in California's lava beds, and at his suggestion McSween's followers came to be known as "Modocs."[7]

Under the immediate control of Deputy Jack Long, the same man who had drunkenly frightened Reverend Ealy, the posse established headquarters in the "round tower," or *torreon*. This was the two-story structure of stone and adobe that had once defended the town against Indians. It stood in the center of town, east of the Tunstall store, in the corral behind the home of Saturnino Baca. Civil War veteran and a leader of the Hispanic community, Captain Baca had tried to steer a neutral course, but he was generally regarded as a Dolan supporter. Half a dozen possemen occupied the *torreon* night and day, and Baca "ordered my family to cook their grub for them."[8]

In the last week of June, Dolan's fighters opened their offensive against the Modocs. Jack Long led the first foray. At daybreak on June 27, the posse appeared in the San Patricio plaza. The Regulators were still in the hills, but the invaders flushed George Washington, who tried to escape across an open field but, when bullets tore up the ground around him, threw down his Winchester and surrendered. Terrified, he spilled out everything he knew about the Regulators.

Leaving Kinney and his followers to hold the town, Long took five men up the Ruidoso Valley to check out Newcomb's ranch. Returning, they spied horsemen across the river and, supposing them to be Kinney's band, turned in their direction. A burst of gunfire at seventy-five yards halted Long's party. One bullet struck Long's horse in the flank, another the mount of a companion. The enemy wheeled and galloped into the bordering hills.

Long had run into eleven Modocs. In addition to Scurlock, Bonney, Bowdre, French, and other familiar figures, the party included McSween and ex-Sheriff Copeland, together with three Hispanics. The firing brought Kinney's horsemen at the gallop, so Scurlock and his men scampered up a mountain and deployed for defense. Kinney tried to take the position, but could not get close enough without dangerously exposing his force. Long dispatched a courier for help, and Peppin sent to Fort Stanton for a military posse.

Late in the afternoon, Captain Henry Carroll and a company of cavalry reported to Long. The Regulator force had already withdrawn into the mountains south of the Ruidoso. Accompanied by Sheriff Peppin, the soldiers took the trail. It doubled back to the river, led eastward to Frank Coe's ranch, and then swung to the north and west. Through the next day and night, Carroll pushed the chase. Early on June 29, a courier overtook him with orders from Dudley to return to the fort.[9]

The encounter near San Patricio marked the second collision between the fighting forces of the two factions. Like the fight in Lincoln on April 30, it drew no human blood. The two dead horses, however, afforded a pretext for adding McSween's name to the official wanted list. Anyone's bullets might have hit the horses, but Jack Long swore an affidavit charging McSween with assault with intent to kill. Ironically, the warrant for his arrest issued from the court of Squire Wilson, who was once again, thanks to a special election, justice of the peace in Lincoln.[10]

Also, the episode at San Patricio coincided with a development of far-reaching consequence, for Dudley's recall of Captain Carroll marked the end of the army's participation in the Lincoln County War. From the beginning, the military high command had carried out the president's instructions to intervene with the greatest trepidation and reluctance. On June 8, the army's judge advocate general had written an opinion holding Dudley's activities under those instructions to be unconstitutional.[11] Before this had any effect, however, higher authority interposed. The army appropriation act emerged from Congress with a rider banning the use of federal troops as a *posse comitatus*. Orders forbidding further aid to civil officers in Lincoln County reached Dudley after Captain Carroll had taken the field in support of Peppin and Long. Dudley quickly sent couriers to find the command and to call off the pursuit of the Regulators; then, he served notice of the end of military involvement in civil affairs.[12]

The fight at San Patricio had given momentum to Dolan's offensive, and Peppin made haste to organize still another thrust at the Modoc bastion. Cleverly, he gathered a posse of fifteen Hispanics. McSween had won Hispanics to his cause, and Peppin intended to get them involved on his side, too. Confronted with a legal summons from the sheriff, as one of the possemen hinted, they had little choice but to go along. Deputizing José Chavez y Baca as leader, Peppin sent the force to San Patricio before daybreak on July 3.

This time, the Regulators were not in the hills but posted on the rooftops of San Patricio. "Those dobes had little breastworks around the tops," related George Coe, "and we got behind those and punched out loopholes." Riding into the plaza in the early morning gloom, the attackers ran into a storm of bullets. "We were scattered around all over town," said Coe. "Two or three of us got on top of every house. It was too dark to see to shoot accurately, but we killed a horse or two and think we wounded a man." They had. As the posse backed hurriedly out of range, Julian López dragged a smashed arm.

Deputy Chavez y Baca sent to Lincoln for help. Dolan, Jack Long, and John Kinney responded with about a dozen men. By the time they arrived, however, the fugitives had withdrawn. The possemen followed, but four miles east of town they confronted Scurlock and his men deployed along the crest of a ridge. A well-aimed volley from the heights downed two horses and sent the pursuers hurrying back to San Patricio.

There, ostensibly searching for more Modocs, they vented their aggravation at the townspeople. With Dolan giving orders and Kinney prominent in carrying them out, possemen kicked in doors or pulled them off their hinges, searched homes, and castigated men as pimps and sons-of-bitches and women as whores. When they rode away, they left the town a shambles and the citizens thoroughly terrorized.[13]

The posse returned to Lincoln with two captured horses, scooped up as they closely pressed the Regulators east of San Patricio. One chanced to be Sue McSween's mare, Pet. When she saw Pet led in front of her home, she inferred that Mac had been shot, grabbed a shotgun, and ran screaming down the street to Dolan's store. There she confronted Peppin, Long, and the entire posse. "She must have her 'Pet,' talk to 'Jemmy,' or someone must die," recorded a witness. Drawn by the commotion, Dolan came to the door and faced Sue, but regrettably, the outcome of the encounter is lost to history.[14]

From the Dolan store, Sue McSween made her way to the home of Saturnino Baca. Confronting him at his front door, she accused him of sending the Chavez y Baca posse to San Patricio to kill her husband. "Madam," Baca replied, "that is not my business, I am not an officer of the law." And also, Sue shouted, they were thieves and had stolen Mac's mare. Baca waved his hand at her and told her to go away. "Very good, very good, Captain," Sue declared as she turned to leave, "I have plenty of money and men to kill you and all your family."[15]

After the second fight at San Patricio, the Regulators continued down the Hondo to Chisum's ranch. "We went down to visit Old John and to rest on the Fourth," recalled George Coe. Chisum was not there. Indeed, he had vanished shortly after the murder of Brady, and to this day no one has discovered where he went. In his absence, however, the ranch hands prepared a big dinner, and everyone made ready to celebrate Independence Day.

During the morning, Frank and George Coe, Billy Bonney, and several others rode over to Ash Upson's store to buy candy for Chisum's niece. On the return, a twelve-man posse jumped them, and they exchanged shots in a running fight back to the ranch. "The two sides fought around the ranch most of the day," recalled George Coe, "but the ranch was a good defensive work and no harm was done." The feast proceeded as planned, while the posse sent to Lincoln for help. By the time reinforcements arrived, grumbled one, "McSween's mob had escaped."[16]

Trailed by the full posse, "McSween's mob" feinted northward up the Pecos, then abruptly cut to the west and once again came to rest in the friendly hills behind San Patricio. The pursuers gave up the chase and headed for Fort Stanton, where Johnny Riley cut enough beeves out of a contract herd for the army to stock their larder.[17]

McSween sensed that the time had come for a showdown. Now that the enemy could no longer call for soldiers when a battle went against them, a conclusive test of strength might bring victory. At San Patricio, McSween succeeded in recruiting enough sympathizers to give him an army of between fifty and sixty men; then, he set forth for Lincoln.

McSween's gamble depended entirely on the military nonintervention enjoined by Congress in the *posse comitatus* act. Despite unequivocal orders, however, Colonel Dudley wavered. The entreaties of afflicted citizens were hard to resist. After Peppin's posse sacked San Patricio on July 3, more than two dozen women walked the twenty-seven miles to Fort Stanton to tell of their ordeal. "In the name of God and the constitution," they appealed to "the noble and good heart" of Colonel Dudley for military protection. Dudley sent an officer to investigate, as he had sent the post surgeon to tend the shattered arm of posseman Julian López.[18]

On July 12, Sheriff Brady's widow appeared with an equally pathetic tale. Doc Scurlock had tried to shoot down her eldest son. "They have murdered my poor husband," she sobbed, "and not satisfied with this they now want to kill my boy." "It was a sad scene to witness the grief and fears of this poor woman," the colonel reported. Although Scurlock later denied the charge under oath, Dudley sent a soldier to stand guard on Mrs. Brady's farm.[19]

Dudley's responses to these appeals, which were token at best, betrayed the intense strain that the escalating violence imposed on the officers at Fort Stanton. His orders were explicit and unmistakable. Any aid beyond affording sanctuary at the fort to people who wanted it violated his orders. Yet the excesses of two gangs of gunman claiming status as law officers terrorized the citizenry, and women and children stood in constant danger. The temptation to rationalize slight breaches of his orders, drafted in an office distant from the realities of Lincoln County, was irresistible. As Dudley complained on July 13, "The present status of affairs in the county is simply shameful and disgraceful. . . . The officers at Stanton are mortified that they can do nothing under present law to protect the innocent."[20]

Events moved swiftly to a climax that placed the innocent in grave jeopardy. On Sunday evening, July 14, with Peppin's possemen scouring the countryside for Modocs, McSween led his little army into Lincoln itself. About fifteen climbed to the roof of his house and knocked firing ports in the parapet, then joined another twenty in occupying José Montaño's store and preparing the rooftop there for battle. With her husband out of town, Mrs. Montaño and the family cowered fearfully in one room. Five men entered the house of Juan Patrón a few paces east of Montaño's; Patrón, too, was absent, having fled to Las Vegas for safety. The balance of the force, almost twenty, lodged in Isaac Ellis's store on the eastern edge of town.

Jack Long and five possemen still held the *torreon*. McSween viewed this property as his, as part of the tract he had bought from Dolan for the new church. Early on July 15, accusing Captain Baca of allowing an improper use of the *torreon*, McSween ordered him to vacate his home within three days. Mindful of Sue

McSween's recent threat to have him and his family killed, Baca at once appealed to Colonel Dudley to send soldiers for his protection. Mrs. Baca had just given birth to a son, he explained, and she was accustomed to a convalescence of forty days.

Instead of assigning a guard, Dudley sent Dr. Daniel Appel, post surgeon, to investigate. In an unsuccessful effort to mediate the dispute, Appel visited the McSweens in their home. He found them alone, but defiant and ready for a fight. The Bacas, McSween declared, were harboring his enemies on his property, and if they did not leave within three days he would burn them out. He had been out in the hills long enough, McSween added. He had now returned to his home, and his enemies would not again drive him out alive.[21]

Only a few hundred feet to the west, at the Wortley Hotel, Dolan and Peppin waited eagerly for their own army to converge on Lincoln and accept McSween's challenge. Late in the afternoon, riding out of town in his ambulance, Dr. Appel observed Dolan there. Some four hundred yards up the road toward the fort, the doctor met part of Peppin's posse under Buck Powell and John Kinney. They had been out looking for Modocs. One of the posse recalled that the wind was blowing "a regular hurricane," kicking up so much dust that one could hardly see. Appel told them that all the McSween fighters were in Lincoln, where they had Long and his men cornered in the *torreon*. "There's no way for you boys to get in there," the doctor warned. "They are everywhere except at Murphy and Dolan's store and the old restaurant across the street [Wortley's Hotel]." The posse galloped down the road to Lincoln. Shortly afterward, Appel heard gunfire.[22]

The firing marked the opening of the Five-Day Battle—the climactic test of strength that McSween had engineered to decide once and for all whether he or Jimmy Dolan would prevail.

That McSween had flung the challenge and Dolan accepted it reflected the confidence that each had in his own strength.

McSween counted a formidable force of around sixty fighters, a third more than the opposition could muster so long as the soldiers stayed in their barracks. The core consisted of a dozen or more first-rate gunmen, men like Middleton, Scurlock, Bonney, Waite, French, and Bowdre—courageous, daring, skilled with firearms, and committed to the cause by five months of shared adventure and hardship. The rest, less experienced at fighting, lacked no less commitment. McSween also enjoyed more public sympathy than Dolan, especially from the Hispanic community, which almost solidly favored his side and contributed a majority of the men who followed him into Lincoln. Finally, McSween's adherents drew inspiration from a conviction of righteousness. Not only were they little people fighting a tyrannical monopoly, they justified their course as lawful. With a mixture of sincerity and cynicism, they looked on the commissions and warrants from two justices of the peace as giving their cause the sanctity of law and themselves the character of officers of the law.

McSween's state of mind fortified the challenge. It was an odd combination of defiance and despair. As he told Dr. Appel, he would run no longer. He would not again be driven from his home alive. Gunfighting was not his style of combat; nor was dashing about the countryside by day and camping in the open by night his style of living. Hotheads such as Bonney and Scurlock doubtless fed McSween's defiance, as did Sue herself. Her actions after the second fight at San Patricio revealed her excited and belligerent temper. In retrospect, however, she blamed the "fool-hardy boys" he rode with for influencing Mac to do many things he regretted.

Sue also remembered her husband's lethargic and resigned mood in these climactic days of battle. So did the preacher's wife. "He seemed to think he was doomed," recalled Mary Ealy. With determination and fatalism, McSween plunged into the Five-Day Battle.[23]

Momentum as much as deliberate intent carried Dolan into the fray. Peppin's posse had been on the offensive for a month, chasing weaker Modoc bands all over the county in an effort to serve their warrants. Learning that the fugitives had taken refuge in Lincoln, the possemen simply dashed in without knowing, or caring, that they confronted a superior force.

Peppin's ranks included talented gunmen as bold and dauntless as Middleton and Bonney, chiefly John Kinney and his outlaw gang. Peppin even numbered the ubiquitous Jesse Evans among his following. In Mesilla, in late June, Evans had stood trial for stealing Indian stock and had won acquittal; then, on Rynerson's recommendation, he had been released on bail in the Tunstall murder case.[24]

The Seven Rivers cowboys, about twenty in number, were also good fighters, and they gave Peppin's posse its only reputable tone. However blindly partisan, they were basically industrious citizens, not averse to bending the law but not imbued by the cynical contempt for the law that stamped Evans and Kinney. The Seven Rivers contingent included the usual crowd of small cowmen animated by hatred of John Chisum—Captain Johnson, Marion Turner, Milo Pearce, Sam Perry, Joe Nash, and the brothers John and Bob Beckwith, Wallace and Bob Olinger, and Jim and John Jones.

Like the Regulators, the "law and order party" fought secure in the knowledge of the law's backing. Peppin's badge stood for the authority of the territorial and federal governments, and his arrest warrants issued from the territorial and federal courts. The self-righteousness of these Dolan fighters was captured in a letter Bob Beckwith wrote to his sister Josie on July 11, telling of the posse's efforts to apprehend McSween's "cowardly mob." "God will be with us," he assured her, "and those murderers will not touch a hair on our heads."[25]

As still another reassuring strength, Dolan knew that he had the sympathy of powerful men in Santa Fe, including the governor and the United States district attorney. He also counted the army's sympathy among his assets.

What Dolan doubtless failed to appreciate fully was the distinction between the army's sympathy and the army's ability to help him. That a genuine emergency would not bring troopers galloping to the rescue seemed inconceivable. Colonel Dudley's token responses to the humanitarian pleas showered on him as the war built to a climax suggested that he had not been altogether immobilized, and his well-known aversion to the "outlaws" and "desperadoes" who fought for McSween signaled a wish to help if only the rationale could be found.

What neither leader seems to have considered was the peril to which a battle in Lincoln itself would expose the townspeople.

Many of the residents had fled, but the little adobe houses still sheltered innocent people, including enough women and children to raise the humanitarian specter that had so troubled Dudley and his officers ever since they had been ordered back into their fort. In that specter resided both dilemma and rationale.

8

The Five-Day Battle

AT DUSK on July 15, amid a swirling dust storm, Dad Peppin's posse clattered into Lincoln from the west. In front of the Wortley Hotel, where Dolan and Peppin waited, blustering Charlie Crawford fired his pistol into the air, and the men reined into the hotel corral. Dismounting, they fired about a dozen shots at the McSween house, splintering slats on the drawn shutters.

To the east, in the center of town, a dozen or more McSween men ran out of the Montaño store and raced up the street toward the McSween house. From the *torreon*, Deputy Long shouted for them to halt. They answered with gunfire, which Long's men returned. Joining Mac and Sue, these Regulators fired off a fusillade of shots that spattered the corral and hotel and sent the posse scurrying for cover.[1] The sound of battle carried through the driving wind to Dr. Appel's ambulance on the road to Fort Stanton and announced the opening of the Five-Day Battle.[2]

McSween commanded two crucial advantages over his enemy: strength and position. He outnumbered the Dolan–Peppin forces roughly sixty to forty men, and his followers were well fortified in strongpoints throughout the town.[3] To serve their warrants, the possemen had to attack these positions, exposing themselves to heavy casualties at almost no risk to the defenders. From McSween's viewpoint, the warrants that his side had accumulated over the months for the arrest of nearly all the men in Peppin's posse justified a fighting defense.

92

At their base in the Wortley Hotel, Dolan and Peppin pondered their problem. One of them, probably Dolan, came up with an ingenious solution. If only they had a cannon, the mere threat of a bombardment might prompt the enemy's surrender. On July 16, as sporadic gunfire laced the deserted street, a courier rode to Fort Stanton with a penciled message from Peppin requesting Colonel Dudley to lend him a howitzer.

Surprisingly, in view of the ban on any form of military intervention, Dudley gave the request serious consideration and even called his officers together for a long discussion. With regret, he decided that he had to refuse. In his reply to Peppin, however, Dudley dropped the neutral stance that he had affected since April. "I do not hesitate to state now," he wrote, "that in my opinion, you are acting strictly within the provisions of the duty incumbent upon you . . . and were I not so circumscribed by laws and orders, I would most gladly give you every man and material at my post to sustain you in your present position, believing it to be strictly legal."[4]

Dudley entrusted this message to Private Berry Robinson. Approaching Lincoln at dusk, with the setting sun at his back, the black trooper ran into a volley of rifle fire. The bullets tore up the earth and frightened the horse, which reared and threw its rider. Robinson recovered and remounted, and as Dolan vigorously motioned him on, he galloped to the cover of the hotel. The fire had come from riflemen posted at the portholes on the McSween roof. Possemen at the Wortley had shouted at them to quit shooting, that their target was a soldier, but they had continued to fire.

Although Peppin got no howitzer, the blunder of the men on the McSween roof proved almost as helpful. Predictably, the firing on a U.S. soldier enraged Colonel Dudley and reinforced the sentiments he had expressed in the message that Private Robinson carried to Peppin. Next day, moreover, Dudley sent a board of officers to Lincoln to investigate "this infamous outrage." Their findings confirmed that the bullets had come from McSween rifles.[5]

That afternoon, McSween rifles further damaged McSween's standing in Dudley's estimation. The day before, Peppin had sent five men to the hills south of town to clear the rooftops of McSween gunmen. On the morning of the seventeenth, Charlie Crawford and Lucio Montoya concluded that the Modocs had evacuated town and started down from their position. A sharpshooter in the Montaño store took careful aim and squeezed the trigger. The ball hit Crawford in the stomach and smashed his spine. "Fernando Herrera shot Charlie Crawford with a 45–120–555 Sharpes," recalled a contemporary, who ranked the shot "among the great examples of marksmanship."[6]

Within view of his friends in the Wortley Hotel, Crawford lay grievously wounded on an open slope under a burning sun. McSween gunmen continued to fire at him, and no one dared to go to his aid. Dr. Appel, one of the investigating officers, decided to help. Accompanied by another officer and two soldiers, he went to the fallen posseman. Strangely, although clearly recognizable as soldiers, the rescue party drew fire from the Montaño store. Bullets zipped over their heads and plowed into the hillside. They retrieved the wounded man, who died a week later in the Fort Stanton hospital. But again, McSween fighters had blundered, for the officers reported to Dudley that for a second time the army uniform had been fired upon.[7]

Reverend Ealy and his family had good cause to remember this day, Wednesday, July 17. After Sue McSween's return from the East, they had moved into the living quarters of the Tunstall store. All day, the sounds of gunfire and the shouts and screams of the combatants intruded into their rooms. Barricading the windows with trunks, they dragged mattresses to the floor and cowered in terror as the battle raged outside.

After dark, a knock at the door roused Ealy from his bed. Two men said that Ben Ellis, son of the store proprietor, had been shot in the neck while feeding his mule in the corral of the Ellis store. Ealy must come at once or Ben would bleed to death. Fearfully, the doctor followed the men to the back of the store and down to an open flat, bathed in moonlight, bordering the river. The plan was to get into the trees along the Bonito and follow the stream down to the Ellis store. The guides, Ealy recalled, "passed the flat unharmed, but when I tried to pass [behind the *torreon*] up came three guns bristling in the moonlight all pointed at me.

Bang, bang, bang, every ball struck an adobe house, Jesus's house, near my head. I turned and ran back." Next morning, Ealy, with his wife and children as protection, boldly marched down the middle of the street to the Ellis store and sewed up the wound. But "the cow boys stole my needle before I finished my work."[8]

On Thursday, July 18, the fourth day of battle, the firing tapered off. As Jack Long recalled, "both sides were comparatively quiet and few shots fired. Neither party knew what the other was doing."[9] But the citizens who had not fled the town quailed in their homes. "All possessed of terror," said José María de Aguayo. "You could not see in the town any person except Nigger Joe [Dixon] and myself," he related, "because my children were crying, because they were hungry and I had to go about and look for milk."[10]

None shrank more fearfully than Saturnino Baca. With the *torreon* next door and the Montaño store a short distance down the street, he and his family felt their lives in deadly peril, especially with Mrs. Baca still recuperating from childbirth on July 11. Then at noon on Thursday, Baca received another missive from McSween commanding him to vacate immediately or be burned out. Once again, Baca sent a frantic appeal to Dudley for help.[11]

Baca's plea came on top of other supplications reaching the fort that day. One in particular had touched the officers. A woman who had walked all the way from Lincoln begged Captain Purington to stop the fighting. She had been unable to go out of her house for water or wood. Her children were cooped up inside too, blocked from venturing out because of bullets flying in all directions.[12] Her stories and others merely confirmed what Dr. Appel and his fellow officers had observed in Lincoln the day before.

Baca's behest proved critical. Early on the evening of July 18, Dudley summoned the five officers of his command to his quarters. For half an hour they discussed the situation in Lincoln and the danger to women and children, and they quickly decided that humanity demanded some form of military intervention. The orders required by the recent congressional legislation unequivocally prohibited intervention in civil affairs, but Dudley persuaded himself that a carefully neutral posture might serve the purpose without violating the orders. Mindful of the risks in the decision, all the officers signed a document recording their concurrence.[13]

Dudley's motives have been debated ever since. His enemies charged that he rushed in with the fixed purpose of helping Peppin, and indeed in response to a plea from Dolan on July 18 to come to his aid. Dudley argued that he went solely to protect women and children. All his officers backed him in this explanation. Neither he nor his officers had any personal stake in the outcome of the struggle. They leaned toward Dolan and Peppin simply because they represented more substantial institutions of law than McSween. But for a week, evidence had piled up of the grave danger in which the battle had placed defenseless citizens, and the officers agonized over the plight of helpless women and children. Moreover, they foresaw the public outrage that would fall on the army if any were harmed while the troops remained aloof at Fort Stanton.

Dudley may have thought that he could have it both ways, that he could protect noncombatants without interfering in civil affairs. More likely, he looked to a big show of neutrality to provide a defense against official reproach. Without much question, Dudley went to Lincoln chiefly for the reason he said he went, and he could not properly have resolved his dilemma in any other way.[14]

Dudley could assemble only a small command. Half of his troops were scouting the Guadalupe and Sacramento mountains for Indians, and the fort could not be left unguarded. The column he led to Lincoln on the morning of July 19 consisted, besides himself, of four officers, eleven black cavalrymen, and twenty-four white infantrymen. Bringing up the rear, tended by infantry, were a small twelve-pounder mountain howitzer and a rapid-fire Gatling gun.[15]

The blue column's approach to Lincoln at about 10:00 A.M. interrupted long-range sniping that had been under way since daybreak. Sheriff Peppin had conceived a vague plan for moving against the McSween house, and he had sent some possemen to the river to make certain that no one escaped from the rear of the house. But by midmorning, he had done nothing more. He was sitting in a privy at the edge of Wortley's corral when one of his men shouted that Colonel Dudley wanted to see him. Walking through the hotel to the street, Peppin confronted the colonel, astride his mount at the head of the column. Dudley declared that he had not come to assist either side, only to protect women and children; but if Peppin or anyone else fired on his command, he would return the fire.[16]

As the troops marched on down the street, the people in the McSween house watched apprehensively. A short time later, they saw three mounted cavalrymen come back up the street to the Wortley, then pass back to the east accompanied by Sheriff Peppin. Observing Peppin guarded by soldiers, Sue McSween recalled, "we all became alarmed." McSween hastily scribbled a note to Dudley: "Would you have the kindness to let me know why soldiers surround my house. Before blowing up my property I would like to know the reason. The constable is here and has warrants for the arrest of Sheriff Peppin and posse for murder and larceny."[17]

The Shields' little daughter took the note and left to find Dudley. She returned with the colonel's reply, signed by his adjutant. It said that no troops surrounded McSween's house and added that if McSween wanted to blow up his house, Dudley had no objection provided soldiers were not endangered.[18] What McSween had meant to write, of course, was that before the soldiers blew up his house with their artillery, he had a right to know why. Whether Dudley understood this but chose to ignore it, or truly believed that McSween threatened to blow up his home, is not apparent.

For McSween and his friends, the advent of soldiers, coupled with the sight of Peppin riding the street under military escort, led to an obvious conclusion: Dudley had come to help Peppin. They would have been doubly alarmed had they known just how much Dudley had already helped Peppin.

After pausing at the Wortley, Dudley had proceeded to near the center of town, where he found an open space slightly east of and across the street from the Montaño store. Its renter, George Washington, readily consented to its use as a campsite. The men pitched tents for the officers and strung a picket line for the cavalry horses. Dudley sent three troopers for Peppin to make certain that he knew where the soldiers had camped.[19]

Dudley wanted no one in Lincoln to misunderstand his purpose. He sent three infantrymen for Peppin again, and also summoned Isaac Ellis, and to both he repeated his declaration of neutrality and his warning against any fire that imperiled his command. As Peppin turned to leave, Dudley exclaimed: "God damn you understand me if one of your men wound one of my men I will blow you above the clouds." Dudley also sent patrols from house to house, and into the surrounding foothills, to give like notice to everyone and to offer the protection of his camp to any who wanted to come to it.[20]

Yet before camping or even dismounting, Dudley had stepped out of his passive role. Learning that the Montaño store harbored McSween gunmen, he had the howitzer unlimbered, loaded, and aimed at the front door; then he sent word that if any bullets came his way he would blow the house down. The startled defenders, with blankets thrown over their heads to hide their identity, promptly abandoned the building and hastened down the street to the Ellis store, where they united with their comrades.[21] Dudley then swung the howitzer toward the Ellis store, and the entire force evacuated that bastion too. Peppin and some possemen came running down the street in time to see them on the hills across the Río Bonito to the north. A brief exchange of gunfire marked their withdrawal.[22]

Dudley's handling of his artillery decisively altered the balance of power. It caused two-thirds of McSween's men to flee the town. Abruptly, Peppin gained a two-to-one numerical advantage over McSween. Moreover, Dudley's threat to blow above the clouds anyone whose fire came near his soldiers favored Peppin. Possemen could fire at the McSween house without violating Dudley's warning; McSween's defenders could not return the fire without risk to the soldiers. As Jack Long later remarked, "there was a more confident bunch inside the McSween house than was to be found outside it, until after the soldiers arrived."[23]

As Peppin's men gathered for the kill, Dudley engaged in an acrimonious exchange with one of Lincoln's leading citizens,

Squire Wilson. Dudley's board of officers had determined that McSween gunmen had fired on Private Robinson on the sixteenth, and in a fit of legalism the colonel had decided that his visit to Lincoln afforded opportunity to act on the findings. He had the justice of the peace brought to camp and instructed him to issue a warrant for McSween's arrest on charges of attempting to kill the soldier. When Wilson resisted, Dudley blustered about placing him in double irons and reporting him to the governor for failing in his duty. Easily intimidated, the old man did as he was told, took affidavits from Dr. Appel and the other two officers of the board, and after much labor handed a warrant to Sheriff Peppin.[24]

By noon, Peppin's ring had tightened around the remaining Regulator stronghold. At first, the sheriff himself had tried to give direction to the attack on the McSween house. Twice, however, he received summonses from Colonel Dudley and then had to leave for a third time when the McSween forces fled from the Ellis house to the north side of the Bonito. This time he returned only as far as the *torreon*, where he stationed himself for the rest of the battle.[25]

Peppin had assigned Deputy Marion Turner, a Seven Rivers stockman, to try to serve warrants on the men in the McSween house. As Peppin began his second hike to Dudley's camp, twenty to thirty possemen began to position themselves around the McSween house—in three little adobes on the south and west, in Squire Wilson's jacal, and against the walls of the McSween house itself.

Meanwhile, Turner, Milo Pearce, and Bob Olinger approached the front of the McSween house, while others crept to the windows along the west wall. With butcher knives, Turner and his men pried loose the shutters covering the front window of the southwest room and tore them from the wall. They smashed the window panes with rifle barrels and used them to push in stacks of adobe bricks serving as barricades. From the cover of the wall, Turner shouted into the window that he had warrants for McSween's arrest. McSween replied that he would not surrender, and that he had warrants for the posse's arrest. Turner demanded to see them. Jim French answered: "Our warrants are in our guns, you cock-sucking sons-of-bitches."[26] After a standoff of ten or fifteen minutes, Turner and his companions withdrew.

No one had expected the McSween defenders to give up to Turner. The attempt to serve the warrants was a mere formality, the pretext for moving to the attack. Already Peppin had decided to burn the enemy out of their stronghold, and one of the men who accompanied him to the Ellis store, Bob Beckwith, brought back a pail full of coal oil, drawn from a drum at the store. At the McSween house, he handed it to Jack Long, the deputy in charge of the possemen behind the house.[27]

Inside the house, Sue McSween announced her determination to go talk with Colonel Dudley. After discussion, her husband consented, and down the street she marched. She saw preparations underway to fire her house, and at the *torreon* she accusingly confronted Peppin. He angrily told her that if she did not want her house burned she must make the men inside come out, that he was tired of chasing them and intended to have them this day dead or alive.[28]

Distraught, Sue faced Dudley next to his tent and asked why his troops had come to town. He gave her the stock answer: to protect women and children. That explanation, Sue declared, was "too thin." Huffily, Dudley said that he was not accustomed to associating with women who used such vulgarisms as "too thin."

Sue implored Dudley to save her husband from death and her home from burning. But Dudley loftily maintained that he could not interfere with the sheriff in the discharge of his duty. McSween harbored known outlaws, he pointed out, and was resisting a legally constituted posse armed with legally issued warrants for their arrest. They could stop the battle at any time simply by giving up to the law. Certain that this would ensure her husband's death, Sue begged Dudley to allow Mac to surrender to him rather than to Peppin. Dudley refused.

As for preventing the burning of her house, Dudley professed puzzlement inasmuch as McSween had written that he intended to blow it up himself. He had no objections, Dudley said, so long as soldiers were not injured. Sue expressed disbelief and asked to see the paper. Dudley refused, saying that she would tear it up if she got her hands on it. Finally, he let her see it, but instructed a sergeant to shoot her if she made any false move.

From there, the conversation degenerated into mutual insults. Dudley scored McSween as a man of no principle, as shown by his cruel attempt to evict the convalescing Mrs. Baca, and implied that any woman married to him must be of low character. Sue charged Dudley with using the U.S. Army to assist thieves and murderers in their lawless schemes and with condemning her husband to certain death. Neither were novices at invective, and both gave as good as they received.[29]

At the McSween house, meanwhile, Peppin's men went grimly about their task. Accompanied by a deaf-mute known only as Dummy, Deputy Jack Long tried to fire the house. It had two kitchens, one at each end of the U-shaped structure. Long and Dummy went into the northeast kitchen, the one serving the Shield residence. They poured coal oil on the floor, covered it with kindling from a woodpile outside the door, and lit the fuel. Billy Bonney watched from the next room but did not fire, possibly because Mrs. Shield was present, carrying furniture from the house and stacking it along the picket fence to the east. The fire burned for about ten minutes, then went out.[30]

Unknown to Peppin's men behind the McSween house, Regulators George Coe, Henry Brown, and Joe Smith had concealed themselves in the Tunstall store. Posseman Andy Boyle, who had briefly watched Long's unsuccessful incendiary efforts, came out of the gate in the east fence and found himself under fire from the west window of the store. A bullet grazed his neck, and he ran around the corner to the cover of the adobe wall at the rear of the house.

Next, Long and Dummy emerged from the same gate and encountered the same fire. They dove for the nearest cover, which happened to be a privy at the northeast fence corner. The open vault, dug into the river bank, faced to the north, and the pair found safety there. At almost the same time, Buck Powell jumped into the refuge. The three men dared not leave. As Coe said of the "little house," when no other target could be seen, "we riddled it from top to bottom." Until after dark, Long, Powell, and Dummy stood in the sink. "It was not a good place to set down," Long explained.[31]

After dodging Coe's bullets, Andy Boyle made his way to the McSween stable at the northwest corner of the property. With the aid of some possemen there, Boyle collected the makings of another fire, this time in the northwest kitchen used by the McSweens. As Boyle related, "I set it on fire with a sack of shavings and chips and used what timber there was on top of the stable to make it burn. It burned very slowly all afternoon from one room to another turning in a circle around the house."[32]

Shortly after 2:00 P.M., a column of smoke formed over the McSween house. Peppin saw it from the *torreon*, Dudley and the soldiers from their camp. The McSween men who had fled the Montaño and Ellis stores also saw it, and eight or nine decided to go to their leader's aid. About 4:00 P.M., they appeared on the slopes north of the river and opened fire on the possemen. From the top of the *torreon*, Peppin fired back, and Dudley had his howitzer and Gatling gun rolled forward and pointed in their direction. They hastily backed off.[33]

As Boyle noted, the fire traveled slowly, room by room, through the adobe house. Few details of what transpired inside the house on that day have come to light. Sometime during the afternoon, the flames touched off a small keg of gunpowder, which prompted later reports that McSween had indeed tried to blow up his own house. Apparently, Tom Cullens was wounded or killed, and possibly one other. Shortly after the fire took hold, Mrs. Shield and her children and the school teacher, Miss Gates, sought refuge with the Ealys in the Tunstall store.[34]

Sue McSween remained until 5:00 P.M. She, who could have contributed so richly to history, left almost nothing unwarped by time and bitterness. A few scraps convey the mood in the house: "The boys talked to each other and McSween and I were sitting in one corner. The boys decided I should leave. They were fighting the fire in my sister's house [the east wing]. McSween said he guessed that that was better. . . . The Kid was lively and McSween was sad. McSween sat with his head down, and the Kid shook him and told him to get up, that they were going to make a break." Sue left, also going to join the Ealys next door.[35]

When Sue reached the Tunstall store, she found possemen preparing to burn it too. The firing of the McSween men from the west window had prompted this decision, and the Ealys were carrying their possessions outside. At their behest, Dudley had sent a wagon and some soldiers to move the belongings to the Patrón house. After the first load, however, Reverend Ealy had uttered some insulting words about Dudley, and he had petulantly refused further aid. Only after Mary Ealy sent a note of apology did the wagon make a final trip, loaded with Sue's organ, Ealy's books, and a sack of flour. The Ealys, Miss Gates, and Sue McSween spent the night at the Patrón house.[36]

Shortly after the Ealys had been moved, Colonel Dudley wandered into the Baca corral surrounding the *torreon*. Meeting Peppin, Dudley observed that if the posse did not quit destroying property, the soldiers would have to intervene. Peppin replied that he did not wish to destroy property, but he meant to have the McSween men out of the two buildings. Whether or not Peppin gave orders in response to Dudley's warning, the posse made no further attempt to fire the Tunstall store.[37]

As darkness fell, the climax approached. Flames consumed all but the northeast kitchen, where the defenders gathered. "The house was in a great blaze lighting up the hills on both sides of the town," recalled Dr. Appel. Firing intensified, and balls whistled over the military camp. Captain Purington remarked that "if the poor devils in that house could live through such a fire and get away they were certainly entitled to freedom."[38]

The "poor devils" had the choice of trying to escape or of burning when the fire ate into the kitchen. About 9:00 P.M., shortly after dark, they made the break. Although the flames lit the sky and the open space between the McSween house and the Tunstall store, the back yard lay deep in shadows cast by the kitchen and the adobe walls on the north and west. The possemen at the door in the back wall, only a few steps from the kitchen door, could make out almost nothing in the yard.[39]

One by one, the men in the kitchen slipped out, gathered in

the yard, and crept to the gate in the fence. In single file, they started into the open. Not until illuminated by the flames did the escapees catch the attention of possemen, who opened a heavy fire from behind the wall and elsewhere. The first five out the gate broke into a run. These were Jim French, Harvey Morris, Tom O'Folliard, José Chavez y Chavez, and Billy Bonney. Morris fell dead at the gate, but the rest dodged through the hail of bullets and lost themselves in the darkness of the river and its sheltering trees.

The firing drove McSween and the others back into the shadows. Some crouched against the walls, while others sought refuge in a chicken house in the northwest corner of the yard. About five minutes later, a few tried once again to break through the gate, only to be driven back by a deadly fire.

Ten minutes passed. Then McSween called out: "I shall surrender." Robert Beckwith answered: "I am a deputy sheriff and I have got a warrant for you." Accompanied by John Jones, Joe Nash, and Dummy, Beckwith entered the yard and confronted McSween at the kitchen door. McSween yelled: "I shall never surrender."

"When McSween said he would not surrender," related Andy Boyle, who was at the door in the adobe wall, "every one of them commenced to shoot. Robert Beckwith fell first, McSween on top of him and two Mexicans right beside of them. Two more Mexicans went into the chicken house, and two more fell between the door and the back house."

Boyle called this shootout "the big killing." It was a wild and confused melee in which both sides shot blindly at close range in the darkened yard behind the blazing house. Beckwith caught the first ball, in the corner of the left eye, and died instantly; another hit him in the wrist. Five bullets slammed into McSween. Vicente Romero and Francisco Zamora fell dead next to McSween. Young Yginio Salazar crumpled with a bullet in the back and one in the shoulder. Though severely wounded in the arm, Ignacio Gonzales got away in the confusion, as did Florencio Chavez and José María Sanchez.[40]

As the McSween house defenders made their break, so did those in the Tunstall store. George Coe, Henry Brown, and Joe

Smith ran into the corral behind the store and confronted an eight-foot adobe wall. Tunstall's bulldog, chained in a corner, charged at Brown, who drew down on him with his rifle. "Henry," shouted Coe, "let that old dog alone and let's get out of here." Beer bottles had been thrown in a mound against the wall. The three men leaped to the top of this, then vaulted over the wall and ran to the river.[41]

McSween's back yard swarmed with jubilant possemen, shouting and firing their weapons in celebration. Painfully wounded, Yginio Salazar regained consciousness, but feigned death. "John Kinney took my gun away from me after I was shot down and kicked me," Salazar recalled. "I was conscious, but just laid there." After the yard cleared, he crawled to the river and made his way to the home of a friend below town, where he was treated next day by Dr. Appel.[42]

Daylight on July 20 revealed the carnage of the night before. The five bullet-riddled bodies still lay in the yard behind the smoking ruins of McSween's house. Several chickens picked at McSween's corpse. "I drove them away myself," said Colonel Dudley, "and ordered a bed quilt that was lying in the yard spread over the body." After the coroner's jury had assembled and reached its verdict, Sheriff Peppin had friends of Zamora and Romero come for their bodies, and those of McSween and Morris were moved to the Tunstall store. Beckwith was removed by friends and arrangements made, with Dudley's permission, for burial in the Fort Stanton cemetery. That afternoon, Sebrian Bates, the McSweens' black servant, dug a grave east of the store, next to Tunstall's grave. No ceremony marked McSween's burial.[43]

At the Tunstall store that morning, even as the bodies of McSween and Morris were laid out in another room, Peppin's victorious warriors crowded into the main entrance. Drawn by a loud commotion inside, Colonel Dudley and Dr. Appel entered. Dry goods and merchandise littered the counters and the floor. John Kinney was there. So was Jesse Evans, stripped to his underwear and trying on a new suit. The officers watched the chaotic scene for about five minutes before returning to camp.[44]

That afternoon, Dudley struck camp and led his command back to Fort Stanton.

For all the thousands of shots fired, the Five-Day Battle produced remarkably few casualties except in the final few moments of furious bloodletting. Charlie Crawford received a mortal wound on the morning of the seventeenth, and Ben Ellis was dangerously wounded that night. On July 19, bullets from George Coe's party in the Tunstall store grazed several possemen, and on this day or earlier Tom Cullens and possibly one other were killed or mortally wounded inside the McSween house. The breakout on the night of the nineteenth cost the lives of McSween, Morris, Zamora, Romero, and Beckwith; Salazar caught two painful bullets, one of which he carried in his body for the rest of a long life; and Ignacio Gonzales nursed a shattered elbow.

The pattern of casualties suggests that neither side pressed the Five-Day Battle very aggressively until the showdown on the last day. No one provided much leadership, either tactical or inspirational. It was not so much a mismanaged conflict as one almost altogether unmanaged. It followed an erratic course undirected from on high and responsive to the impulses of individual fighters.

McSween came to town on July 14 without any apparent plan other than not again to be driven from his home. He led a force that outnumbered Peppin's and held defenses that could be taken only at great cost, but his dispositions betray no foresight or purpose. Once Dolan and Peppin accepted the challenge, McSween could not control his men in the Montaño and Ellis stores. The possemen in the Wortley Hotel, and especially in the *torreon*, effectively cut off communication between the various McSween strongholds.

Nor did McSween's resolve remain firm. As Sue noted, no one in the McSween house fired during July 18. And even on the nineteenth, with the posse closing in for the kill, there is no evidence of defensive fire except from the Tunstall store. In the morning, Deputy Turner and his companions spent about fifteen minutes at a window of the McSween house trying to serve warrants without drawing any fire. In the afternoon, Long and Boyle methodically went about the task of setting the house ablaze without any interference from the defenders. Indeed, Billy Bonney watched from the adjoining room as Jack Long tried to kindle his fire in the northeast kitchen. Nor did McSween's uncertainty bring forth leadership from his fighters, unless Bonney, as hinted by Sue, rose to the occasion during the final hours in the McSween house. Doc Scurlock, John Middleton, and Charlie Bowdre, McSween loyalists from the beginning, badly failed their chief. With close to forty gunmen, they abandoned the Ellis store on the flimsiest provocation and sought safety in the hills north of town. A handful made a half-hearted attempt to relieve McSween in the afternoon, but allowed themselves to be driven off by a few shots from George Peppin's Winchester and, possibly, the threat of Dudley's artillery.

Alexander McSween failed the test of leadership that he himself had forced. His hesitant course reflected the ambivalence that had marked his behavior from his first appearance in Lincoln. His complex makeup seems to have masked a struggle between ambition for power and wealth and ambition to promote the public welfare, a struggle that gained its ultimate resolution only on the back doorstep of his blazing home.

Nor did McSween's executioners exhibit much leadership. After the troops reached Lincoln, Sheriff Peppin spent the entire day in the *torreon*. Aside from ordering the McSween house set afire, he gave no direction to the attack. Dolan spent the day in one of the little adobes opposite the McSween house and exerted no influence on the course of battle. Nor did Deputy Turner, who returned to the Wortley Hotel after failing to serve his warrants. The decisive figures were Jack Long and Andy Boyle, who on their own initiative persisted at great risk in firing the McSween house, and Boyle, Nash, Pearce, Dummy, Jones, and Beckwith, who stood up against McSween and his comrades in the final shootout.

Of all the players in the drama, however, none acted in as truly critical a role as Colonel Dudley. On the silent and smoking battlefield of Lincoln, he left the makings of a controversy that burst over him and the army. Inflamed by his own quarrelsome disposition, the dispute centered on whether, actively or passively, he had decided the outcome of the fight. Almost a year later, an army court cleared him. History has not been so generous.

Dudley's mere appearance in Lincoln, coupled with notice that he would return the fire of anyone whose bullets came his way, shifted the tactical advantage from McSween to Peppin. As four days of shooting had shown, McSween could not be dislodged from his defenses without unacceptable risk. Now, Peppin could attack, but McSween could not shoot back without the danger of hitting a soldier.

Next, Dudley's menacing deployment of his artillery shifted the numerical odds from McSween to Peppin. The flight of the men in the Montaño and Ellis stores lost McSween two-thirds of his little army. From roughly sixty to forty in McSween's favor, the odds jumped to about forty to twenty in Peppin's favor. This development also aided Peppin in greatly contracting the battle-field. Now his men had only the McSween house and Tunstall store to worry about, and they could move freely about the rest of the town in safety. Dudley justified his handling of the artillery as elementary precautions for self-defense in case of attack, a technicality that scarcely diluted his responsibility for the decisive event of the battle.

In view of this action, the McSween forces could not be faulted for believing that the soldiers had come to help Peppin, a belief that later expanded to include their active participation. Occupants of the McSween house and Tunstall store recalled soldiers standing about and even helping to fuel the blaze, and Billy Bonney and José Chavez y Chavez told of three soldiers firing on them from the southwest corner of the Tunstall store during the deadly break for the river.

In fact, Dudley gave strict orders that no soldiers were to leave camp unless authorized. They had no reason to disobey, certainly not to risk their lives in a fight that did not remotely concern them. Enough left on routine assignments from Dudley, however, to constitute a conspicuous military presence and to give rise to the conviction of the McSween people that the army supported the enemy. Adding to the impression and explaining some of the testimony, several possemen wore old military jackets or trousers.[45]

Dudley needlessly invited criticism by bullying Justice of the Peace Wilson. The warrant for McSween's arrest that Dudley forced Wilson to issue had no effect on the events of the day. Peppin already had warrants for McSween and virtually all of the Regulators. He did not need another warrant to claim legal sanction for his attack on the McSween forces. Dudley's enemies made much of this episode, as if he sought the warrant to justify his presence, but its principal significance was to betray the colonel's sympathies and convict him of bad timing and bad judgment. He need not have chosen this particular day to make an issue of the matter.

Dudley's bombast toward Sue McSween further damaged his credibility and gained him an enemy of formidable powers. She also confronted him with a dilemma to which he proved entirely insensitive. He had come to town to protect women and children. The McSween house contained three women and five children. He might have seized on this pretext to accept McSween's surrender as Sue had pleaded. He was technically correct, of course, in declining to interfere with the sheriff. But he had already intervened in civil matters simply by marching into Lincoln, and the added risk could not have been so great if explained by the wish to end bloodshed. He surely knew that if McSween surrendered to the sheriff, he would be killed on one pretext or another before he could come to trial. As further rationale, and as McSween himself pointed out in a note to Dudley, the precinct constable, one of the Regulators, had legal warrants from the justice of the peace for the arrest of Peppin and most of his posse. What better course than to stop the fighting and let the courts decide? Instead, he climbed on his high plane of noninterference, leaving Sue, her sister, Miss Gates, and the children to seek safety elsewhere and McSween and three others to perish in the final shootout.

On top of all the other accusations, Dudley found himself charged with abetting and even participating in the looting of the Tunstall store on July 20. In truth, he briefly watched Peppin's men ransack the store without protesting. But unless Jesse Evans walked out in a new suit, which is uncertain, the store was not actually looted before the troops returned to their station in the afternoon. The plunder of the contents occurred that night and the next day, and some of the very noncombatants Dudley had come to protect shared the adventure with the jubilant possemen.[46]

Although the military court of inquiry that probed Dudley's conduct swept away all the allegations and even bestowed generous compliments, the evidence presented to the court gives him a different place in history than in military law. Even though prohibited by orders, Dudley went to Lincoln for the right reasons. Once there, by his words he showed his partiality for Peppin, and by his deeds he gave decisive assistance to Peppin. However technically persuasive it was to a military court, the rationale for these words and deeds rings hollow in history. Yet, ironically, even the most passive role could not have avoided influencing the battle in favor of Peppin. Dudley could have brought about a different result only by abandoning all pretense of noninterference and simply stopping the fight. This is what he should have done.

Dudley's erratic behavior in Lincoln is consistent with his official conduct throughout the Lincoln County War. He alternated wildly between responsible command and capricious, self-defeating impulse. Only one witness at the court of inquiry, probably the least reliable, testified to Dudley drinking on July 19,[47] but it would be surprising if he did not have a sizable flask in his saddle bag and even more surprising if he did not imbibe liberally from it during the day. Dudley's eccentricity usually found its inspiration in a bottle, no less on July 19, 1878, than on any other day.

A master at self-justification, Dudley easily convinced himself of the rectitude of his every action in Lincoln. That his actions truly traced a bewildering course escaped him entirely. He deeply, and correctly, believed that he went to town for unimpeachable reasons. His grand show of neutrality convinced almost no one of his neutrality, but him it did convince. Neutrality justified his refusal to save McSween and to interfere with the impending looting of the Tunstall store. A military technicality rationalized a departure from neutrality in the handling of his artillery, a legal technicality in the browbeating of Justice Wilson, and a sudden impulse to avoid further destruction his warning against burning the Tunstall store. In Dudley's mind, all fell logically and defensibly into place, and he genuinely believed that he had behaved responsibly and humanely.

So, perhaps, did the other participants on both sides, although it is difficult to credit Jimmy Dolan with high-minded motives. In all his mental density, Peppin surely believed his role to be correct and lawful. The Seven Rivers cowboys also convinced themselves of their public-spirited purpose. By contrast, Jesse Evans and John Kinney were there simply for whatever they could get out of it, and by whatever means. In truth, in this noisy fight no one behaved very admirably. Of all the events of the Lincoln County War, the Five-Day Battle most dramatically reveals it to have been a war without heroes.

9

The
Wrestlers

THE LINCOLN COUNTY WAR should have ended in Alexander McSween's back yard on the night of July 19, 1878. The war was a struggle to determine whether an existing monopoly or an aspiring monopoly would dominate Lincoln County. Neither, it turned out, would achieve that distinction, for both collapsed in the rubble of war. With McSween's death and Dolan's bankruptcy, nothing remained to fight about.

The war did not end. It had taken on a life of its own, independent of its commanders. Even before the Five-Day Battle, the armies had outrun their leaders. After the battle, although the Regulators and Peppin's posse dissolved as formal organizations, the old hostilities kept public sentiment polarized. Most of the fighters on both sides stayed in the county, spreading crime, violence, and dread from the Pecos to the Sierra Blanca.

Former Regulators contributed prominently to the turmoil. Colonel Dudley complained of Doc Scurlock, Jim French, Charlie Bowdre, and "that bunch" strutting openly around Lincoln and darkly declaring their intent to assassinate him for his supposed complicity in McSween's death. They slept in front of Juan Patrón's house, where Sue McSween stayed, because she feared that Dolan, or Dudley, plotted her murder. "I guess we owed it to the wife of old penny pincher Mac," recalled Jim French, "but she never even thanked us."

A year or two later, French wrote to Sam Corbet: "Do you remember the night we was guarding outside her house and the

Pole cat walked across your chest and wakened you up and you let out a yell you could hear a mile away and wakened Mrs Mac in the house and scared her so she thought Jim Dolans boys had come to kill her sure enough."[1]

The "McSween ring," as Colonel Dudley styled these men, also menaced Saturnino Baca, whom they held largely responsible for persuading Dudley to bring the soldiers to Lincoln on July 19. Dudley took them seriously when they threatened to burn out Baca in retaliation for the burning of the McSween house, and he stationed a guard at Baca's home. This, of course, violated his orders, and he had to withdraw the guard when reprimanded by higher headquarters. Baca found refuge at Fort Stanton.[2]

Indian Agent Frederick C. Godfroy also took fright at the Regulators. Possibly in an effort to get his own man substituted for Godfroy, McSween had brought charges of fraud and corruption against the agent, and a special investigator had been sent to examine the ties between him and Murphy, Dolan, and Riley.[3] After McSween's death, Godfroy had gained the notion, perhaps not without reason, that the Regulators were out to kill him.[4]

They almost did. On August 5, the Indian agency formed the setting for the last action of the Regulators as a body. Their motives are obscure. They may indeed have been after Godfroy because of his feud with McSween. Another report had them en route to recover stolen stock. Frank Coe explained, unconvincingly, that they wanted to visit the grave of Dick Brewer, who had been buried at the agency after the Blazer's Mills fight of April 4. Most likely, they went simply to steal ponies belonging to the Indians.

The band that approached the agency at South Fork numbered almost twenty. It included Scurlock, Bonney, Middleton, Bowdre, French, and others of the Anglo contingent, together with about ten Hispanics. The Anglos paused to drink from a spring while the Hispanics continued toward the agency. Within sight of the buildings, the latter encountered a party of Indians and firing broke out.

At the agency issue house, Godfroy and his clerk, Morris Bernstein, were doling out rations to some Indian women. Hearing the gunfire, they hastily mounted and galloped out to investigate. Bernstein, in advance, rode into the midst of the battle and was shot down by Atanacio Martínez, the Lincoln constable who had occasionally ridden with the Regulators since the first hostilities in February. With bullets zipping around him, Godfroy turned and raced back to the agency.

A few soldiers happened to be at the agency, and with the agent they sprang to the defense. The confused firing that followed killed Billy Bonney's horse, and he escaped injury only by mounting behind George Coe and galloping across an open glade under heavy fire. The Anglo group circled the agency to the corral and made off with all the horses and mules.

Godfroy found Bernstein's body lying face down with four bullet holes in it. His pockets had been emptied and his rifle and pistol taken.[5]

The theft of government stock gave Colonel Dudley the excuse to put a detachment of troopers on the trail of the culprits, but they scattered and easily escaped. For the next few months, although frequently appearing in Lincoln, they spent much time at Fort Sumner, where they collected stolen horses to sell in the Texas Panhandle. Fred Waite, John Middleton, and Henry Brown decided to leave New Mexico for good. Bonney remained, with the faithful O'Folliard fawningly at his side, to assert growing leadership among former Regulators whose pursuits turned more and more to open outlawry. On September 6, the Kid and several others stole fifteen horses from Charles Fritz's ranch, east of Lincoln, and added them to the herd they eventually drove to the Panhandle.[6]

Lincoln County struggled not only with the legacy of the fight between McSween and Dolan. Far worse, it plunged into a desperate battle against outlaws from other parts of the West. With the army neutralized and Peppin afraid to venture beyond sight of Fort Stanton, desperadoes rushed from elsewhere to take advantage of the absence of any authority to uphold law and order. Citizens shut themselves in their homes or abandoned them altogether.

The horrors that swept the county in the wake of the Five-Day Battle, however, were chiefly the work of a gang that traced its origins to Peppin's posse. They called themselves the *Wrestlers*, a term doubtless corrupted from *rustlers*, and at first most were probably men who had come to Lincoln County with John Kinney. They may have organized for the specific purpose of seizing Tunstall's cattle as a reward for serving Peppin. Around the time of the Five-Day Battle, John Selman and a handful of cohorts came up from Texas and threw in with the Wrestlers. With a trail of lawlessness and violence leading back to desertion from the Confederate army in 1863, Selman had compiled a record of vicious criminality that made Kinney and Evans look like gentle neophytes. Selman soon asserted leadership over the Wrestlers and made their escapades a reflection of his own malignancy.[7] Through August and September, the Wrestlers, who also called themselves Selman's Scouts, laid waste the valleys of the Bonito, Ruidoso, and Hondo. They maimed or killed men, insulted or raped women, and drove off horses and cattle. They broke open and plundered homes in Lincoln, burned Clenny's store in San Patricio, and put the torch to Frank Coe's ranch on the Hondo.

The bandits also paid their expected visit to the Tunstall ranch. Early in August, Godfrey Gauss, Tunstall's erstwhile chuck wrangler, rushed to the Feliz to get Tunstall's cattle, but Jimmy McDaniels and eight Wrestlers got there first. They cleaned out the ranch and drove the herd down to the Pecos. They "taken everything," whined Sam Corbet, "even old Gauss's clothes."[8]

On one memorable day, September 28, the Wrestlers blazed a horrifying trail of murder, fire, rape, and destruction down the Bonito and the Hondo. Near Fort Stanton, they brutalized the Hudgens family at Murphy's old brewery. In Lincoln, they tried to seize the Ellis store, but were driven off by gunfire. Down the valley, at Bartlett's mill, they dragged the wives of two mill workers into the brush, stripped them naked, and as Dudley put it delicately, "used them at their pleasure." At the nearby farm of José Chavez y Sanchez, they rode up to three men cutting hay in the fields, two of whom were Chavez's young sons, and opened fire. All three fell riddled with bullets. Down the Hondo, at Martín Sanchez's farm, they demanded watermelons. "His boy, about twelve or fourteen years old," related Coe, "carried the watermelons up for them and before they left they shot him down." He fell with bullets in his head, chest, and belly.[9]

Dr. Appel's civilian assistant, Dr. William B. Lyon, volunteered to go to the Sanchez farm and treat the boy. A courier met him with word that the boy had died. Lyon stopped at the Chavez place, where he "found the whole family in a most pitiable condition—the father and mother almost crazed with grief, and all in a state of constant terror." Along the road, Lyon saw deserted fields, and the few travelers moved with dread. "On meeting a stranger on the road both parties clear for action," he reported.[10]

The Wrestlers left their mark on the Pecos, too, and in fact they made their winter headquarters at Seven Rivers. All three mail carriers between Fort Sumner and Fort Stanton served notice that they would not risk the "perfect reign of terror" along the road, and Roswell postmaster Ash Upson closed the post office and sought safety in Picacho. Roswell's leading citizens appealed to Dudley for protection. "Men are shot down like so many dogs," they said, "in parties of two or three. Women are outraged, and their children driven from their homes. Entire settlements have been compelled to abandon their Ranches, Crops, and flee from the country for safety."[11]

The violence that swept Lincoln County in the aftermath of the Five-Day Battle differed in kind and intensity from any that had gone before. Even in the bloodiest days of the war between McSween and Dolan, no such barbarity had been inflicted on anyone, much less on inoffensive people going about their daily business. Only in the Horrell War of 1873 was there precedent, and that had been mild by comparison. The code sanctioned killing for cause, with the definition of cause left to the killer. The code did not sanction random, mindless, purposeless slaughter, destruction, and pillage. And the code did not sanction rape, an offense of great rarity in Lincoln County. How the code came to be suspended for a month or two can only be explained by the depravity of a few offenders. Most of the outlaws, even those who rode with John Selman, stuck by the code. But the few who did not, including Selman, spread truly appalling havoc and produced a crisis that cried out for decisive military action.

Colonel Dudley fumed in impotence. José Chavez y Sanchez, at Fort Stanton to buy coffins for his two murdered sons, sat in Dudley's parlor and poured out his anguish. That such wanton killing could occur "in the presence of two sheriffs and plenty of troops" struck Dudley as outrageous. "I respectfully and earnestly ask in the name of God and humanity," he implored his superiors, "that I may be allowed to use the Forces at my command, to drive these murderers, horse-thieves, and escaped convicts out of the country."[12]

Dudley's instincts were correct, as they were on July 19 when he led his soldiers into Lincoln. Peppin could do nothing. "The Sheriff is as powerless as a child," Dudley observed.[13] Only the U.S. Army had the power to combat such rampant savagery.

As early as mid-August, pressures had begun building for military intervention. A delegation of county officials trooped to Santa Fe to plead with Governor Axtell for help in getting the army involved again. In forwarding their petition to President Hayes, the governor declared that armed bands totaling two hundred men overran southeastern New Mexico, inflicting murder, arson, rape, and robbery on the populace. Men had been murdered, he said; women and young girls, "mere children," had been ravished, and property stolen. New Mexico had no militia, and its treasury was too lean to organize one. Only federal troops could "end this horrible state of affairs."[14]

But the *posse comitatus* law kept the soldiers penned up in their fort. The gates could be unlocked in only two ways. The president could declare a state of insurrection and then authorize troops to serve as a *posse comitatus*, aiding the sheriff in apprehending criminals and bringing them before the courts. Or the president could declare both insurrection and martial law, which would substitute military power not only for the police but the courts as well.

Such extreme and politically distasteful solutions were unlikely to be seriously considered by the president unless they were forcefully urged by the territorial governor. And Axtell, while calling for military intervention in Lincoln County, had so far lost credibility as to have no influence with the administration in Washington. In fact, although he did not know it, by late August Axtell was a lame-duck governor.

117

10
Ben-Hur
Wallace

GOVERNMENT INVESTIGATOR Frank Warner Angel came back to Santa Fe in the middle of July 1878, on the eve of the Five-Day Battle. Although what he had learned in Lincoln County biased him in favor of McSween, he told Governor Axtell that against him he had found "not the scratch of a pen" in evidence. Charged also with investigating the Colfax County War, Angel next journeyed to Cimarron. There, the persuasive Frank Springer, a principal in that conflict, convinced him of the governor's villainy. Angel returned to Santa Fe, penned a long series of intimidating "interrogatories" for Axtell to answer, and headed for Washington.[1]

Angel's report, submitted in October to Secretary of the Interior Carl Schurz and Attorney General Charles Devens, scored Axtell on eleven out of twelve allegations relating to the Lincoln and Colfax county wars. The governor's ill-considered actions in removing Justice Wilson and Sheriff Copeland and appointing Sheriff Peppin formed the basis for charges of favoring Dolan, usurping judicial functions, abusing appointive and removal powers, and even directly and indirectly supporting outlaws and murderers. He stood acquitted only of the accusation that he was a Mormon plotting to make New Mexico a Mormon territory.

Axtell deserved better. His handling of Lincoln County troubles had indeed been badly flawed, the result of poor judgment and uncritical acceptance of the opinions and advice of partisans. But his course was not mendaciously or corruptly motivated, and the language in which Angel described the offenses partook more of hyperbole than of fact. Compared with his predecessors, Axtell had been a good governor.

Even so, he was to be the sacrificial lamb. Angel had already formed his conclusions by the time he reached Washington, D.C., in late August. A meeting with Secretary Schurz, the cabinet officer to whom territorial governors reported, doomed Axtell. On August 31, Schurz advised President Hayes that Angel's oral report had convinced him of the need for a change in Santa Fe, and "the sooner the better." As a candidate for the post had already said he would serve, "we ought to have him on the spot as speedily as possible."[2]

The candidate was Lew Wallace, and ever since Hayes's inauguration he had anxiously awaited the president's summons to high office. His law practice in sleepy Crawfordsville, Indiana, afforded none of the adventure and romance that he craved, and he found vicarious compensation in literary pastimes. One novel had proved moderately successful, and now he labored on another, a sweeping saga of biblical times whose hero he named Ben-Hur.

Wallace expected reward for valuable services to the Republican cause in the disputed presidential election of 1876. A diplomatic post in Bolivia held no appeal. The territorial governorship of New Mexico seemed little better. But perhaps fearing no further offers, when he was sounded out in August 1878, he said that he would accept.[3]

On September 4, the word went forth to Crawfordsville. Rescued at last, Wallace hastened to Washington for a briefing by Angel; then, he faced west. On the night of September 30, stiff, sore, and utterly exhausted, he "crawled off" the buckboard that had brought him from the railhead in Colorado and took refuge in the Exchange Hotel.[4]

New Mexico had gained no ordinary party hack such as presidents usually sent to this remote territory as a reward for political services. At fifty-one, Lew Wallace looked back on a career of genuine distinction, one that testified to uncommon merit. Service in the Mexican War had kindled in him a martial ardor that burned ever more brightly with advancing age. In the Civil War he rose rapidly to high rank. But at Shiloh, General

Wallace took longer to get his division to the battlefield than General Ulysses S. Grant thought warranted, and chances for military fame and glory fell victim to Grant's search for a scapegoat. Wallace never regained the prestige and authority that he had enjoyed before Shiloh, and the resulting sense of injustice proved to be a lifelong obsession. His quest for vindication, sometimes tactless and self-defeating, irritated General and later President Grant as well as General William Tecumseh Sherman, Grant's friend and also a Shiloh commander. In 1878, Sherman headed the army, and Governor Wallace needed, but did not get, his friendly cooperation.

Wallace looked and acted like a governor. A thick, short beard and brushy mustache covered much of his face, while his hair fell carelessly across a high forehead. Eye glasses perched on the bridge of his nose. "Tall and slender," wrote a newsman who interviewed him on the eve of his departure for New Mexico, with "the weather-beaten face and military bearing indicative of the trained soldier, a piercing black eye, and decision of character written in every lineament of his countenance. An active life in the field has left its traces on his face and sprinkled his raven hair with gray. His manner is frank and courteous and his conversational power great."[5] Lawyer, politician, soldier, scholar, philosopher, musician, artist, author, sportsman, restless adventurer, and ambitious public figure, Lew Wallace brought to his post a sharpness of intellect, a range of abilities, and a breadth of interests unrivaled by any predecessor.

At once, Governor Wallace plunged into his new duties. He had been sent to New Mexico to clean up Lincoln County, and within five days of taking the oath of office he had gathered evidence to support bold measures. From Colonel Edward Hatch, commander of the military district, he obtained the dispatches of Colonel Dudley at Fort Stanton. Judge Bristol reported that the fall term of district court could not be held in safety; and anyway, the citizens were too terrorized to function as witnesses or jurors. U.S. Marshal John Sherman declared himself powerless to serve federal arrest warrants.

Citing these opinions, Wallace telegraphed his recommendations to Secretary Schurz on October 5. With the army, the sheriff, the marshal, and the courts impotent and the territory without a militia, he said, only one recourse remained: martial law. He urged Schurz to see the president and seek a proclamation placing Lincoln County under martial law, suspending the writ of habeas corpus, and establishing a military commission to try all offenders.[6]

The Hayes administration reacted swiftly, but met Wallace only halfway. To use troops in apprehending criminals seemed defensible; to use them to try, convict, and sentence criminals was not politically acceptable. In a fence-straddling proclamation of October 7, therefore, President Hayes declared Lincoln County to be in a state of insurrection and commanded all dissidents to disband and return to their homes by October 13. After that date, the army could again lawfully furnish posses to civil authorities.[7]

This was hardly the martial law for which Wallace had asked, and he thought the measure unresponsive. "To refer the matter to the civil authorities is childish," he wired Schurz with a fine disregard for presidential protocol. Lincoln County suffered as much from a paralyzed court as from a paralyzed sheriff; for troops to help in catching criminals served no purpose if the courts could not try and punish them. The judiciary could not be expected to function, he declared, "when courts must sit surrounded by bayonets, and juries deliberate in dread of assassination." The only solution was "to make war upon the murderous bands," and that meant martial law.[8]

But Wallace made the best of what he had been given. No one seemed quite sure of the next move. On October 26, therefore, he took it upon himself to lay before Colonel Hatch a proposed program for employing the army to pacify the war zone. Hatch obligingly framed instructions for Colonel Dudley that reflected Wallace's thinking as well as his own orders from Washington to disperse "unlawful combinations" that had failed to heed the president's command. Dispatched the very next day, October 27, Hatch's orders required Dudley to provide the sheriff with military posses upon request, but also, even in the absence of requests, to take the initiative in rounding up and confining criminals.[9]

Even before these orders went out, Wallace had persuaded

himself that the president's proclamation was working. Little more than a week after he had branded it childish, he informed Schurz that it had produced a "sufficient effect" and that he hoped martial law could be avoided.[10] Except for generally favorable press coverage, Wallace had no evidence on which to base his new assessment, but he had suddenly acquired good reason for wishing it so. Rumors flew that political enemies sought to head off his confirmation in the U.S. Senate, and he wanted to be able to say that he had already done what he had been sent to New Mexico to do.

Although Schurz thought Wallace's alarm unfounded, worry over his confirmation probably motivated the governor's next move. Needing a show of success to offset the opposition, Wallace simply declared success. Two dispatches from Colonel Dudley reported no recent crime or violence, so on November 13 Wallace issued his own proclamation announcing the end of disorders in Lincoln County and inviting residents to resume their normal occupations. To foster the return to peace and normalcy, Wallace extended a "general pardon" to all offenders not already indicted by a grand jury.[11]

The governor's proclamation met with the disapproval of New Mexico's newspapers. "Of course the Governor is desirous of being confirmed," editorialized the *Mesilla Independent*, "and the most peaceful aspect of affairs will be the more conducive to that result." In fact, a lull in "the murdering of people in cold blood" had occurred, conceded the *Mesilla News*, but peace had not returned, and "the people are living in daily expectation and fear of a recurrence of lawlessness." Only the sight of bluecoats on the roads and in the settlements restrained new outbreaks of violence. Reports from Colonel Dudley throughout late November and early December sustained the opinions of the press.

The amnesty attracted even more criticism. The *New Mexican* thought it "granted undeserved grace" to malefactors; the *News* branded it "outrageous;" and the *Independent* pronounced it both illegal and improper. "The bad element," according to the *Independent*, "along with the good are invited to return and still apply their nefarious vocations." Again, Dudley's dispatches substantiated the charge. Men who had fled the county rather than face military arrest now returned, secure in the protection of the governor's pardon.[12]

Wallace drew criticism not merely for his proclamation. "As to Lincoln County," he had wired Schurz on the very day he took office, "I shall go see the people immediately." Yet he did not go, and from all sides his procrastination earned reproach. The newspapers took up the cry. Late in December, Wallace lamely explained that he could have gone to neither town nor fort without arousing bad feeling at the other, "so I stayed away from both, and am well satisfied that I did so."[13]

In truth, Wallace either convinced himself of the accuracy of his proclamation or simply lost interest in Lincoln County, or both. The explanation probably sprang in large part from a competing preoccupation. He had resumed work on his novel. Each night Wallace withdrew to an inner room of the ancient Palace of the Governors and, in the glow of a "student's-lamp," spun more adventures for the fictional Ben-Hur. Nudged by the vicarious immediacy of the Holy Land, Lincoln County receded to the far corners of his mind.[14]

Meanwhile, in Lincoln County, events tended to support Wallace's first evaluation of the president's proclamation. The sheriff and his deputies could call on troops to help in arresting criminals, but the absence of effective judicial machinery made the effort futile. Judge Bristol would not hold district court in Lincoln until April, if then. In the meantime, Justice of the Peace Wilson presided over the only court in which offenders could be arraigned and bound over for trial. Ignorant and confused as ever, he handed down rulings that defied law and logic and generally favored the McSween faction. Colonel Dudley fumed in frustration over Wilson's habit of dismissing charges against men whom the troops had gone to great trouble to help in apprehending and bringing into court. In one instance, Dudley reported, Wilson acquitted a man of larceny but made him pay court costs and return the property he had stolen. For the sheriff and the army alike, such caprice destroyed all incentive to try to run down criminals.[15]

For other reasons, too, the army proved less effective than

Wallace had hoped. The instructions governing the troops left considerable uncertainty about how large a role they could play in restoring order, but commanders preferred the narrowest possible interpretation. In practice, they generally acted only on the request and in the presence of a civil officer. When Captain Henry Carroll helped a Roswell constable arrest the principals in a knife-wielding drunken brawl, the issue arose of which civil officers to assist. Wallace argued that the secretary of war's original orders permitted a comprehensive definition—territorial, county, and township. But the army stuck to a limited interpretation. Only federal marshals and county sheriffs, or their deputies, would be aided. As the U.S. marshal refused to name a deputy in Lincoln County until peace was restored, that left Sheriff Peppin, and he had all but abdicated months earlier.[16]

On still another score the army disappointed Wallace— Colonel Dudley. Not only did his role in the Five-Day Battle make him anathema to the McSween faction and thus a focus of local contention; he was also the key to the governor's hopes for ending the troubles in Lincoln County. Without his active cooperation, success seemed elusive. Yet, unthinkingly, Wallace had managed to anger that vain and temperamental controversialist and to become embroiled with him in a bitter public feud. Until one or the other departed, Lincoln County could expect no solution.

11
Colonel
Dudley

COLONEL DUDLEY led his column back to Fort Stanton on the afternoon of July 20, 1878, and promptly sat down to write an official report. In wordy detail, he described all the happenings of July 19–20 in Lincoln.' He put the best face on his own motives and actions, of course, but nothing could hide the reality that he had violated an act of Congress and military orders issued by the secretary of war himself.

Despite his report, Dudley's foray into Lincoln earned him no reprimand—indeed, no official notice at all. In the absence of any public protest, the army chain of command shrank from giving prominence to so politically volatile an issue as military involvement in domestic disorder.

Dudley would probably have escaped official scrutiny altogether except for Sue McSween. The distraught widow loudly proclaimed him the actual murderer of her husband; then, she conceived the notion that he intended to murder her, too. Terrified, she had men like Middleton and French guard her residence at night, and finally, in September, she fled to Las Vegas, where her sister's husband, David Shield, had set up a new law practice.

In Las Vegas, Sue found an ally. Recently arrived from Oregon, Huston I. Chapman was a excitable and verbose young lawyer with one arm and, despite bad health, a talent for hyperbole fully the equal of Dudley's. Sue engaged him to help in settling the McSween estate, but Chapman quickly took up her cause against Dudley. In a letter of October 24, 1878, he informed Governor Wallace that he could prove Dudley "criminally responsible" for McSween's death. Moreover, he said, Mrs. McSween had left Lincoln because of Dudley, and she now feared to return even though her affairs there needed attention.[2]

Wallace thought Chapman's accusations "incredible." Because Dudley would play a central role in cleaning up Lincoln County, however, the accusations were disquieting. Wallace sent the letter to Colonel Hatch for comment, and he, with military correctness, endorsed it to Dudley for comment.[3]

Dudley reacted with typical bombast. Disdaining even to comment, he enclosed eight affidavits that attacked Sue McSween as ruthless, dishonest, and scandalously immoral, but which dealt only briefly and superficially with the events of July 20. Saturnino Baca, for example, declared that Sue had come to Lincoln from a whorehouse in Kansas. Sheriff Peppin averred that he had seen her "in actual criminal contact with a well known citizen." Francisco Gómez, eighteen when he helped to build the McSween house in 1877, testified to frequent sexual encounters with Sue in the brush along the river. He had resisted, he said, but she persevered "in such a palpably lewd and libidinous manner" that he surrendered.

The affidavits make titillating reading, as they did when they reached Santa Fe in November 1878. How much truth they contained cannot be known, although one wonders who at Fort Stanton made young Gómez, who was probably illiterate, utter words like "palpably lewd and libidinous." Dudley intended the affidavits to portray Sue as a woman of such low repute as not to be taken seriously. The truth of the allegations, however, is beside the point. Sue's morals had nothing to do with Chapman's complaints. Even though Wallace must have recognized how unresponsive the reply was, he shrugged it off as "perfectly satisfactory."[4]

Wallace next proceeded, unwittingly, to antagonize Dudley further. He had drafted his amnesty proclamation but had not released it when Chapman visited him in his Santa Fe office. The lawyer served notice that, at the next term of district court, he and McSween's friends intended to begin criminal proceedings against Dudley for murder and arson. Thinking to provide Dud-

ley a defense against such harassment, Wallace pulled his proclamation from a pigeon hole of his desk and inserted a phrase ex-
tending the amnesty to all army officers.[5] However generously
motivated, this addition, as Wallace should have seen, could be
read in more ways than one.

Issued on November 13, Wallace's proclamation stunned
Dudley, who reacted with mindless spontaneity. Though not ignorant of the governor's motivation, he chose to interpret the intended favor as a slander on him and his officers. He struck back
in a rambling "open letter" that rejected the extension of the amnesty to the military and blasted Wallace for the implication of
criminal guilt that, in his view, it threw over the Fort Stanton
officers. Published in the Santa Fe *New Mexican* on December 14,
the polemic was both a grave official impropriety and a personal
insult to the governor of the territory.[6]

Even before publication of the open letter, Wallace had decided that Dudley had to go. Huston Chapman had written him
two long and emotional letters from Lincoln. Although full of
partisan excess, they clearly showed that Dudley had aroused
enough local antagonisms to unfit him for his post. On December
7, the governor advised Colonel Hatch that the time had come to
send to Fort Stanton an officer with no prior involvement in the
hostilities or connections to the principal personalities. Hatch
backed away from so delicate an issue, as did his superiors all the
way to the top. But General-in-Chief William Tecumseh Sherman
met it head-on. He refused to injure Dudley's reputation by relieving him for no other reason than the whim of a mere civil
official, and Secretary of War McCrary backed him. A vindicated
Dudley filed the papers for future reference and chalked up another grievance against the governor.[7]

Dudley quickly found other grievances. Aside from the insult to army officers, Wallace's proclamation of November 13 created serious problems for Dudley and his command. He had just
received orders to aid in putting down the insurrection proclaimed by President Hayes. Yet here was Wallace with his own
proclamation declaring peace and order restored in Lincoln
County. Did that mean the army should no longer support civil
authorities? Lawyer Chapman thought so, and he did little to

promote peace by counseling Lincoln residents to shoot any army officer who tried to arrest them. Wallace attempted to clear up the confusion by stating that the peace and order he had proclaimed depended on continued military intervention, but that explanation failed to put the issue to rest.[8]

Dudley scoffed at the notion that the troubles had ended. After a lull, they had resumed with fresh intensity, in part because of the governor's proclamation. Promised amnesty, many who had fled the county now came back. Moreover, sheriffs and army officers hesitated to make arrests, "not knowing who is pardoned and who is not." "If His Excellency Governor Wallace thinks peace and order prevails in Lincoln County," Dudley wrote in mid-December, "he is the worst fooled official I ever saw."[9]

In addition to rampant rustling and general lawlessness throughout the county, the old Dolan-McSween rivalries broke out anew, largely because Sue, with Chapman in tow, had come home to Lincoln. They took up residence in the old Baca home, from which the captain and his family had at last been evicted. Together, they kept up a shrill agitation against Colonel Dudley and drew up legal papers to charge him, Peppin, and Jack Long with murder and arson. The return of prominent Regulators like Doc Scurlock and Billy Bonney heightened the danger of new violence. Dudley made matters worse by placing Fort Stanton off limits to such "murderers and rustlers," whom he identified by name even though they had not been convicted of any crime, and among whom he included Huston Chapman.[10]

Dudley also incurred abuse as a result of the misbehavior of one of his officers, an immature youth with a thirst for whiskey that ultimately cost him his commission. Lieutenant James H. French commanded a military posse sent to Lincoln to help Sheriff Peppin. On the bitterly cold night of December 13, he took some of Peppin's arrest warrants and went in search of Jim French, Doc Scurlock, and others. At the house occupied by Sue McSween and Huston Chapman, the lieutenant forced an entry, engaged in a profane shouting match with Chapman, and stripped to the waist to settle matters with one arm tied behind his back—a manly deference to Chapman's single arm. Chapman brought charges against French in Justice Wilson's court, but a board of officers exonerated him in military eyes, and Dudley sent him to an assignment safely distant from the county seat.[11]

Sue's attorney had not only succeeded her husband as a leading feudist, but he brought to the role a hysteria that made him more dangerous. "Chapman," reported Dudley, "is credited with doing more at the present time to keep the community in a state of excitement than any other man in the county, not excepting Jim French, Kidd, or any of that clique." Ben Ellis later observed that Chapman was "a 'rule or ruin' sort of fellow whom nobody liked."[12]

On the very night of Lieutenant French's rampage, another incident occurred that deepened fears of renewed factionalism. John Copeland, former sheriff and leading McSween supporter, got into a drunken altercation with young Johnny Mes, a Dolanite. Copeland settled the dispute by firing a bullet into Mes's lungs and another into his bowels. Fearing retaliation by Mes's friends, Copeland turned himself in at once. Next morning, Justice Wilson acquitted him of attempted murder. The anger kindled on both sides prompted the gathering of a mob of Copeland's allies to finish off Mes and his "nurse," John Hurley, another Dolan henchman. To prevent this, Colonel Dudley had the wounded youth brought to the Fort Stanton hospital.[13]

Dudley thought Copeland's acquittal reprehensible. The shooting, he said, "was a most cowardly and dastardly act." Copeland was "a big, stout, powerful man; the party shot a beardless boy only nineteen years old." Justice Wilson's action once more demonstrated what a "perfect farce and disgrace" his court had become and dramatized the need for a new justice of the peace, one "whose soul and body does not belong to one party."[14]

Along the Pecos, too, disorders continued. Wrestlers infested this area, and the Seven Rivers cowboys who had fought with Peppin continued to reaffirm their double identity as rustlers and responsible stockmen. One of the few honest ranchers complained that all his neighbors were competing to see who could steal the most stock, and they did not want anyone nearby who would not join in their activity. He feared for his life if he remained at his home. Another rancher told Colonel Dudley that honest men could either throw in with the thieves or flee the country. Captain Henry Carroll and his cavalry company had been stationed at Roswell since early November, but bandits concerned them less than frozen feet and frozen rations.[15]

A stolid, unimaginative officer who had come up from the ranks, Captain Carroll was also conscientious, and he wanted to strike at the rustlers infesting his district. Sue McSween, now handling the Tunstall estate, had sent Charles Scase to look for the Tunstall cattle. He found them on the lower Pecos, in the possession of Wrestlers. Likewise, Emil Bowers, a Hunter and Evans herd boss, thought some of his employer's stock could be found in the same place. With a commission as special constable from Roswell's justice of the peace, he presented himself to Carroll for a *posse comitatus*. The issue of giving military aid to constables had not yet been resolved, so Carroll referred Bowers's application to Dudley; then, without awaiting a reply, Carroll formed a posse and rode down the Pecos with the constable.

For three weeks, Carroll and his men scoured the frozen valley of the Pecos as far south as Pope's Crossing, in Texas. They found cowboys such as the Jones brothers and Marion Turner, veterans of Peppin's posse, posing as aggrieved stockmen, but in addition they turned up evidence of these same men altering brands and otherwise tampering with other people's cattle.

The troops also came upon the remains and other debris of a family of nine Hispanics, slaughtered in October by John, Jim, Tom, and Bill Jones and John Collins. The victims had supposedly killed a friend of the Jones family, and their demise was engineered under the guise of a law-enforcement action. Carroll's troopers found the skeleton of one, an eighteen-year-old boy, propped against a tree. The skull had fallen off and lay nearby with a cigar in its mouth, an exhibition of the Wrestlers' macabre humor.

After marching more than five hundred miles, Carroll's command returned to Roswell on February 23 with almost three hundred stolen cattle retrieved from the Wrestlers. Hunter and Evans and others claimed about half, but 140 head belonged to the Tunstall estate and ultimately came under Sue McSween's control. They cost the estate dearly, as much in search and herd fees for

140 head as McSween had originally paid for the entire lot of 209 at Sheriff Brady's public auction.[16]

One person who was fully as anxious as Sue McSween to withdraw his cattle from the perils of the Pecos was Thomas B. Catron. His agent (and brother-in-law), Edgar Walz, persuaded Dudley that the Catron herd, formerly Dolan's, merited a military escort out of the danger zone because it was destined for the Mescalero and San Carlos Indian agencies to fulfill beef contracts. Jimmy Dolan accompanied Walz to the Pecos and, with half a dozen soldiers from Captain Carroll's command, returned with almost twenty-one hundred head. While inspecting the cattle with the chief herder, Dudley discovered to his anger and chagrin that he had helped move "about the finest herd of young stock cattle in the country." It contained hardly ten head of beeves; and it was destined not for Indian agencies, but for Catron's new ranges at Murphy's former ranch, Fairview. Young Walz, Dudley vowed, would never again get a chance to dupe him.[17]

The chief herder who arrived at Fort Stanton with the Catron herd on February 15, 1879, was William Campbell. Although he was about to play a key role in the Lincoln County War, he remains a shadowy character. An associate of Dolan, Jesse Evans, and others who had opposed McSween, he had a hair-trigger temper and a streak of meanness that made even his friends afraid to cross him. He also had some sort of relationship to Colonel Dudley, who did not ordinarily consort with the likes of Campbell. As far back as early November, Dudley had summoned Campbell to Fort Stanton for an unexplained conversation. With a huge brown mustache, Campbell looked fierce, and so did his cowboys. Dudley considered them a bunch "I would not like to run against with a few men."[18]

By mid-February, Lincoln finally had a new sheriff. Peppin had submitted his resignation in December, but George Kimball did not qualify until early February. A sensible, steady man intent on doing his job fearlessly and without favor, Kimball represented a great improvement over both Copeland and Peppin. For the first time since William Brady, Lincoln had a decent and competent sheriff.

By mid-February, too, with Dolan's return from the Pecos

accompanied by Billy Campbell and Jesse Evans, Lincoln played host to prominent figures of both the old warring factions. Bonney and O'Folliard were also in town. Increasingly acknowledged as the leader of the McSween remnants, Bonney told Sam Corbet that he was tired of fighting, tired of running from the Dolan outfit, and tired of running from law officers with warrants for his arrest.[19] Both sides wanted the old feuds put to rest, but Chapman's constant agitation kept them alive and even exaggerated.

Billy Bonney put out a peace feeler. Early on February 18, he sent a message to one of Dolan's adherents at Fort Stanton, asking whether the Dolan people proposed peace or war. The reply came back that they would come to Lincoln in the evening and talk over the matter.[20]

To the number of fifteen or twenty, the antagonists gathered in town on the night of February 18, exactly one year after the killing of Tunstall. Principals on the McSween side were Bonney, Tom O'Folliard, Joe Bowers, and young Yginio Salazar, now recovered from the wounds received in McSween's back yard on July 19. On the other side were Dolan, Campbell, Jesse Evans, Billy Mathews, and others. Edgar Walz was there too, and he stated that the two groups took station behind facing adobe walls before hesitantly advancing into the street to parley.[21]

Hard words opened the talk. Jesse Evans said the Kid could not be dealt with and would have to be killed on the spot. Billy replied that they had met to make peace and he did not care to open negotiations with a fight. Tempers cooled, and the exchange ended in general handshaking and a more or less formal peace treaty. The pact, reduced to writing, stipulated that no one on either side would kill anyone on the other without first withdrawing from the treaty, that no army officer or soldier would be killed for any past offense (probably a reference to the McSween partisans' threats against Dudley and Purington), that neither party would give evidence in a civil prosecution against the other and would render all possible aid in resisting arrest, and that anyone who failed to live up to the agreement would be executed.[22]

With peace declared, the newfound friends embarked on a boozy celebration. Noisily, and growing drunker and drunker, they staggered from one drinking place to another. Shortly before 10:00 P.M., they called at the home of Juan Patrón, who had arrived that evening from Las Vegas with Huston Chapman. Why they went there is not clear; possibly, it was merely a drunken impulse. But they had no sooner entered than Campbell drew his pistol and aimed it at Patrón, who avoided death only by jumping behind some of the party.

Leaving Patrón's, the celebrants lurched up the dark street to the west. In front of the courthouse, they chanced to meet Huston Chapman, unarmed and his face swathed in bandages to ease the pain of a severe toothache. Campbell challenged him and demanded his name. "My name is Chapman," was the reply. "Then you dance," commanded Campbell, drawing his pistol and shoving it against Chapman's chest. He did not propose to dance for a drunken crowd, Chapman answered, adding: "Am I talking to Mr. Dolan?" "No," interjected Jesse Evans, "but you are talking to a damned good friend of his." With the rest of the group, Dolan stood about ten feet behind Campbell. At this juncture, Dolan drew his pistol and drunkenly fired a round into the street. The shot produced an instinctive tightening of Campbell's trigger finger. "My God, I am killed," exclaimed Chapman as Campbell's bullet punched into his chest and knocked him to the ground, dead, with his clothes set afire by the powder flash of the revolver.[23]

The shooting of Chapman did not dampen the festivities. Leaving the lawyer's body blazing in the middle of the street, the revelers headed for Cullum's eatery for an oyster supper. On the way, Campbell remarked that he "had promised his God and General Dudley that he would kill Chapman, and he had done it." He added that now he was "going to the post and kill Charlie Scase," the man Sue McSween had sent to Seven Rivers to look for the Tunstall cattle. "I promised General Dudley that I would not kill Scase in the post, but now I am going to kill him wherever I find him."[24]

Over Cullum's oysters, Dolan and Campbell held a consultation, then handed a pistol to Edgar Walz and asked him to go place it in Chapman's hand so that the killing could be explained

133

as self-defense. When Walz refused, Billy Bonney volunteered. With the pistol, he went outside, proceeded directly to his horse, and rode out of town.

Aside from his reluctance to invite another murder charge, Bonney had good reason to leave town. Sheriff Kimball carried a warrant for his arrest and, observing him walking the street during the day, had gone to Fort Stanton for a military posse to help in taking him. With a lieutenant and twenty cavalrymen, the sheriff reached town shortly before midnight. A search of several houses failed to turn up the Kid, but the troopers discovered the body of Chapman lying in the street, with his clothing in ashes and his upper body severely burned. Justice Wilson admitted knowing about the killing, but said he could find no one to help move the body. The soldiers carried it to the courthouse.[25]

Wilson could find no help because Lincoln's populace quaked behind their adobe walls. Already apprehensive over the gathering of so many veterans of past hostilities, they now shuddered in fright that Chapman's killing would set off another battle between McSween and Dolan gunmen. Citizens united to plead with Dudley for military protection, and Sheriff Kimball obliged with the necessary documentation. Dudley sent troops, and he himself went to town for the first time since July 19, 1878. He found himself greeted as the savior of Lincoln. People who only recently had vied with one another in denouncing the colonel made a public meeting ring with expressions of gratitude and respect.[26]

The slaying of Chapman proved to be a milestone in the Lincoln County War. Although it removed an inflammatory influence and failed to provoke new hostilities, it did reopen old wounds, terrify the people, and serve notice that the war had not yet ended. Also, it finally persuaded Governor Wallace that he had better get down to Lincoln and try to accomplish the purpose for which he had been sent to New Mexico. And that visit, it turned out, would give even greater significance to the Chapman killing.

Aside from its importance, Chapman's murder is laden with mystifying questions and dark hints of conspiracy, and evidence has yet to surface that points to a satisfying explanation. Did one side or the other, or both, set out deliberately to kill Patrón and

Chapman? The editors of the *Mesilla Independent* thought so. Of the peace conference, they wrote that "the whole thing was a sham, gotten up to throw people off guard in order, as Campbell said, to 'make a killing.'"[27]

Dolan's part is puzzling. He gave contradictory and implausible accounts. In one, he denied even being present. In another, he professed not to have learned that Chapman had been shot until he arrived at Cullum's eating place. Yet one of the witnesses told a newspaper editor that Dolan had fired a shot from his Winchester into Chapman's prostrate form. Dolan countered that he had not carried a Winchester that night.[28]

Campbell's well-documented remark about his God and General Dudley is damning to Dudley and tantalizing to the historian. Dudley did have an association of some sort with Campbell, as indicated by the former's summons of the previous November and by his friendly inspection, with Campbell, of the Catron herd brought up from the Pecos. In addition, Governor Wallace collected some scraps of evidence, of unknown reliability, showing that on the night of the killing, after returning to Fort Stanton, Dolan obtained a "loan" of fifty dollars from Dudley and then passed it on to Campbell. Finally, Campbell's threat against Charlie Scase, uttered at the same time as the God and Dudley remark, had some substance, for Scase sought military protection at the fort. Apparently, he and Campbell had crossed each other on the Pecos recently, and Campbell had vowed to kill him. Dudley made protection contingent on bunking in a barracks with black soldiers. Scase found this intolerable and fled the area altogether.[29]

Campbell's offhand remark about Dudley has never been satisfactorily explained, nor has Dudley's association with Campbell. One can only ask what motive Dudley could have had that was so compelling as to warrant his complicity in murder. The only known motive was to end Chapman's hysterical vendetta against him, and it draws some credibility from the charges of murder and arson that the lawyer had filed against Dudley in Justice Wilson's court. Coincidentally or not, on February 20, less than two days after Chapman's murder, Wilson dismissed the charges because Chapman was no longer around to press them.[30]

While suspicious, this circumstantial evidence is not enough to convict, and in the final reckoning Chapman's harassment seems to provide insufficient grounds for the risks involved in a murder pact with Campbell. In fact, Campbell may simply have tossed off a careless, drunken remark, without any more meaning for Dudley than for God.

And for that matter, what were Campbell's motives? All of the Dolan crowd had ample cause to detest Chapman and, given the low value set on human life, to kill him. If they plotted his murder, however, why did it take place in the middle of town, on almost the same spot where Brady was shot down? Could the gain justify the hazard of so public a murder? And if deliberate, as the *Independent* charged, how did the conspirators know that Chapman would return from Las Vegas on that very night, and why did they get themselves so drunk they could hardly walk before carrying out the deed?

Until more evidence comes to light, the Chapman slaying is most plausibly seen as a drunken accident. The carousers met Chapman by accident, and in their stupor they killed him by accident. This explanation makes Dolan's confused testimony believable. He was so drunk that he may well have stood by while Campbell shot Chapman, and may even have put a bullet into the corpse himself, and still not have understood that a shooting had occurred until he later sat down over oysters.

Years later, Edgar Walz gave the event a tone that rings true for the time and place. When commanded to dance, Chapman refused, said Walz, "so one of the boys shot him through the heart and he fell over against me, dead. There was really no malice in this shooting. Life was held lightly down there in those days."[31]

12

The Governor
and
the Kid

IN THE OPENING WEEKS of 1879, more than three months after informing Secretary Schurz that he would go at once to Lincoln County, Governor Wallace had not gone to Lincoln County. He attended to the trivia of office, complained of the moldering old "palace" that housed the executive chambers and of the bankrupt treasury that deprived him even of sufficient stationery, and labored late into the night over the manuscript of *Ben-Hur*. Early in February, he journeyed to the Colorado railhead to meet his wife Susan and son Henry and to conduct them back to Santa Fe.[1]

Pressures mounted for Wallace to visit Lincoln County. Newspapers criticized his delay. Huston Chapman lectured him in stridently insulting language. Colonel Dudley, who had been openly contemptuous of the governor since the eruption of their public feud in November, lost no opportunity to draw attention to his continuing absence from the scene of the troubles. One respected Santa Fean wrote to Wallace from Fort Stanton that "nothing but a personal visit and a stay of some week or ten days, will enable you to form a correct idea of the true standing & bearing of the matter."[2]

Still, Wallace procrastinated. By mid-January, he had decided that April would be soon enough, and he arranged with Judge Bristol to accompany him when he held the spring term of district court in Lincoln—*if* he thought he could safely preside in Lincoln.[3]

Then, in late February, came word of the senseless slaying of Huston Chapman, dramatizing the gathering of some of the most violent of the old feudists and stirring a climate of near panic in the county. Wallace reacted with bewildering ambivalence. He branded Colonel Dudley's dispatch of troops to Lincoln as a "ridiculous action" likely to alarm the populace unnecessarily, but he then notified Colonel Hatch that conditions in Lincoln County might be so bad as to require "the instant proclamation of martial law." At the same time, the governor submitted to Secretary Schurz a "plan of campaign" that looked to the federal courts instead of military commissions to suppress outlawry, and he told Hatch that he hoped for a civil rather than a military solution. In truth, because the conflicting reports reaching him from Lincoln County provided no basis for informed decision, Wallace did not know what to do. The Chapman affair and the furor it set off finally roused the governor from his lethargy. He could continue to ignore Lincoln County only at his political peril. Although uncertain of the remedy, Wallace would dally no more. He would go to Lincoln himself.[4]

Wallace reached Lincoln on March 5, 1879. He had traveled from Santa Fe with Colonel Hatch, who intended to inspect Fort Stanton and then proceed to El Paso. Hatch took station at the fort, while the governor established himself in rooms in Lincoln provided by merchant José Montaño.

High on Wallace's agenda, fixed even before leaving Santa Fe, was getting rid of Colonel Dudley. Wallace had tried and failed in December, and he had spoken to Hatch about it several times since. Hatch, an amiable, competent officer with a superb combat record in the Civil War, liked Wallace and stood ready to oblige him in nearly any way that he was asked. For Dudley, at the same time, Hatch nursed a contempt rooted in a personal feud that reached back nearly a decade. If Dudley's removal could be engineered without damage to his own interests, Hatch could be expected to cooperate wholeheartedly. On the eve of his departure from Santa Fe, he had warned his superiors to expect another official request from the governor, this one not easily to be brushed aside.[5]

Wallace and Hatch undoubtedly worked out the details during the journey to Lincoln. In order to lend credibility to the scheme, however, Wallace first had to talk with Lincoln's citizens, which he did on March 6. Although they had just held a public meeting to pour out their gratitude to Dudley, Wallace had no trouble in finding men to provide the ammunition he needed.

In order to bring criminals to justice, Wallace wrote to Hatch on March 7, he had to have witnesses to swear affidavits as the basis for legal proceedings, and these he could not obtain because people feared retaliation through Dudley's misuse of military power. They held him responsible for McSween's death, and they also believed him to be somehow involved in Chapman's murder. Wallace did not know the truth of these allegations, he said, but he had become convinced that the fears of the citizens were not irrational. Whether innocently or not, Dudley had become "so compromised by connection with the troubles in this county that his usefulness in the effort now making to restore order is utterly gone."

Wallace took his request to Fort Stanton and presented it to Hatch. With documentation in hand, Hatch reacted as intended. On March 8, he issued an order relieving Dudley from command. Then he and Wallace joined in a merry feast that inevitably partook of a celebration. Afterward, the governor returned to Lincoln, called a public meeting, and boasted that he had accomplished "the best day's work ever done for the citizens of Lincoln County."[6]

Colonel Dudley erupted in almost incoherent rage. He had been unjustly relieved and his reputation smeared without any chance to offer a defense or even to know what the specific accusations were or who had made them. The records of the fort and twenty witnesses within a ten-mile radius could "annihilate totally" every charge against him. Yet neither Wallace nor Hatch would take time to talk with him, even though they passed the afternoon of March 8 at "a convivial dinner given at the post." The secretary of war himself had ruled that Dudley should not be relieved on petition of the governor. Even so, Dudley telegraphed the adjutant general of the army, "I am disgraced without a hearing and deprived of even preparing a defense." In a follow-up letter, and in a long personal letter to General Sherman, Dudley poured out his indignation and demanded a court of inquiry.[7]

Dudley's reaction was predictable and his reasoning not lacking in merit. He had indeed been abruptly dumped without a chance to defend himself or to confront his accusers. He had been charged with grave criminal offenses by unnamed men with a history of wildly fluctuating opinions, and the governor himself would not more than inferentially associate himself with the allegations. Neither Hatch nor Wallace even talked with him about Lincoln County, much less asked for any explanations. From Dudley's viewpoint, he had been treated shabbily, in a manner insulting to one of his rank and service, and he was right.

Yet so were Wallace and Hatch. Whether or not he was criminally culpable, Dudley had in fact become so entangled in local animosities that he could take hardly any official action not perceived by someone as motivated by partisanship. However unfairly, that public image disqualified him for the task that Wallace had set for the troops at Fort Stanton. Even more critical, now that the governor had taken personal control of the campaign to restore order to Lincoln County, the commander of Fort Stanton had to be an officer with whom he could work in harmony. On that score alone, as Wallace and Hatch both clearly understood, Dudley had to go. And at once; the campaign had opened, and it could not be suspended while the issue climbed the chain of command to General Sherman and Secretary McCrary for decision.

Having played his role as planned, Colonel Hatch departed for El Paso on March 11. He left Wallace with just what he needed—a commander cheerfully responsive to his every wish. With Captain Purington on leave, command devolved on the next senior officer, Captain Henry Carroll, the tenacious troop leader who had recaptured the Tunstall cattle from the Wrestlers. Of modest ability but respected and well liked by the citizens, he proved to be an ideal choice to work closely with Wallace.[8]

The governor launched his campaign with an energy and flair that somewhat made up for his five months of dawdling. His objective was to purge the county of bad men. He hoped to accomplish this by arresting and trying all he could catch and driving the rest out by their example.

One measure he pressed on Captain Carroll was simply to arrest everyone herding cattle who could not prove ownership by registered brand or bill of sale. The cattle were to be turned over to Probate Judge Florencio Gonzales and entrusted by him to John Newcomb, on whom Wallace conferred the title of "Keeper of Cattle."

But the main goal was to round up the outlaws who had terrorized the county for a year. From informants in Lincoln, notably Squire Wilson, he learned who the worst offenders were, and on March 11 he furnished Carroll with the names of thirty-five men to be sought out and arrested. The list was a veritable Who's Who of the Lincoln County War, including Regulators Bonney, Waite, Scurlock, Bowdre, French, and others; Seven Rivers warriors such as the Jones boys, John Beckwith, Marion Turner, Andy Boyle, and Buck Powell; John Selman and the Wrestlers; and Jimmy Dolan and Billy Mathews. "Push the 'Black Knights' without rest," Wallace urged Carroll, "and regardless of boundary lines."[9]

Wallace especially wanted the men involved in the Chapman murder. Unlike others on the list, they could not go free simply by pleading the governor's amnesty. That crime had occurred after his proclamation. Immediately upon arriving in Lincoln, he had heard that Kid Bonney and Tom O'Folliard were at Las Tablas—"Board Town"—some twenty miles northwest of Lincoln, and that Dolan, Evans, Campbell, and Mathews were at Murphy's old ranch, Fairview. At Wallace's request, Colonel Hatch sent two detachments to find the culprits. Las Tablas failed to yield the Kid and O'Folliard, but the troopers returned from Fairview with Evans, Campbell, and Mathews and lodged them in the Fort Stanton lockup.

Mindful of the need for witnesses as well as defendants, Wallace had specifically exempted Jimmy Dolan from the sweep. "His larger money interest in the county," Wallace hoped, "would make him pliant for use as a witness." With his friends confined, Dolan rushed to Lincoln to surrender and to continue his four-month effort to ingratiate himself with the governor. Wallace took his parole on condition that he remain within the limits of Fort Stanton. Almost at once, however, he violated parole, and Wallace had him placed under close guard—although in the comfortable setting of the post library rather than in the cells that held Campbell, Evans, and Mathews.[10]

While Wallace toyed with Dolan, Captain Carroll diligently searched out the fugitives on the list that the governor had compiled for him. With methodical persistence, he kept his patrols scouring the country and rounding up leading fighters of the old McSween and Dolan factions as well as rustlers and other desperadoes who had rushed to Lincoln County when all pretense at law enforcement collapsed after McSween's death. By the end of March, Wallace had a dozen imprisoned, and a week later a correspondent of the *Mesilla Independent* observed that the Fort Stanton guardhouse had become "a 'Bastille' crowded with civil prisoners."[11]

With these men Wallace faced the same stubborn obstacle that had thwarted him from the first. Efficient military action could corral offenders, but the civil machinery remained ineffective to dispose of them. The problem surfaced on March 6 with the arrest of Evans, Campbell, and Mathews. Hatch sent word to Wallace to make certain that the sheriff was at the fort to greet them with arrest warrants when the detachment returned from Fairview Ranch with the prisoners. But warrants could not be issued without supporting affidavits, and "The truth is," Wallace confessed, "the people here are so intimidated that some days will have to [pass] before they can be screwed up to the point of making the necessary affidavits." Therefore, the governor had to take the responsibility for requesting that the prisoners be confined without warrants "Hold them I beg of you," he pleaded. "To let them go now is to lose everything at the beginning of the struggle."[12]

As Wallace knew, such a stratagem could only delay the legal process, and not for long at that. Lincoln's only practicing attorney lost no time in signing up Evans, Campbell, and Mathews as clients and then instituting habeas corpus proceedings. Wallace made haste to instruct Justice Wilson that he lacked authority to issue writs of habeas corpus, but Judge Bristol had no such handicap, and he would be in Lincoln soon for the April term of district court.[13]

As the hope faded that Dolan would testify against his friends, another prospective witness unexpectedly turned up. A messenger brought Wallace a letter, dated March 13, from another participant in the debauch that had ended with Chapman's killing. The writer explained that he had come to Lincoln to make friends with the old enemies, "so as to be able to lay aside my arms and go to work." "I was present when Mr. Chapman was murdered and know who did it," he wrote. But "I have indictments against me for things that happened in the last Lincoln County War, and am afraid to give up because my enemies would kill me." If those indictments could be annulled, he would tell all. "I am called Kid Antrim," he concluded, "but Antrim is my stepfather's name."[14]

Wallace lost no time in seizing on the offer. The messenger who brought Bonney's proposition took back a reply. "Come to the house of old Squire Wilson," the governor directed, "at nine (9) o'clock next Monday night alone. . . . Follow along foot of the mountain south of town, come in on that side, and knock at the east door. I have authority to exempt you from prosecution, if you will testify to what you say you know."

Billy did as instructed. On the night of March 17, in Squire Wilson's rude jacal next to the courthouse, the distinguished soldier-statesman and man of letters confronted the smooth-faced young outlaw destined for immortality in the folklore of the West.

In 1902, Wallace described the meeting in a vivid detail doubtless colored by two decades of savoring by an incurably romantic mind. In truth it was a dramatic scene—the cramped, gloomy room flickering in lamp light, the tensely expectant governor and justice of the peace, the soft knock at the door. As Wallace remembered it, the Kid entered warily, with rifle in one hand and pistol in the other. Only after he was assured that no one else was present did he relax and lower his weapons.

Whether it was so dramatic as remembered, the exchange did produce agreement. Wallace would contrive a fake arrest of the Kid and confine him in Lincoln until district court convened.

The Kid would identify the killers of Chapman for the grand jury, and in return Wallace would pardon him, or see that he was not prosecuted, in the murders of Sheriff Brady and Buckshot Roberts.

The agreement almost fell apart. The very next day, March 18, Jesse Evans and Billy Campbell persuaded their guard to desert and, with his help, broke out of the Fort Stanton lockup. They quickly lost themselves in the mountains. Even in protective custody, Billy could readily visualize himself shot down by these two before he could relate his story to the grand jury. "Please tell you know who that I do not know what to do, now as those Prisoners have escaped," he wrote to Squire Wilson. But Wallace sent back reassurances, and on March 21 Sheriff Kimball rode into Lincoln with Billy Bonney and Tom O'Folliard.[15]

Wallace accorded his prisoner preferred treatment, confining him under guard in Juan Patrón's home rather than in the cellar jail. He also visited him on at least one occasion, when Bonney poured out a long and useful narrative of outlaw personalities and activities.[16] That the patrician governor looked upon his lowly conspirator with condescencion, however, may be inferred from a report to Secretary Schurz. "A precious specimen nicknamed 'The Kid,'" he wrote, "whom the Sheriff is holding here in the Plaza, . . . is an object of tender regard. I heard singing and music the other night; going to the door, I found the minstrels of the village actually serenading the fellow in his prison."[17] The governor might also have reflected on how much the incident revealed about the stature his "precious specimen" had already attained in the eyes of many citizens.

Although Billy Bonney stood ready to testify in the Chapman killing, Wallace needed still more witnesses. He had hoped that the steady accumulation of bad men in the Fort Stanton lockup would begin to restore confidence, but it did not, especially after the escape of Evans and Campbell dramatized military imperfections. "'Say nothing,' seems to be the policy," observed the *Independent*. "The man who dares to raise his voice against the acts of murderers, or attempts to expose their crimes, at once becomes the mark for the assassin's bullet." Judge Bristol thought that this attitude was a serious obstacle to resolving Lincoln County's problems through the civil courts. The people, he wrote to Wallace, "consider their lives would be in peril if they should disclose criminal acts," and, he conceded, "there seems some ground for their fears."[18]

To the witness problem Wallace added a growing disenchantment with the army. He and Captain Carroll got along well. "He appears to be the man for the place," Wallace informed Hatch. But on March 20, Captain Purington returned from leave. He ranked Carroll, and Hatch assigned him to command. As post commander before Dudley, Purington had shown partiality for the Dolan faction even more openly than Dudley, and Wallace considered him almost as objectionable as Dudley. Purington promptly confirmed Wallace's fears by finding somewhere in army regulations an excuse for resisting almost everything he wanted to do. "The military," Wallace complained to Schurz ten days after Purington's arrival, "do not enter heartily into the work requested of them."[19]

A partial answer was for the governor to form his own army, and by the end of March he had organized a militia company, the Lincoln County Rifles. Ultimately, it numbered about thirty, virtually all of whom were Hispanic and mostly former McSween supporters. For example, José Chavez y Chavez, the Kid's companion in the breakout from the McSween home, enlisted as a private, as did the ever-present George Washington.

Wallace made Juan Patrón captain of the company. With engaging ways, respected by Anglos and Hispanics alike, he served the governor efficiently and loyally.

The Lincoln County Rifles performed some hard service, such as an expedition to Fort Sumner in search of Scurlock and Bowdre. The latter had flown, but they arrested Scurlock and brought him in. They also made repeated but vain attempts to find Evans and Campbell. However much the Rifles justified their expense, they were poor substitutes for the regulars. Critics labeled them the "Governor's Heelflies" and, as Squire Wilson noted, "make fun of them Generaly when they meet them."[20]

At the end of March, Wallace's mounting troubles led him back to a familiar nostrum—martial law. He could get few witnesses, and the men held illegally at Fort Stanton seemed likely to go free on writs of habeas corpus. Under Purington, the army cooperated halfheartedly if at all. Moreover, even if court met, hardly anyone untainted by old rivalries could be found to serve as jurors. Virtually every man of competence, Wallace concluded, "is yet all alive with prejudices and partialities." In these circumstances, martial law seemed to be the only answer. Habeas corpus could be suspended and the drawbacks of civil court avoided by trying all offenders by military commission. On March 31, therefore, the governor appealed by telegraph to Secretary Schurz and President Hayes to proclaim martial law at once.[21]

Like previous petitions for a military solution, this one came to nothing. Within four days, in fact, Wallace was briskly moving toward a civil solution. On April 4, he advised Schurz that if the approaching session of district court turned out to be a failure, there would then be no recourse but martial law. And on the same day, he wrote to Judge Bristol, urging the necessity for a spring term of court in Lincoln.[22]

Again, therefore, civil measures would be tested. With Wallace pleading for a judicial effort, and with the Fort Stanton guardhouse overflowing with prisoners awaiting court action, Judge Bristol finally overcame his doubts and fears and resolved to hold a spring term of court for Lincoln County.

13

War's End

ON APRIL 13, 1879, Judge Bristol, District Attorney Rynerson, and other officers of the Third Judicial District Court arrived at Fort Stanton. Governor Wallace was on hand to greet them.

But Governor Wallace remained in Lincoln only for the opening of court and the selection of jurors. Leaving for Santa Fe on April 18, he explained that he had to prepare himself to testify in the forthcoming Dudley court of inquiry.[1]

The explanation rings hollow. It may simply have been an excuse, or rationalization, to get out of Lincoln. He had been there through six weeks of tiring, exasperating, and even dangerous labor, and he undoubtedly yearned to get back to his writing desk in Santa Fe. Or he may have sensed impending failure, the harvest of an uncooperative prosecuting attorney, a weak and timid judge, terrified or partisan witnesses and jurors, and the governor's own amnesty proclamation, which afforded a plea in bar of prosecution for most of the eighteen men held at Fort Stanton. To distance himself from judicial proceedings that promised so little return on his investment in labor and prestige might have held some appeal.

For several weeks, Wallace had been searching for someone to act in his behalf in energizing what he feared would be Rynerson's lackadaisical prosecution. Lincoln's only attorney, Sidney Wilson, was too lucratively busy representing the prisoners in habeas corpus proceedings. Wallace had also appealed to New Mexico Attorney General Henry L. Waldo, one of the territory's ablest lawyers, but he was occupied in preparing to act as Colonel Dudley's counsel in the court of inquiry. The choice, finally, fell on Ira E. Leonard of Las Vegas.

Ira Leonard had fled Missouri to New Mexico for his health. Asthma still troubled him, and he felt poorly much of the time. But his affliction diminished neither his energy nor his ambition. In Missouri, he had been a judge. He wanted to be a judge again; more specifically, he wanted to sit on the bench occupied by Warren Bristol. He had therefore interested himself in Lincoln County's troubles, had assiduously cultivated Governor Wallace, and had succeeded Huston Chapman as attorney for Sue McSween.

To Wallace, Leonard seemed ideal. The two thought alike. "Dangerous diseases require heroic treatment," declared Leonard, "that's what is needed now." To Leonard, Wallace looked for the heroic treatment.[2]

As Wallace may have foreseen, nothing heroic characterized this term of court. Fear and intimidation still stalked the town. Witnesses hung back. Partisans on both sides pursued the old interests of McSween and Dolan. The grand jury, with Isaac Ellis as foreman and every member a McSween adherent, flung out indictments with wild abandon. Judge Bristol, anxious to get out of Lincoln, pushed them hard. He showed "the timidity of a child," Leonard complained, "and stood in fear of the desperate characters."[3]

In contrast, by his languid prosecution, Rynerson earned the favor of the desperate characters. "He is entering into his work with no spirit," observed Leonard's companion George Taylor, a civil engineer who also happened to be a cousin of President Hayes, "and leaves all the work for the Judge only interfering to raise obstacles in the way of bringing the rascals to justice."[4]

The rascals, Taylor noted, had no animosity toward Rynerson, but plenty toward Leonard. A note addressed to him and posted in a tree warned him to leave the country or "they would take my scalp and send me to hell." Several days later, on the night of April 24, two men galloped down the street in front of the house where Leonard and Taylor lodged and fired two bullets at their bedroom window. They dove for their arms, but the gunmen vanished in a cloud of dust. "There is no telling when the scoundrels will make a rush on us," said Taylor, "they are thirsting for revenge and plunder."[5]

Others endured the menace as well. Leonard's friend John McPherson, serving as a deputy sheriff, was herding horses in the Capitan foothills when a bullet punched through his hat brim and grazed his forehead. And Sheriff Kimball received an ominous message crudely composed around a diagram of a coffin: "you son of a bitch you had as well pass in your chips for you have not got many days before you will Git one of these Boxes."[6]

Despite Rynerson's obstruction, the grand jury returned no less than two hundred indictments against some fifty men. The case of most concern to Leonard and Wallace, of course, was the Chapman murder. True to his promise, Billy Bonney testified, and Billy Campbell, Jesse Evans, and Jimmy Dolan were duly charged with murder or accessory to murder.[7]

Rynerson's conduct of the case, however, raised doubts about Wallace's ability to make good his end of the bargain with the Kid. The governor had spoken either of an exemption from prosecution or a pardon. Whatever Wallace's promises, Rynerson clearly intended to prosecute. "He is bent on going for the Kid," Leonard wrote to Wallace, and "he is bent on pushing him to the wall. He is a Dolan man and is defending him by his conduct all he can."[8] Far from dropping the prosecution, the district attorney brought up the case and obtained a change of venue to Doña Ana County, where jurors would be less likely to sympathize with the likable young fellow.[9]

With the grand jury entirely made up of McSween followers, most of the indictments fell on Dolanites. Besides Dolan, Campbell, and Evans, the grand jury indicted Peppin and nineteen of the Seven Rivers warriors for the murder of Frank McNab at the Fritz ranch a year earlier, Marion Turner and John Jones for the murder of McSween, and John Selman and eight Wrestlers for stealing cattle and horses as well as for their murder rampage the previous September. Finally, on the sole testimony of the McSweens' black servant, Sebrian Bates, the jurors indicted Peppin, John Kinney, and Colonel Dudley for arson in the burning of the McSween house, and Kinney for breaking into the Tunstall store. Of all the men singled out by the grand jury, only Tom O'Folliard and Sam Smith, charged with the theft of Charles Fritz's horses in September, were McSween followers.

None of the indicted men came to trial at this session of court, and most never did. Even before court convened, Judge Bristol released fifteen of the Stanton prisoners on habeas corpus petitions. Few others named in the indictments were anywhere near Lincoln, and those who were simply pleaded Governor Wallace's amnesty and heard Judge Bristol dismiss their cases. A few chose to fight the charges—Jimmy Dolan, for example, and Colonel Dudley. Certain that they could not get justice in Lincoln, both won changes of venue to other counties.[10]

Almost no one seemed to think the court term a success. Captain Purington groused about the partisan grand jury and their favored treatment of the Kid and other McSween followers. The press, too, pronounced the session a failure, with the *Independent* commenting sourly on the injustice of holding some men in the Stanton guardhouse "while Kid and Scurlock perambulated at leisure." Ira Leonard complained not only about Rynerson, but more and more stridently about Judge Bristol.[11]

Leonard's sniping at Judge Bristol, of course, did not represent an entirely disinterested opinion. It accompanied the beginnings of a campaign to unseat Bristol and to substitute Leonard. Squire Wilson got up a petition advocating this switch, and Governor Wallace lent his prestige to it. George Taylor wrote to his cousin, President Hayes, pronouncing Bristol "a very weak man" who shrank from using the law to put down the violence, and instead "temporizes with these outlaws." But Taylor stopped short of urging the appointment of Leonard. Not for another year, moreover, did Wallace get around to proposing Leonard's name for Bristol's post, and by then it was too late.[12]

On May 9, 1879, a little more than a week after Judge Bristol adjourned district court, the Dudley court of inquiry convened at Fort Stanton. Colonel Galusha Pennypacker presided, flanked by Major Nathan W. Osborne and Captain Henry R. Brinkerhoff. A court of inquiry has no power to convict or to sentence; it merely inquires whether sufficient evidence exists to justify a court-martial. A "recorder" therefore functions as the equivalent of a prosecutor. Captain Henry H. Humphreys held this post, but assisting him was none other than Ira Leonard. Dudley objected strenuously, pointing out that Leonard was Mrs. McSween's attorney and also a prospective witness, but the court overruled him. No less strangely, Dudley's counsel was New Mexico Attorney General Henry L. Waldo, who followed the custom of most public officials by pursuing private practice on the side.

As early as February 1879, after the Chapman slaying, Ira Leonard had appointed himself as Dudley's prosecutor and persecutor. Shortly before leaving Las Vegas on his fatal last journey to Lincoln, Chapman had confided to Leonard his fear of harm from Colonel Dudley and Lieutenant French, the tippling young officer who had burst into Sue McSween's parlor on December 13 and tried to pick a fight with Chapman. To Leonard, therefore, Chapman's death seemed a self-fulfilling prophecy, and less than a week later he wrote to Governor Wallace expressing the conviction that Dudley and French somehow lay behind "this dastardly assassination." In fact, he said, he looked forward to acquainting Wallace with some circumstances that "constitute to me 'proof as strong as holy writ' of their implication in it."[13]

Leonard did not stop there. He drew up formal "charges and specifications" against Dudley and, on March 4, mailed them to the secretary of war. According to Dudley, Leonard did this as Sue McSween's paid attorney, which is plausible, for the document contained particulars that must have come from her. In it, Dudley was accused of aiding in the murder of McSween, the burning of his house, and the looting of the Tunstall store, and also of vague evils growing out of the open letter to Wallace, the slander of Sue McSween, and the misconduct of Lieutenant French. Significantly, while enclosing a newspaper account that connected Dudley with the murder of Chapman, Leonard did not include this offense among his charges. Possibly, on reflection, he decided that his "proof as strong as holy writ" might not stand up in court.[14]

Leonard's unsolicited "charges and specifications" formed the basis of the official inquiry into Dudley's conduct. They reached the War Department at about the same time as Dudley's demand, in the wake of his removal from command, for a court of inquiry.

No one in Washington knew why Dudley had been relieved or what alleged offenses a military court should consider. Although not in proper military form and failing even elementary standards of legal precision, Leonard's document filled a need, and it went out with the orders authorizing a court of inquiry.

When the court convened at Fort Stanton, Leonard did most of the recorder's work. He presented the case against Dudley, questioned witnesses, and cross-examined defense witnesses. During the early sessions, he thought he had Dudley on the run. "I tell you," he wrote to Wallace on May 23, "we are pouring the 'hot shot' into Dudley so fiercely that his face for the last three days has strikingly resembled the wattles of an enraged turkey gobbler."[15]

But the euphoria soon turned to gloom. Ruling after ruling of the court thwarted Leonard or favored Dudley. This was due in part to the court's yearning to whitewash Dudley, but in larger part to the adroitness of Dudley's counsel. In Waldo, Leonard more than met his match. The attorney general was an able and respected lawyer whose eloquence was exceeded only by his sarcasm. Witness after witness crumpled under his withering attacks.

Governor Wallace took the stand first. He did not make a good showing. Waldo had no difficulty in exposing weaknesses and contradictions in the testimony, while also attacking his motives with telling effect. "His testimony," Waldo told the court, "is of the most trashy and worthless quality imaginable," and his "lips should have blistered to a crisp and peeled to the bone when they uttered the foul and mendacious accusation" against Dudley.[16]

Other witnesses against Dudley did even worse, especially Sue McSween and the blacks, Sebrian Bates and George Washington. A blatant racist, Waldo characterized Bates's testimony as "reeking with the foulest distillations of perjury, vapored forth at every breath of the slimy, crawling reptile that gave it utterance." And Washington "ranks only next to Bates in the robust vigor of his mendacity." As Waldo noted, much of Leonard's case rested on the testimony of these two, and his charge that it was concocted under the guidance of Leonard and Sue McSween is persuasive.

Over a span of almost two months, sixty-four witnesses testified, and their memories of what happened varied according to their attachment to Dolan or McSween. In general, witnesses appearing in behalf of Dudley sounded more convincing than those put forward by Leonard, although both sides excelled at prevarication.

Between Waldo's courtroom skill and the court's desire to protect one of its own, Dudley emerged victorious. On July 5, 1879, the court concluded that none of the allegations brought by Leonard and Wallace had been proved, and therefore proceedings before a court-martial were unnecessary.

On the face of the evidence, no other finding seems defensible. Careful analysis and comparison of the testimony shows Dudley to have contributed decisively to the conditions that led to McSween's death, but the evidence has to be tortured in order to convict him of any offense in military law. The court could justly have faulted Dudley for some of his actions while in Lincoln on July 19, 1878, especially his handling of the artillery, but none constituted a crime. On the other hand, as the court noted, he marched into Lincoln "for the most humane and worthy motives and of good military judgment under exceptional circumstances."

Higher authority took a long time to review the record of the Dudley court of inquiry. Not until the end of 1879 did the military bureaucracy come forth with a final disposition of the case, and then only after nudged by Dudley. The delay hid a disagreement within the army. Colonel Hatch's superior, General John Pope, took issue with the court's findings and drew up papers to bring Dudley before a court-martial. In Washington, however, the judge advocate general of the army pronounced the findings convincing and predicted that an expensive court-martial would reach the same conclusion. Doubtless with some relief, Secretary of War McCrary decided against General Pope. On December 30, 1879, General Sherman directed that all proceedings against Dudley cease and that he be given a new command.[17]

The civil courts took even longer than the military to deal with the legacy of the Lincoln County War, but with similar happy outcomes for most of the defendants.

George Peppin and Jimmy Dolan wound up in Socorro, in another judicial district. Peppin was charged with arson and participation in the killing of Frank McNab, and Dolan with complicity in the killings of Tunstall and Chapman. At the November 1879 term, the district attorney simply declined to prosecute Peppin on either charge. For Dolan, a jury trial was scheduled, but canceled when the district attorney announced that he would not prosecute these cases either. The surviving records do not disclose why, but it is worth noting that the district attorney, J. Francisco Chavez, and Dolan's defense counsel, Thomas B. Catron, were among the most politically prominent and powerful men in New Mexico.[18]

Peppin and Dolan should have been tried. They would not likely have been convicted, but the charges against them, resting upon substantial evidence, deserved to be heard by a jury.

After the sluggish workings of the courts had finally disposed of the indictments growing out of the spring 1878 and spring 1879 terms of district court in Lincoln, virtually every defendant went free. Some, such as the Seven Rivers stockmen, had pleaded Governor Wallace's amnesty. Others, including Jesse Evans, Billy Campbell, and John Selman and the Wrestlers, had fled the territory, with most of them heading for Texas, and their names were finally dropped from the court docket books. Still others—Dolan, Peppin, and Mathews among them—went free when prosecutors decided not to prosecute.

Of all these several score participants in the Lincoln County War, only two actually stood trial: Colonel Dudley and Billy Bonney.

The April 1879 grand jury charged Dudley as well as Peppin with arson in the burning of the McSween house. Since Sue McSween had been prominent in bringing the charge, Dudley persuaded Judge Bristol to order her to appear as a witness when the case came to trial. Dudley also convinced the U.S. attorney general that the charge grew out of the performance of his official duties, and therefore he should be defended by the United States district attorney for New Mexico.

The case came before Judge Bristol in Mesilla in November 1879. Sue McSween, however, failed to appear as ordered. She sent word that Ira Leonard had not called for her, and she asked for postponement to a later term of court. Judge Bristol angrily refused, and she belatedly showed up. After three days of heated legal contention, the jury returned a verdict of not guilty, and the spectators broke into cheers and applause.[19]

The verdict was just. Dudley should have stopped the burning of the McSween house. But he did not set the fire, nor did any of his men; and technically, as he repeatedly protested, his orders unequivocally prevented him from interfering with the sheriff in the performance of his duty.

Billy Bonney fared less fortunately than Colonel Dudley. After his experience at the April 1879 term of court, he needed no one to spell out his probable fate at the hands of Bristol and Rynerson. After testifying in the Dudley court of inquiry, the Kid simply rode out of Lincoln, probably with the full knowledge of Sheriff Kimball. From this point on, he turned to more or less open outlawry. He made several attempts to persuade Governor Wallace to help. But Wallace, undoubtedly rationalizing that the Kid's return to criminal life dissolved any lingering obligations, responded by posting a five-hundred-dollar reward for his capture.[20]

In the election of 1880, Lincoln County acquired a new sheriff, a tall, lanky, heavily mustached former buffalo hunter who had recently immigrated from Texas. Pat Garrett had impressed John Chisum and other big Pecos stockmen with his fixity of purpose and skill with a six-shooter, and they had persuaded him to stand against George Kimball for the sheriff's badge. Garrett won handily, and at once he set forth to capture the reward that Governor Wallace had posted for Billy the Kid.

Just before Christmas of 1880, Sheriff Garrett cornered the Kid and his gang in an old rock house at Stinking Springs, near Fort Sumner. Charlie Bowdre died in the ensuing shootout, but the Kid and his other companions surrendered. Lodged in a cell in Santa Fe, Billy bombarded Governor Wallace with appeals for help. "I have done everything I promised you I would," he wrote on March 4, 1881, "and you have done nothing that you promised me." The governor ignored the pleas and filed them with his other papers.[21]

The trial took place in Judge Bristol's court in Mesilla early in April 1881. Although six men had fired twice as many bullets into Sheriff Brady, Prosecuting Attorney Simon B. Newcomb portrayed the Kid as the murderer. After two days of argument, the jury swiftly agreed. At 5:15 P.M. on April 13, Judge Bristol directed that Bonney be returned to Lincoln and hanged by the neck until dead. On April 30, 1881, Governor Wallace signed the death warrant.[22]

Thus, among fifty or more men indicted for offenses in the Lincoln County War, only Billy the Kid was convicted of any crime. It is easy to feel a twinge of sympathy for him, since he lived up to his part of the bargain with Lew Wallace, and others were as guilty of crime as he. But in fairness to the governor, he could not control District Attorney Rynerson, and he had little opportunity to work out an acceptable form of executive clemency before the Kid turned to open outlawry. After that, little could be done without serious political if not legal consequences. And however many other offenders deserved punishment, including those who shared in the murder of Brady, there is virtually no chance that at least one of the bullets that killed Brady was not fired by the Kid. Only he stood convicted, but there can be no reasonable doubt of his guilt.

While ridiculing the spring 1879 term of district court, the *Mesilla Independent* voiced the hopes of all by concluding that "feeling in Lincoln will perhaps cool down now."[23] Surprisingly, although hardly because of anything Judge Bristol's court accomplished, Lincoln County did "cool down"—a relative term in that wild and violent part of New Mexico.

In the absence of any lurid new sensations to attract public attention, Governor Wallace stepped forward with the only voice willing to pronounce the court term in Lincoln a success. As with his proclamation of November 1878, needing success, he simply declared success. The Dolan and McSween factions were dead, he informed Secretary Schurz on June 11. The amnesty proclamation had produced exactly the desired effect: "to shear the past close off." Had all the men indicted stood trial, he reasoned, the court battles would have been accompanied by "heart burnings, disputes, revivals of old feuds, fights, shootings, bush-whackings, and general turmoil." As it was, most pleaded the governor's pardon, and the old hostilities had been put to rest.

Outlaw gangs remained, Wallace conceded. Most citizens favored eliminating them through martial law. But he ticked off half a dozen reasons for resisting such a measure and trusting instead to the civil courts. At last, and finally, he had discarded this panacea for the territory's troubles.[24]

In fact, the governor's claim of success coincided with the end of the Lincoln County War. It was not a clean, unmistakable end. Peace did not suddenly return. The gangs of which Wallace complained yielded only gradually to the restoration of law enforcement, as did deeply ingrained habits of looking to Winchester and Colt's for the settlement of disputes. For a decade the county suffered more or less crime and disorder. Also, the old factional rivalries left wounds that, as Wallace had predicted, took years to heal. But the danger of a resumption of open warfare between the Dolan and McSween factions, so imminent in the wake of the Chapman murder, subsided through the spring of 1879, and thus signaled, somewhat uncertainly, the close of the war.

Lew Wallace contributed to this result meagerly and only after indefensible delay. For five and a half months after taking office, he pursued an erratic course. He had no firm, consistent approach to the problem that he had been sent to New Mexico to solve. He made policy as he went along, and that not very thoughtfully.

His troubles began with his procrastination in going to the scene of the trouble and investigating in person. They continued with his vacillation over martial law; his abrupt and repeated shifts on this issue must have led President Hayes and Secretary of the Interior Schurz to conclude that the governor did not know what to do.

The amnesty proclamation made matters worse. It proclaimed a peace that did not exist and pardoned the criminals responsible for the war. The declaration of peace not only raised false hopes but confused the army's role by appearing to cancel the very condition—the "insurrection" proclaimed by the president—that gave it legal legitimacy. The amnesty encouraged the return of criminals who had fled and made the governor's subsequent campaign to bring them to justice futile in all ways save as a demonstration of purpose.

And herein lay Wallace's sole constructive contribution to closing down the Lincoln County War. By spending six weeks in Lincoln, by demonstrating personal concern and leadership, and by aggressively attacking the outlaws with the army and his own militia, he helped to revive the institutions of government and to reawaken the confidence of the people in them. That he did finally help in bringing about a resolution, however, does not excuse his failure to do more and to do it sooner.

What he should have done was to go to Lincoln at once and devise a plan of action on the scene. From there, he probably would not have issued his proclamation of peace and amnesty, and he probably would have pressed strenuously for martial law. There, he would have seen the army in its congressionally imposed shackles, with the sheriff helplessly barricaded at Fort Stanton, the courts powerless, the people demoralized and unable to make legal process work, and murder, larceny, rape, and other crimes rampant across the land. As he sensed at first, such extreme affliction called for extreme remedy: martial law. By suspending the usual constitutional safeguards and trying forty or fifty of the chief troublemakers by military commission, Wallace might well have achieved quick and lasting victory. Colonel Dudley would have had to go, as he ultimately did, but by early March the army was already casting about for an officer with the "prudence and intelligence" to take his place in the event of martial law.[25]

Instead of unequivocally pressing for martial law, Wallace muddled through, and eventually the problem, with a slight boost from him, simply went away. Whether a firm and unswerving demand could have moved President Hayes cannot be known. Wallace never forced him to face up to the decision. By vacillating between military and civil approaches, Wallace gave the president and his advisers the excuse they wanted for avoiding such a politically distasteful remedy as martial law.

Wallace's faltering course seems understandable only in terms of that knight of chariot and galley, Judah Ben-Hur. Ever the romantic, the novelist found the mythical adventures of his biblical hero far more engrossing than the ugly reality of Lincoln County. Never was he happier than when lost in *Ben-Hur*, he wrote to his wife, "a perfect retreat from the annoyances of daily life as they are spun for me by enemies, and friends who might as well be enemies." Eagerly he anticipated the words "The End"— "how beautiful they will look to me!"[26]

From all the villainous and vicious gunslingers in Lincoln County, from all the brutal and remorseless killers, from all the scheming and grasping grubbers for money and power, no one emerges as an appealing character. Lew Wallace had the potential. He might have shone forth as the lone hero of the Lincoln County War. Instead, in a choice not necessarily deliberate but ultimately to his enormous benefit, he wrote *Ben-Hur*. And the Lincoln County War ended as a war without heroes.

14
Respectability

EVEN AS GOVERNOR WALLACE boasted of war's end, Lincoln County verged on momentous change. Gold strikes west of Lincoln in December 1879 led to the burgeoning of White Oaks, Nogal, and other mining camps. Although ultimately disappointing, mining quickly overshadowed agriculture and attracted immigration. Population increased, and thus producers and consumers. Agriculture diversified, with alfalfa fields and fruit orchards in particular lessening dependence on the corn crop. Sheep and cattle spread over the hills, as corporate organization and infusions of foreign capital stimulated stock raising. By 1886, almost three hundred thousand head of stock grazed the pastures of Lincoln County. Because of economic growth and diversification, a Lawrence Murphy could never again gain such monopolistic power.[1]

As a result of economic change, Lincoln County began to turn respectable. Churches, schools, newspapers, and other marks of settled respectability took root. Crime and violence, while still common, surrendered gradually to more effective sheriffs and judges and to the community's growing insistence on stability, order, and security.

Not surprisingly, therefore, respectability also overtook many of the Lincoln County warriors of the 1870s. Men who had pursued every crooked, deceitful, devious, and lethal means to attain their ambitions or to gratify their whims now emerged as reputable citizens, even as pillars of the business or political community. They suppressed or rationalized the criminal and immoral behavior of their youth and turned to the task of transforming a wild frontier settlement into a model of staid, orderly community life.

None more so than Jimmy Dolan. Ever resourceful, he climbed from the wreckage of war and bankruptcy to reign as one of Lincoln's most eminent citizens. In July 1879, he married Caroline Fritz, daughter of Charles Fritz of Spring Ranch. This proved critical to Dolan's comeback, for in the final settlement of the Tunstall estate Charles Fritz acquired new properties. In one of the Lincoln County War's strangest ironies, in 1882 Jimmy Dolan became proprietor of the old Tunstall store and hung his name on the building that had once housed his archenemy. In another irony, in the same year Dolan and his partner, William L. Rynerson, acquired the old Tunstall ranch on the Río Feliz and stocked it with five thousand cattle. In 1887, they incorporated as the Feliz Cattle Company. Dolan also dabbled in politics, serving as county treasurer for five years and then winning election in 1888 as senator in the territorial legislature.[2]

Although honored and respected, Jimmy Dolan never prospered or settled into a happy personal life. Caroline died shortly after their second daughter was born. Maria Whitlock came to the household to care for the children, and Dolan married her in 1888. Rumors abounded of his mistreatment of Maria, but the daughters remembered their father fondly. He had one serious problem, the same as Lawrence Murphy: he drank too much. Finally, as Frank Coe recalled, "The saloon men would not let him have whiskey, but the cowboys would give it to him." He died in Roswell in 1898—"from delirium tremens," said Coe—and was buried at Spring Ranch in the Fritz family cemetery.[3]

Others likewise gained respectability. Johnny Riley also went into partnership with Rynerson and raised cattle near Las Cruces. Later, he moved to Colorado and prospered, first as a stockman, then as a hog raiser. He died in Colorado Springs in 1916.[4]

In another irony, Billy Mathews, Dolan's loyal lieutenant and the deputy who attached Tunstall's cattle, reasserted his Homestead Act claim to the Tunstall property on the Río Peñasco and did well as a stockman. By the 1890s, when a vanity press compiled sketches of New Mexico's leading citizens, Mathews could be seen as "a man of high character, ineffable integrity and sterling worth." As for his part in the Lincoln County War, the authors declared, "he fearlessly discharged the duties devolving upon him, counting not the personal cost, and it was largely through his efforts that the matter was terminated so as to preserve the interests of those who were on the side of right."[5]

John Copeland, George Peppin, Yginio Salazar, and Frank and George Coe all lived out long and useful lives. The Coes, especially, exuded respectability. Settling on the middle Ruidoso at a place that came to be known as Glencoe, they founded a dynasty that flourished economically, politically, and socially well into the twentieth century.[6]

Hispanic leaders also led the way to respectability. Juan Patrón, securely eminent after presiding in Santa Fe as speaker of the territorial assembly, gave promise of still greater attainments, even the U.S. Congress. But in 1884, amid confusing circumstances, he was shot and killed in a Puerto de Luna saloon. The murderer, Texan Mike Maney, eventually won acquittal in a court presided over, coincidentally, by Judge (and former governor) Samuel Beach Axtell.[7]

Saturnino Baca lived longer, but more quietly. He held occasional posts of public trust, such as postmaster, county commissioner, and member of the territorial penitentiary commission. He and the handsome, socially prominent Juanita, with their nine children, ranched near Lincoln. In 1889, in a dispute over grazing rights, the captain was shot in the arm and suffered an amputation. Even so, he lived until 1924, when he died at the age of ninety-four.[8]

No one wanted respectability more than Sue McSween. Because of the indelible stain on her chastity created by Lincoln gossip and the Dudley affidavits, she could never have complete respectability, but by her own exertions she won as much as anyone else. In 1880, she married George Barber, a surveyor reading law (in McSween's old law library, which he acquired in the estate settlement) under the tutelage of Ira Leonard.

Together, in 1885, Sue and George Barber plunged into

162

stock raising on the west side of the Sierra Blanca, at Three Rivers. While George practiced law in Lincoln and White Oaks, Sue alone managed the ranch. "She planned and superintended the construction of all the buildings on the place," reported the White Oaks *Lincoln County Leader* in 1888, "designated the location of the fences, corrals, and all the necessary works of this character, at the same time overseeing the cowboys, masons, carpenters and farm hands."[9] She also had crews working to establish grain fields, vegetable gardens, fruit orchards, and berry patches.

Sue Barber's achievement in developing the Three Rivers Ranch stamps her as an uncommonly able, strong-minded, independent, and persevering woman in a time when women were expected to remain meekly obedient in the kitchen. If her role in the Lincoln County War reflected these traits, as the evidence suggests without explicitly documenting, she influenced the course of events more acutely than anyone suspected.

Publicity as well as prosperity came to Sue as her fame spread beyond New Mexico. In 1891, she divorced George Barber, on grounds that he had failed to support her and then had abandoned her; but she continued to revel in the role of a "cattle queen" presiding over a range grazing five thousand head of stock. Finally, in 1902, she sold out and moved into a house that she had acquired in White Oaks. In 1915, the Three Rivers ranch came into the possession of Albert Bacon Fall, whose soaring political star would abruptly crash eight years later in the wreckage of Teapot Dome.

White Oaks had already begun to descend toward its ultimate fate as a ghost town. In a moldering house in a moldering town, Sue McSween Barber herself moldered into old age. Walter Noble Burns interviewed her for his best-selling *Saga of Billy the Kid*, but the book infuriated her. Historian Maurice G. Fulton also worked patiently to pry historically valuable recollections out of the old woman, but his efforts netted a file full of complaining, scolding letters and little more. Sue died in White Oaks in 1931 at the age of eighty-six.[10]

Respectability did not await all of the veterans of the Lincoln County War. Lawrence Murphy was one, although his obituary in the *New Mexican* gave no hint of it. At the age of forty-eight, alcoholism killed him on October 20, 1878, only three weeks after Lew Wallace took the oath as governor. Murphy had suffered from "bilious fevers," reported the *New Mexican*, and the cause of death was "general debility." "Full of manly courage, able, educated, a true man," concluded the editors.[11] Less benevolently, Frank Coe recalled that when Murphy arrived in Santa Fe in May 1878, "he was sick and was put in a hospital and the Sisters of Charity would not let him have whiskey, and that cut his living off. He died in a short time and everybody rejoiced over it."[12]

Billy the Kid was another, although his reward was an immortality far transcending mundane respectability. He had already begun his ascent into legend when Judge Bristol pronounced the death sentence in Mesilla on April 13, 1881. Chained and shackled, Billy was loaded into a wagon for the journey back to Lincoln. Deputized to guard him were three veterans of Peppin's posse in the Five-Day Battle: Billy Mathews, John Kinney, and Bob Olinger. The Kid detested Olinger, a tall, powerfully built bully who took perverse pleasure in tormenting his prisoner. On April 21, Sheriff Pat Garrett confined the Kid in the northeast second-floor room of the newly acquired county courthouse— the old "big store" of Murphy, Dolan, and Riley.

A week later, on April 28, Billy the Kid took another giant leap into legend. Sheriff Garrett had gone to White Oaks to collect taxes. Bob Olinger and J. W. Bell guarded Billy. At noon, Olinger escorted the other county prisoners across the street to the Wortley Hotel for lunch. The Kid asked Bell to take him to the privy behind the building. A friend had hidden a pistol there, and Billy slipped it inside his shirt. Back in the courthouse, while ascending the stairs, he shot and killed Deputy Bell, scooped up Olinger's double-barreled shotgun, and ran to the window overlooking the east yard. As Olinger sprinted across the street, the courthouse custodian, Tunstall's former cook Godfrey Gauss, shouted: "The Kid has killed Bell." Olinger looked up at the window and declared: "Yes, and he's killed me too." Both barrels of Olinger's own shotgun exploded and filled his chest with buckshot, killing him instantly. With Gauss's help, Billy worked for an hour trying to pry off his shackles, but finally rode out of town with only one leg free.

For three months, Pat Garrett and his deputies pursued Billy tirelessly. The trail led to his favorite haunts around Fort Sumner, and finally, on the night of July 14, 1881, to the darkened bedroom of old Pete Maxwell. Garrett crouched next to Maxwell's bed, asking in whispers of the Kid's whereabouts. Coincidentally, at this very moment, the Kid himself entered the room from the porch. Instantly, he sensed something awry but, unaccountably, spoke instead of acted. His soft query, "Quien es? Quien es?" spelled his doom. Garrett fired twice. The first bullet slammed into the chest of his quarry. Billy the Kid crumpled to the floor, dead.[13]

Almost at once, Billy the Kid was enshrined in the folklore of America. Pat Garrett's *Authentic Life of Billy the Kid*, published in 1882, burnished the legend, and a generation of dime novels infused it with adventurous appeal. The legend took on new life and new dimensions in 1926, with the appearance of Walter Noble Burns's *Saga of Billy the Kid*. Pretending to historical accuracy, it contained hardly a hint of fact. A constant stream of books and magazines, fortified by the movies and television, ensured that Billy the Kid, in legend if not in historical truth, would live forever in the world's imagination.[14]

The Lincoln County War did more for the Kid than he for it. For the Kid of legend, the war provided a setting for feats of prowess and adventure and acts expressive of character that would be endlessly chronicled with creative hyperbole. For the Kid of history, the war provided the influences that shaped his personality from adolescence to manhood. By July 1878, his values closely resembled those of the other Regulators, ambiguously reflecting both the noble and ignoble, and sanctioning a future either for good or for bad. Some of the Regulators turned toward good. The Kid turned the other way.

As for Billy the Kid's contribution to the Lincoln County War, it was the same as the other Regulators—no more, no less. Had he never found his way to Lincoln County, the course of the war would almost certainly have remained essentially as history has recorded it.

Already, Billy's Regulator friends had scattered, and some died as violently as he. As members of the Kid's gang, both

Charlie Bowdre and Tom O'Folliard had already, in December 1880, fallen before the guns of Garrett's posse. John Middleton punched cows in Kansas, married an heiress, corresponded complainingly with the elder Tunstall in London, and died in an ambush in 1885. Henry Brown became a Kansas lawman, but he also developed a covert sideline as a bank robber; in 1884, a lynch mob ended both careers.

Other of Billy's companions went straight. His closest friend, Fred Waite, headed home for Indian Territory, served as a tax collector, and died naturally in 1895. Jim French was understood to have sailed for South America. The fierce and feared Doc Scurlock moved his family to Texas, and over the next half-century he worked variously as mail carrier, school teacher, physician, farmer, and bookkeeper, and for amusement he composed an occasional poem. In 1929, a heart attack felled him at age eighty.[15]

Down on the Pecos, in the plains world of Texas cowmen, hostilities subsided between John Chisum and the Seven Rivers stock growers. Chisum's operation rapidly scaled down as he moved most of the herds that he had sold to Hunter and Evans to ranges safely distant from the war zone. Creditors tied him up with lawsuits and hounded him unmercifully. On top of these afflictions, a tumor took root in his neck, which resisted treatment, even surgery. On December 22, 1884, at the Arkansas resort of Eureka Springs, cancer killed John Chisum.[16]

Among Chisum's neighbors, habits of personal violence died slowly. In the wake of the Lincoln County War, they turned against one another. Fiery old Hugh Beckwith had never got along well with daughter Camilla's husband, Will Johnson, whom he now held responsible for inducing his sons Bob and John to fight in Peppin's posse. Bitter over Bob's death in McSween's back yard, the patriarch quarreled repeatedly with his son-in-law. On August 17, 1878, a month after the Five-Day Battle, Hugh lost his temper, seized a shotgun, and filled Johnson with buckshot. Johnson's partner, Wallace Olinger, ran in from the corral, took in the death scene, and promptly shot Hugh in the face with a pistol. The tough old man mounted his horse and rode all the way to the Fort Stanton hospital for medical aid. A month later, after recovery, he mounted his horse again and disappeared forever into Texas.[17]

Hugh's other son, John, ran cows in partnership with Heiskell Jones's oldest son, also named John. Rumor had it that their herd consisted principally of "strays." Whatever its character, in August 1879 the two quarreled over its ownership, and Jones shot and killed Beckwith. Bad blood already existed between Jones and rancher Milo Pearce (another veteran of the Five-Day Battle), and the killing of Beckwith brought it to the surface. Bob Olinger, a friend of John Beckwith, made the quarrel his, too. Pearce lay on a cot on his front porch when Jones rode up, dismounted, and approached. Bob Olinger stepped from the front door, leveled his Winchester, and fired two bullets into Jones's back with fatal effect. One went on to hit Pearce in the thigh and cripple him for life.[18]

Others prominent in the drama of Lincoln County played out their lives elsewhere. After breaking out of the Fort Stanton lockup in March 1879, Jesse Evans prudently headed for Texas. There, in 1880, he killed a Texas Ranger, was caught and tried, and wound up in the penitentiary with a ten-year sentence. In 1882, however, he walked away from a work gang and vanished from history.[19]

John Kinney's rustling days ended in 1883 when Albert J. Fountain's Mesilla and Las Cruces militiamen broke up his gang. Kinney served a short term in the penitentiary before gaining release through legal stratagem. Thereafter, he dabbled off and on at mining in Arizona and died in Prescott in 1919 of Bright's Disease.[20]

An even more checkered career came to John Selman, of Wrestler infamy. After several adventurous years on both sides of Texas law, he won election as constable of El Paso in 1892. In 1895, Selman gained a dubious fame by killing the notorious gunman John Wesley Hardin, only to fall himself a year later in a drunken gunfight with a federal marshal.[21]

Rob Widenmann removed himself from the Lincoln County War in June 1878, more than a month before McSween's death. He received plenty of advice from Lincoln not to return, and he did not. After lingering in Mesilla until autumn, he left New

Mexico forever. He paused briefly at his Ann Arbor home and then journeyed to London for a visit with John Henry Tunstall's family. For a time, Widenmann helped the elder Tunstall prepare papers for his long and unsuccessful attempt to secure indemnification from the United States government for his son's death, but the welcome wore thin, and Widenmann departed under strained circumstances.

Widenmann passed the remainder of his life restlessly unable to succeed in the business world and haunted by dark fantasies of reprisals for his part in the Lincoln County War. He professed to see conspiracy in high places to sanitize the official record in Washington archives and even to eliminate anyone who might expose the truth about official wrongdoing in New Mexico. "Until the Cleveland administration came in," he wrote in 1927, "Schurz and I were under a close system of espionages [as] we well knew, and had we made any move we would, undoubtedly, have been put out of the way." Even in 1927, almost half a century later, he believed that no survivor of the Lincoln County War would "dare to open up the whole matter and give the real causes."[22] He died three years later, at the age of seventy-two, in the New York suburb where he had spent most of his years since returning from England.[23]

Thoroughly traumatized by the war, Reverend Taylor F. Ealy and his family also hastily abandoned Lincoln. They left with the troops on July 20, 1878, passed a miserable week at Fort Stanton, and then journeyed to Las Vegas.

The clergyman's next assignment was Zuñi Pueblo, in western New Mexico, and here he fared even worse, if possible, than in Lincoln. He had no understanding or appreciation of the Indians' culture and set himself singlemindedly to make them all into Presbyterians at once. He failed, of course, and in 1881 the Ealys returned to Pennsylvania to labor in more congenial and fruitful vineyards. The preacher left as a monument to his career not only two generations of contented parishioners, but the profitable T. F. Ealy Baby Powder Company.[24]

Lieutenant Colonel Nathan Dudley took self-righteous satisfaction in his exoneration by a military court in July 1879 and his acquittal of the charge of arson by a civil jury in November 1879.

He expected to return to the command of Fort Stanton to savor his triumph. Colonel Hatch had better sense, however, and assigned him to Fort Union instead.

Hatch also tried to rid the army of Dudley altogether, alleging unfitness for any duty wrought by decades of dissipation. But Dudley's official vindication persuaded the army hierarchy to leave well enough alone. Years later, when he accidentally learned of Hatch's attempt, Dudley smugly called attention to his record in the campaign against the Apache Victorio in 1880. Commanding the mounted component of an expedition that marched a punishing seven hundred miles through the Mexican deserts, he claimed to have been the senior cavalry officer, yet the only one who never once had taken refuge in a wagon or ambulance.

Seniority made Dudley a full colonel and commander of the First Cavalry in 1885 and brought him to retirement in 1889—coincidentally, in the same year that his old antagonist, Edward Hatch, died of injuries sustained in a carriage accident. Dudley lived out a quiet retirement in Roxbury, Massachusetts, and died in 1910, with his last six years sweetened by promotion to brigadier general on the retired list.[25]

Colonel Dudley was not a likable fellow. But neither were any of the other principals in the Lincoln County War. At least he was basically sincere, as few of them were. He wanted to do his military duty as law, justice, and humanity demanded. Personal limitations made that ideal impossible to achieve. In particular, whiskey muddied his thinking and impaired his judgment. So bitter an enemy as Colonel Hatch thought whiskey the key ingredient in Dudley's performance. "If Dudley had not been so constantly under the influence of liquor while at Stanton," he wrote to Governor Wallace, "he might have managed matters very well. I attach the most of his trouble to drink."[26] It was true throughout his life, and it goes far to explain his erratic conduct in the Lincoln County War.

Early in 1880, Governor Lew Wallace wrote "The End" on the final page of his epic novel. In April, he journeyed to New York to arrange for publication. *Ben-Hur: A Tale of the Christ* appeared near the end of the year. Ultimately, *Ben-Hur* made Wallace a wealthy and revered literary figure. More immediately, it won him release from the oppressive post in New Mexico. President James A. Garfield, an old Shiloh comrade, found the tale of Ben-Hur so moving that he gave Wallace the post of minister to the court of the Turkish Sultan in Constantinople, a fitting reward for one who so treasured exotic peoples and places. On May 30, 1881, as Sheriff Pat Garrett scoured the Pecos River country for Billy the Kid, the governor who had arrived in Santa Fe on a springless buckboard climbed aboard a Pullman sleeper and, surely without regret, turned toward new adventures and new realms to conquer.

15

Post-Mortem

THE LINCOLN COUNTY WAR is often viewed as a classic western shootout, the archetypal collision of violent men with clashing interests and ambitions, played out in an untamed frontier land promising fortune to the brave and the bold.

Up to a point, the image reflects the reality, although not in any of the usual formulas favored by screenwriters. The war was not a fight between sheepmen and cowmen, or stockmen and sodbusters, or big cattlemen and little (except for the sideshow on the Pecos), or enclosers and fence-cutters, or vigilantes and outlaws, or corporate moguls and nesters, or Anglos and Hispanics (although there were overtones), or feuding families, or any other of the traditional squareoffs so conspicuous in the Old West of imagination.

But above all else the Lincoln County War was, in fact, a collision of personalities. Quite simply, motivated by a quest for money and power, Tunstall and McSween picked a fight with Murphy, Dolan, and Riley, who responded with every legal and lethal means at their command.

Economic and social conditions in Lincoln County invited and made possible the personal fight. However raw, Lincoln was not a booming, bustling place like the mining camps, railheads, and cattle towns usually associated with frontier violence. Rather, it was a frontier backwater, distant from population centers and deficient in public transportation. This very condition fixed the environment in which a clash of personalities could spark factional strife of the intensity of the Lincoln County War.

The fledgling economy of the 1870s lent itself to monopoly domination. Fort Stanton and the Mescalero Apache Agency offered the only local market for the agricultural products of the area. Supply contracts went to distant entrepreneurs, often on political grounds. But they usually turned to Lawrence Murphy as subcontractor, for only he, through his mercantile and other enterprises, commanded the credit machinery to assemble virtually the entire crop yield and guarantee deliveries according to contract. But for the single significant market afforded by federal contracts, coupled with a cashless economy, the Murphy monopoly would not have existed, and Tunstall and McSween would not have been enticed into the commercial challenge that led to war.

Paradoxically, within six months after the close of the Lincoln County War, the conditions that buttressed the Murphy monopoly changed fundamentally. The gold strikes at White Oaks, Nogal, and elsewhere in the mountains west of Lincoln gave the county a diversified economy as well as increased population. The Lincoln County War of 1878 could not have occurred in 1880.

The struggle for economic supremacy took place in a social setting conducive to violence. Lincoln in the 1870s was a first-generation frontier community, with infant institutions and the social instability characteristic of new settlements on a remote frontier.

All over the American West, law and order suffered in youthful pioneer communities like Lincoln. County treasuries in sparsely settled and economically underdeveloped areas could not afford adequate police and courts. Peace officers tended to be too few and too ineffective to cope with the outlaws who gravitated to such tempting prey, much less with the free-spirited adventurers who peopled every frontier. The man behind the badge practiced a highly personal, capricious brand of enforcement, and, because of vast distances and rudimentary transportation, it rarely reached beyond the immediate vicinity of the county seat. The courts were no more efficient, with judges and prosecutors of doubtful competence and juries unable or unwilling to apply justice evenly. Jails remained to be built, or were makeshift contrivances easily breached.[1]

Often, when conditions became intolerable, vigilantes formed to do what the law could not or would not do. Vigilantes usually came from the upper social levels and represented the conservative forces of the community. Typically, a border community, no matter how new, began at once to resolve itself into a three-tiered social hierarchy: the business and political elite—the "better sort;" laborers, herdsmen, innkeepers, and miners—the "common sort;" and all the others, who included outlaws, drifters, hard cases, and any racial or ethnic minorities that happened to be present.[2] When the better sort and the common sort grew disgusted enough with lawlessness and disorder and strong enough to do something about it, conditions favored a vigilante cleanup. The top two tiers united against the bottom tier.[3]

Lincoln met all the conditions for this generalized vigilante model. Sheriff Brady enforced a haphazard, personal law and rarely operated far from his base. Court came to Lincoln only twice a year, and then it functioned haltingly and unevenly, with mediocre judge and prosecutor and erratic, ill-equipped jurors.

Crime flourished, reflecting patterns characteristic of other frontier areas with small population, token law enforcement, and nascent social and governmental institutions. Cattle rustling was so common as to be looked upon by many as no offense at all. Horse theft, although much more objectionable, was almost as routine. Homicide and attempted homicide occurred with bloody regularity. Assault, drunkenness, and general rowdyism were rampant, although almost never prosecuted.[4] (By contrast, such "big city" crimes as burglary, arson, mugging, and rape rarely occurred. Bank robbery was unknown because banks were unknown. Stagecoach holdups, frequent elsewhere in New Mexico, were also unknown because stagecoaches, in the usual sense, were unknown. Bandits rarely interfered with the mail buckboards that passed for coaches.)

Crime bred violence. Drunken rowdyism bred violence. And Indian depredations bred violence. In fact, Indian hostility, which compelled the pioneer to be always on guard against a

surprise attack, went far toward fixing the violent cast of the frontier mind, in Lincoln as elsewhere. Violence rocked Lincoln
County throughout the 1870s.

At the same time, social organization stratified into the three
typical levels. Indeed, separate hierarchies emerged for Anglo
and Hispanic. Among the better sort were Tunstall, McSween,
Murphy, Squire Wilson, the Ellis family, and Sheriff Brady. Down
on the Pecos, John Chisum and Hugh Beckwith occupied the
social summit, as did Dr. Blazer at South Fork. Juan Patrón, Saturnino Baca, Florencio Gonzales, José Montaño, and Martín
Chavez represented the peak of the Hispanic pyramid. Dolan and
Riley began as common sort, but with Murphy's fall they moved
up to the better sort. Other commoners included John Copeland,
Sam Wortley, George Peppin, the Coe cousins, Dick Brewer, and
Billy Mathews, as well as most of the Seven Rivers warriors on the
Pecos. Jesse Evans and The Boys, the Mes gang of horse thieves,
and assorted losers of both Anglo and Hispanic origin occupied
the bottom tier.

Despite conditions favoring vigilantism, the Lincoln County
War brought forth no vigilantes. The top two levels did not combine against the bottom. Instead, the social hierarchy split vertically, with elements of all three tiers on both sides. Indeed, the
fight was between leading personalities of the better sort, and
men of the lower strata chose sides according to personal interest
or previous alignment. McSween's followers called themselves
Regulators, which historically is a synonym for vigilante. But
they met almost none of the usual tests of vigilantes, and in fact
they portrayed themselves not as extralegal battlers for the law
but as actual arms of the law as represented by the justice of the
peace. Nor did Dolan's fighters view themselves as vigilantes. On
the contrary, except for the brief Copeland interlude, they rode
in the service of the county sheriff, and their ostensible mission
was to enforce the processes of the district court.

In contrast to the Anglo hierarchy, the Hispanic hierarchy
did not divide vertically. Many of the Hispanics wanted no part of
the war, which was chiefly an Anglo struggle. With few excep-
tions, however, most notably Saturnino Baca, those who chose
sides lined up behind McSween. Their motives probably reflected

longstanding resentment of Murphy's tyranny, combined with the assiduous efforts of Tunstall and McSween to win their allegiance and support. Ethnic factors seem to have played only a minor part in the Lincoln County War, which is surprising in view of the ugly ethnic content of the Horrell War and the Tularosa Ditch War.[5]

The Lincoln County War invites comparison with the other great bursts of violence that flashed across the West—Wyoming's Johnson County War, Arizona's Pleasant Valley War, and New Mexico's Colfax County War, among others.

With the Johnson County War, intriguing if superficial similarities emerge. Englishmen, for instance, also figured in this battle between big cowmen and little cowmen. Like Tunstall, the foreigners used surrogates to gain control of ranges under the Desert Land Act. Unlike Tunstall, they could not relax their patrician snobbery enough to win acceptance by the local population. The Johnson County hostilities also involved warring factions that wrapped themselves in a cloak of legality and righteousness, wrought a total collapse of law and order, attracted an influx of outlaws reminiscent of the Wrestlers in Lincoln County, raised the threat of martial law, brought about presidential intervention in the form of a proclamation of insurrection, and featured the employment of federal troops. Johnson County's brawl yielded no more heroes than Lincoln County's; nor victors, either. "Nobody won the Johnson County War," concluded its chronicler.[6]

With the Colfax County and Pleasant Valley wars, Lincoln County had less in common. Colfax County, like Lincoln County, excited the aspirations of the Santa Fe Ring and became embroiled in territorial politics. Governor Axtell lost his job as much for his course in Colfax as in Lincoln County. But the Colfax War was basically a struggle between squatters, both Anglo and Hispanic, and the foreign corporate claimants to the Maxwell Land Grant.[7] Pleasant Valley—a fight between sheepmen and cowmen, rustlers and ranchers, and feuding families—bore even less resemblance to the Lincoln County War.[8]

Whatever the particular origins, progress, and consequences, however, all these wars, and virtually all other explosions of vio-

175

lence on the western frontier, displayed four underlying themes. In these themes, rather than in superficial similarities or differences, the Lincoln County War finds firm links to other wars and to frontier violence in general.

One common strand was liquor. Everywhere on the frontier, nearly all men drank nearly all the time, which made nearly all men more or less drunk most of the time. Drink enhanced self-importance, impaired judgment, generated heedless courage, and encouraged unreasoning resort to violence. Tunstall and McSween rarely, if ever, sampled intoxicants; but the rest of the combatants in the Lincoln County War imbibed deeply and regularly, some even constantly. Whiskey controlled Colonel Dudley, for example, and whiskey caused the slaying of Huston Chapman.

A second theme was the instant accessibility of firearms. Most men carried a Colt's sixshooter or two in holsters or stuffed into their belts, while saddle scabbards held the greatly favored Winchester repeating rifle or carbine, and with varying skill most men knew how to use them. When whiskey or any other cause sparked the instinct to violence, guns could be quickly summoned to the fray, with frequently mortal effect. McSween shrank from firearms, but no one else on either side, including Tunstall, had his aversion to these final arbiters of frontier disputes.

A third theme evident in all the wars was a quest for money and power. Gilded Age America set high store on both, and nowhere higher than on the frontier. The West attracted daring young bravos in search of quick money, and the scramble contributed to much of the West's violence. "Follow the money," advised the veteran biographer of John Chisum, who had discovered that dry and confusing financial records usually held the secret to the ambitions that produced conflicts.[9] Tunstall's dogged pursuit of fortune brought on the Lincoln County War. Tunstall and McSween fought Murphy, Dolan, and Riley over money and power, and all their minions had the same goals.

Finally, and most compelling of all themes, was the code of the West. Avenge insult or wrong, real or imagined, the code decreed. Never retreat before an aggressor. Any degree of violence is permissible, including death. "I'll die before I'll run," vowed practitioners of the code.

If not originated in Texas, the code received its most extreme definition and widest practice there in the bloody Reconstruction years. Some of the West's worst violence exploded in central Texas in the decade after the Civil War. The leading authority on Texas feuds notes that in most states the law requires a man to retreat as far as he can before he kills an assailant. In Texas to this day, because of this heritage, he need retreat no farther than "the air at his back."[10]

The tradition of violent self-redress and self-defense so ardently embraced in Texas flowed northward on the Chisholm Trail, the Western Trail, and the other great cattle trails on which Texas cowboys pushed their herds toward the nation's beef markets. The tradition reached up the Pecos into New Mexico on the Goodnight–Loving Trail. By the early 1870s, it was firmly imbedded in the culture of Lincoln County.[11]

Jimmy Dolan imbibed it deeply. Although a New Yorker, he made a place for himself in the rough-and-tumble world of the code after his discharge from the army at Fort Stanton in 1869, at the impressionable age of twenty-one. In May 1877, Dolan exhibited his devotion to the code by slaying Hiraldo Jaramillo, a youth of twenty. According to the account in the *New Mexican*, which Dolan probably wrote himself, he acted in the best tradition of self-defense. Rumor, however, said that he killed Jaramillo as a favor to his friend George Peppin.[12]

Predictably, as commanded by the code, Dolan, when challenged by Tunstall and McSween, retreated no farther than "the air at his back." At Blazer's Mills, Buckshot Roberts dramatized his adherence to the code in spectacular, and suicidal, fashion. Tunstall may have tried to defend himself when jumped by Morton, Evans, and Hill. In his own way, even McSween invoked the code. All the Lincoln County fighters, in fact, practiced the code.

In addition to the four common themes, the Lincoln County War boasts a fifth theme, a spectacular and enduring ornament that gives it front rank among notable frontier conflicts: Billy the Kid. He played a moderately important though hardly crucial role in the war, but in the image of posterity he has come to dominate it and, like a huge but appealing giant, to bestride the entire landscape of the Old West of popular imagination. Amid the savagery of gangsters like Selman's Wrestlers, Billy the Kid shines brightly as the Lincoln County War's lone "social bandit." The test is not whether the social bandit, like Robin Hood or Jesse James, robbed from the rich and gave to the poor, but rather whether people thought he did and thus accorded him the status of folk hero.[13] In his own time, however undeservedly, Billy the Kid won this accolade, especially from the unsung Hispanic plowmen and herdsmen of Lincoln County. No other frontier fight can boast a personality that has had so powerful an impact on the world's imagination.

As one of the West's most celebrated eruptions of violence, the Lincoln County War occupies a prominent place in the larger story of frontier violence and American violence in general. In recent years, these have been topics of deep national concern.

In the middle 1960s, the United States plunged into a decade-long paroxysm of violence—the interminable Vietnam bloodletting, political assassinations, black revolt in the ghettos, antiwar protest, ferment on the radical left, and the "red power" movement of American Indians. The violence, in turn, set off a national soul-searching to plumb the origins of this dark strain in the American psyche. Seeking precedent and explanation, pundits and scholars alike turned to the frontier West. In the violent world of Jimmy Dolan, they sought understanding of the violent world of Lyndon Johnson and Richard Nixon.

Among students of frontier violence, two schools of thought emerged. The first, representing the conventional wisdom of half a century, held that the frontier was an extraordinarily violent place—the haunt of ferocious Indians, desperadoes, and criminals of every stripe who killed, maimed, robbed, and spread such terror as to brutalize pioneer society. Over the span of two centuries, the argument ran, the values and attitudes of the tumultuous western border infected American culture and planted a predisposition to violence deeply in the national character. Instinctively, Americans turned to force for the redress of grievances, foreign and domestic; and at the same time they cultivated a passion for firearms that made the force frequently deadly. In the frontier experience, therefore, lay the explanation of the frenzied violence that seized the United States in the late 1960s and early 1970s.[14]

Other students rejected this interpretation as the offspring of myth rather than history. The frontier, they contended, suffered no more violence than other parts of the United States, possibly even less. A citizen ran greater risks to life, limb, and pocketbook in Philadelphia, New York, and Boston than in Denver, El Paso, and Dodge City. Indeed, the modern proclivity for violence may owe more to the urbanizing experience than to the frontier experience, for the prevalent crimes now are city crimes rather than the crimes common to the frontier. In this rendering, frontier violence is a result, not a cause, of a violent streak that has animated the American mind from the beginning.[15]

The debate remains unresolved, mainly because of an absence of reliable statistics from earlier times. Even so, the studies that grew out of this trying decade shed much light on the nature of violence in frontier society and in the larger society of the nation. They clearly demonstrate that, whether more or less violent than elsewhere, the frontier was assuredly a violent place. They contribute to an understanding of frontier violence in general and sketch a backdrop for the bloody drama of Lincoln County.[16]

The blood and the drama are fact, not the imaginings of popular scribblers. The Lincoln County War was a significant case study in frontier violence. It reveals the mentality of the generations that conquered the wilderness and pushed the frontier to the far edge of the continent. It illuminates the heritage of Americans as a people inclined to violent pursuit of ambition and violent resolution of problems. It was also a momentous episode in the development of territorial New Mexico as well as an exciting story of vivid characters in collision.

But beyond all the analyses of meaning, the Lincoln County War's most enduring legacy to the world may well be as a launchpad for the rise of an unknown youth of sunny disposition and deadly trigger finger into one of the mightiest legends of all time.

Notes

Abbreviations

AAAG	Acting Assistant Adjutant General
AAG	Assistant Adjutant General
ACP	Appointments, Commissions, Promotions
AGO	Adjutant General's Office
BIA	Bureau of Indian Affairs
CO	Commanding Officer
DFRC	Denver Federal Records Center
DM	Department of the Missouri, Fort Leavenworth
DNM	District of New Mexico
HHC	J. Evetts Haley History Center, Midland, Texas
HL	Huntington Library, San Marino, California
Hq.	Headquarters
IHS	Indiana Historical Society, Indianapolis
LR	Letters Received
LS	Letters Sent
NARS	National Archives and Record Service, Washington, D.C.
NMSRCA	New Mexico State Record Center and Archives, Santa Fe
RG	Record Group
TANM	Territorial Archives of New Mexico
UAL	University of Arizona Library, Tucson
UNML	University of New Mexico Library, Albuquerque
WPA	Works Progress Administration

CHAPTER 1

1. Frederick Nolan, ed., *The Life and Death of John Henry Tunstall* (Albuquerque: University of New Mexico Press, 1965), p. 153. Tunstall's voluminous letters to his family in England are remarkably revealing of Tunstall the man and entrepreneur. Typescripts are in the Maurice Garland Fulton Collection, UAL. They contain little that is not included in Nolan's published version. Fulton copied the originals and returned them to the family. Nolan worked from originals in possession of the family. The following paragraphs are based on Tunstall's letters home from Santa Fe, chap. 5.

2. Nolan, *Life and Death of Tunstall*, p. 88.

3. Ibid., pp. 95, 133.

4. Ibid., p. 158.

5. Ibid., p. 141.

6. Ibid., p. 115.

7. Ibid., p. 180.

8. I am indebted to Donald R. Lavash, historian at the NMSRCA and biographer of Sheriff William Brady, for the little that can be gleaned from official records of the antecedents of the McSweens. The marriage certificate records McSween's age in 1873 as twenty-nine, which would have made 1844 his year of birth. This agrees with the age he gave on his will on February 25, 1878. According to Lavash's findings, however, church records on Prince Edward Island give his birth date as June 15, 1837. Lavash's research also discloses that Sue Homer joined the First Presbyterian Church of Atchison on April 29, 1873, three and one-half months before her marriage, but that the church's membership book has no mention of McSween or the marriage—an oddity, given McSween's claim to have been a Presbyterian minister.

Most of what has been assumed about the McSweens came from Sue herself, whose remarriage after Alex's death gave her the name Barber. Her contributions to the history of Lincoln County were made chiefly in a series of letters during the late 1920s to Maurice Garland Fulton and in many visits he made to her home in White Oaks, New Mexico. The letters, and scraps of Fulton's recordings of what she told him, are in the Fulton Collection, UAL. Also useful is an interview she gave to J. Evetts Haley in White Oaks on August 16, 1927, HHC. Sue was in her eighties, and what she said suffered from bad memory and, probably, deliberate distortion.

9. Marion Turner to Ed., Roswell, April 18, 1878, *Las Vegas Gazette*, May 4, 1878. Marion Turner assuredly did not write this literate letter. From original documents known to be of his authorship, it is clear

that he verged on illiteracy. Most likely, it was written for Turner by Marshall A. (Ash) Upson, Roswell postmaster and sometime journalist who later ghosted Pat Garrett's history of Billy the Kid.

10. Carlota Baca Brent, interview with Frances E. Totty, December 6, 1937, WPA files, folder 212, NMSRCA.

11. J. J. Clancy to Maurice G. Fulton, Anton Chico, N.M., November 26, 1932, Fulton Collection, box 1, folder 4, UAL. See also miscellaneous material in Patrón biographical notes, Mullin Collection, HHC.

12. Nolan, *Life and Death of Tunstall*, p. 191.

13. Ibid., p. 193.

CHAPTER 2

1. A good picture of Lincoln County emerges from the censuses of 1870 and 1880, NMSRCA.

2. Frederick Nolan, ed., *The Life and Death of John Henry Tunstall* (Albuquerque: University of New Mexico Press, 1965), p. 192.

3. True Bill of Grand Jury, Lincoln County, October 12, 1875, *Territory v. A. H. Mills*: Manslaughter, Criminal Case file no. 163. Lincoln County, District Court Journal, Fall 1875 term, pp. 29, 59, 73–74. Ibid., Fall 1876 term, pp. 215–16, 222. Murphy to Axtell, Lincoln, December 5, 1876, enclosing petition, TANM, roll 98, frame 842. Executive Record Book No. 2, 1867–82, p. 277, TANM, roll 21, frame 466. All in NMSRCA.

4. Nolan, *Life and Death of Tunstall*, p. 193. Tunstall got his facts confused. He was under the impression that the murder had occurred only recently. Actually, it had taken place in September 1875, but because of Mills's flight the trial and conviction did not transpire until October 1876, about two weeks before Tunstall's arrival in Lincoln. The pardon was issued early in December 1876.

5. Robert A. Casey, interview with J. Evetts Haley, Picacho, N.M., June 25, 1937, HHC.

6. Although burdened with modern connotations and without roots in the history of territorial New Mexico, *Hispanic* or *Hispano* is the term that seems most satisfactory.

7. Frank Coe, interview with J. Evetts Haley, San Patricio, N.M., August 14, 1927, HHC. Lincoln's history is detailed in John P. Wilson, "Lincoln: A New Mexico Epic," a report, unpublished at this writing, prepared for the State Monuments Division of the Museum of New Mexico, Santa Fe, May 1986. I am greatly indebted to this report and to many informative letters from its author.

8. Rev. Taylor F. Ealy to sister Mary, Lincoln, March 4, 1878, in Norman J. Bender, ed., *Missionaries, Outlaws, and Indians: Taylor F. Ealy at Lincoln and Zuni, 1878–1881* (Albuquerque: University of New Mexico Press, 1984), p. 23. I have used the original Ealy Papers in Special Collections, UAL, but where possible citations will refer to this book.

9. Yginio Salazar, interview with J. Evetts Haley, Lincoln, N.M., August 17, 1927, HHC.

10. In addition to the Robert A. Casey interview, cited in n. 5, another of the children, Lily Casey Klasner, tells of life at Casey's Mill in *My Girlhood among Outlaws*, ed. Eve Ball (Tucson: University of Arizona Press, 1972). See also James D. Shinkle, *Robert Casey and the Ranch on the Rio Hondo* (Roswell, N.M.: Hall-Poorbough Press, 1970).

11. The Blazer Family Papers are in Special Collections, UAL.

12. Lawrence G. Murphy richly merits a serious biography, for he was a significant and colorful figure in New Mexico's territorial history. This sketch has been drawn in part from his obituary in the *Weekly New Mexican* (Santa Fe), October 26, 1878; from the Murphy biographical notes, Mullin Collection, HHC; and from Philip J. Rasch, "The Rise of the House of Murphy," Denver Westerners, *Brand Book*, 12 (1956), pp. 53–84. I have also examined Murphy's regular army enlistment papers in RG 94, ACP Files, NARS. An excellent characterization by one who knew him is in Klasner, *My Girlhood among Outlaws*, p. 94. My account also rests heavily upon extensive reading in the official records of Fort Stanton, the Mescalero Apache Indian Agency, the New Mexico Superintendency of Indian Affairs, and the Headquarters, District of New Mexico, all in NARS and all available on microfilm. Much useful information is contained in Lawrence L. Mehren, "A History of the Mescalero Apache Reservation, 1869–1881" (Master's Thesis, University of Arizona, 1969); and Wilson, "Lincoln: A New Mexico Epic."

13. A detailed picture of Murphy's operation emerges from a close study of his ledger books for 1871 and 1872, Special Collections, UAL. Subsequent store accounts appear as Exhibit 11 of McSween's deposition in Frank Warner Angel, "Report on the Death of John H. Tunstall," Department of Justice, 1878. The Angel Report, hereafter cited as such, is in the Records of the Department of Justice, NARS. I have used a copy in the Victor Westphall Collection, NMSRCA.

14. These charges find support in many of the depositions in the Angel Report, as well as in Indian Bureau records, especially RG 75, Special Case 108, Reduction of the Mescalero Reservation, NARS.

15. Depositions of Florencio Gonzales and George Van Sickle, Angel Report. The pattern of Murphy's land dealings emerges in Lincoln

County Record Book A, a sort of catchall for recording land and property transactions during the early 1870s, in the Lincoln County Courthouse, Carrizozo, N.M. I have used photocopies generously lent by Harwood P. Hinton.

16. Deposition of Juan Patrón, Angel Report.

17. The records of the Third Judicial District Court, NMSRCA, bear out this conclusion. Murphy was a frequent litigant; the usual action was a civil charge of "assumpsit"—breach of contract.

18. Both Mullin and Fulton found a belief prevalent among Lincoln old-timers of Murphy's homosexual proclivities; and see also Capt. James F. Randlett to Adjutant General, Fort Stanton, July 22, 1873, RG 94, Adjutant General LR (Main Series), 1871–80 (M–666, roll 120), NARS. Randlett identified a prominent local official whom "it is said and so believed by everybody I know, holds a relation to Murphy the most unnatural and disgustingly brutal."

19. The monthly balances in his Santa Fe bank account fell from between thirty and fifty thousand dollars in 1873 to between five and eight thousand in 1874 and subsequent years. Ledger Book 2, Records of the First National Bank of Santa Fe, Archive 177, Special Collections, UNML.

20. George Coe, interview with J. Evetts Haley, Ruidoso, N.M., June 12, 1939, HHC. Coe, who ranched with his cousin Frank on the Hondo, is a much-quoted authority on the Lincoln County War, with most citations to his book, *Frontier Fighter, The Autobiography of George W. Coe*, as related to Nan Hillary Harrison (Boston and New York: Houghton Mifflin Co., 1934; 2d ed., Albuquerque: University of New Mexico Press, 1951; Lakeside Classics ed., ed. by Doyce B. Nunis, Jr., Chicago: R. R. Donnelly and Co., 1984). The book suffered from the intervention of Harrison and is not nearly so valuable as the Haley interviews. Both Coes had poor memories for events and chronology, but they are good for local color and characterizations of people.

21. Klasner, *My Girlhood among Outlaws*, p. 94. See also Dolan biographical notes, Mullin Collection, HHC.

22. *Daily New Mexican* (Santa Fe), November 20, 1876.

23. Frank Coe, interview with J. Evetts Haley, San Patricio, N.M., August 14, 1927, HHC.

24. Deposition of Agent W. D. Crothers, July 21, 1875, in RG 75, Special Case 108, Reduction of the Mescalero Reservation, NARS.

25. The best account of the origins of the movement of Texas cattle into New Mexico is J. Evetts Haley, *Charles Goodnight: Cowman and Plainsman* (Norman: University of Oklahoma Press, 1949). For counts of

cattle coming up the Pecos, see *Daily New Mexican* (Santa Fe), August 2, 1872, and January 26, 1874.

26. *Las Vegas Gazette*, November 25, 1875, quoted in William A. Keleher, *The Fabulous Frontier: Twelve New Mexico Items* (Albuquerque: University of New Mexico Press, 1962), p. 60.

27. The basic biographical work on Chisum is Harwood P. Hinton, "John Simpson Chisum, 1877–84," *New Mexico Historical Review* 31 (July 1956), pp. 177–205; (October 1956), pp. 310–37; and 32 (January 1957), pp. 53–65. Hinton is working on a full-scale biography of Chisum.

28. Haley, *Charles Goodnight*, p. 235. This characterization emerges in Hinton, "John Simpson Chisum." See also the approving portrayal in Klasner, *My Girlhood among Outlaws*.

29. James P. Jones, interview with J. Evetts Haley, Rocky Arroyo, N.M., January 13 and 14, 1927, Panhandle Plains Historical Museum, Canyon, Texas.

30. Hinton, "John Simpson Chisum," p. 192.

31. Lee Scott Theisen, ed., "Frank Warner Angel's Notes on New Mexico Territory, 1878," *Arizona and the West* 18 (Winter 1976), p. 344.

32. All these stockmen are treated in more or less detail in biographical notes in the Mullin Collection, HHC. Some are characterized in Klasner, *My Girlhood among Outlaws*. An idealized picture of the Jones family is Eve Ball, *Ma'am Jones of the Pecos* (Tucson: University of Arizona Press, 1969).

33. Hinton, "John Simpson Chisum," pp. 190–91.

34. Quoted in C. L. Sonnichsen, *Tularosa: Last of the Frontier West*, 2d ed. (Albuquerque: University of New Mexico Press, 1980), pp. 22–23. Sonnichsen's discussion of the code is excellent. I have also drawn heavily on Sonnichsen's discussion of the "theory and practice of feuding" in *I'll Die Before I'll Run: The Story of the Great Feuds of Texas* (New York: Devin-Adair, 1962). chap. 1.

35. Klasner, *My Girlhood among Outlaws*, pp. 110–11, 216.

36. This theme is prevalent throughout the historical literature of Texas and New Mexico, but see especially Sonnichsen, *Tularosa*, pp. 24–25.

37. Philip J. Rasch, "The Tularosa Ditch War," *New Mexico Historical Review* 43 (July 1968), pp. 229–35. McKibben to AAAG, DNM, Fort Stanton, May 29, 1873, with six attachments; Lt. John W. Wilkinson to Acting Post Adjutant Fort Stanton, Blazer's Mill, June 2, 1873; McKibben to AAAG, DNM, Fort Stanton, June 13, 1873; "Report of the Grand Jury in regard to an affair between U.S. troops of Fort Stanton &

Citizens of Tularosa in which a citizen was killed by troops &c.," July 2, 1873, RG 393, LR Hq. DNM, NARS (M1088, roll 20).

38. James P. Jones, interview with J. Evetts Haley, Rocky Arroyo, N.M., January 13—14, 1927, Panhandle-Plains Historical Museum, Canyon, Texas.

39. William Jones, interview with J. Evetts Haley, Rocky Arroyo, N.M., January 13, 1927, Panhandle-Plains Historical Museum, Canyon, Texas.

40. *Daily New Mexican* (Santa Fe), January 2, 1874. The *New Mexican* got its account from Juan Patrón, who was in Santa Fe. He gave the casualties as Isidro Patrón, Dario Valizan, José Candelaria, and Isidro Padilla killed; and Apolonia García, Pilar Candelaria, and a nephew of Dario Valizan wounded.

41. Robert A. Casey, interview with J. Evetts Haley, Picacho, N.M., June 25, 1937. For secondary accounts, see Philip J. Rasch, "The Horrell War," *New Mexico Historical Review* 31 (July 1956); and Wilson, "Lincoln: A New Mexico Epic," chap. 5. The records of the Departments of War and Interior are full of official correspondence on the Horrell War, much of which I have consulted without citing here.

42. Capt. James F. Randlett to Maj. W. R. Price, Roswell, September 18, 1873, RG 393, LR Hq. DNM, NARS (M1088, roll 19). Not all these depredations could be charged to the Mescaleros, as the Comanches were also involved. Clearly, though, the agency Indians were deeply implicated.

43. Robert A. Casey, interview with J. Evetts Haley, Picacho, N.M., June 25, 1937, HHC.

44. *Daily New Mexican* (Santa Fe), 15 January and 21 May 1875; A. M. Gildea to Maurice G. Fulton, May 9, 1930, Fulton Collection, box 2, folder 2, UAL; depositions of Jacob B. Mathews, Marion Turner, E. H. Wakefield, Jerry Hockradle, and James J. Dolan, in Report of Inspector E. C. Watkins, Report no. 1981, June 27, 1878, RG 75, Records of the BIA, Inspectors' Reports, 1873—80, NARS (hereafter cited as Watkins Report). Watkins concluded: "I think the evidence shows conclusively that in the matter of horse stealing, Mr. Chisum is far ahead of the Indians and that a balance should be struck in their favor."

CHAPTER 3

1. Howard R. Lamar, *The Far Southwest, 1846—1912: A Territorial History* (New Haven: Yale University Press, 1966; 2d ed., New York: W. W. Norton, 1970), chap. 6. Another balanced view is Robert W. Larson,

"Territorial Politics and Cultural Impact," *New Mexico Historical Review* 60 (July 1985); and Larson, *New Mexico's Quest for Statehood, 1846−1912* (Albuquerque: University of New Mexico Press, 1969), chap. 9. Although these are authoritative accounts, the history of the Santa Fe Ring remains to be adequately probed. No one has documented its membership, organization, techniques, and purposes to show that it existed as an entity rather than simply as a group of men individually pursuing similar ends in similar ways.

2. All the historical literature of New Mexico's territorial period gives prominent attention to Catron; but see, especially, Victor Westphall, *Thomas Benton Catron and His Era* (Tucson: University of Arizona Press, 1973).

3. Tunstall letter of April 28, 1877, in Fulton Collection, UAL; portions excerpted in Frederick J. Nolan, ed., *The Life and Death of John Henry Tunstall* (Albuquerque: University of New Mexico Press, 1965), pp. 212−13.

4. The flow and disposition of the elder Tunstall's money can be traced in his son's letters home in Nolan, ed., *Life and Death of Tunstall;* in the McSween−Tunstall account, Exhibit 11 to McSween's deposition, Angel Report; and in McSween's bank account (Ledger Book 2) and his bank's cash book and letter book, Records of the First National Bank of Santa Fe, Archive 177, Special Collections, UNML.

5. Frank Coe, interview with J. Evetts Haley, San Patricio, N.M., March 20, 1927, HHC.

6. Nolan, *Life and Death of Tunstall,* pp. 209, 214. Much information is in the Brewer biographical notes, Mullin Collection, HHC.

7. Nolan, *Life and Death of Tunstall,* p. 210. See also pp. 203 and 215. Investigator Angel noted: "given to boasting" and "veracity doubtful when he speaks of himself." Lee H. Theisen, ed., "Frank Warner Angel's Notes on New Mexico Territory, 1878," *Arizona and the West* 18 (Winter 1976), p. 368. See also Widenmann biographical notes, Mullin Collection, HHC. Exhibit 11 to McSween's deposition in the Angel Report, a list for 1877 of McSween's credits and debits in account with Tunstall, shows McSween making an occasional payment to Widenmann—and also to Brewer—on behalf of Tunstall.

8. In partnership with Frank Freeman, Jacob B. Mathews had homesteaded on the Peñasco. Tunstall paid him 530 dollars for improvements and a quitclaim. Sam Corbet to John P. Tunstall, October 31, 1879, Fulton Collection, box 14, folder 4, UAL, explains the connection between young Tunstall and Mathews. The quitclaim is listed on Corbet's accounting of the Tunstall estate assets, Mullin Collection,

HHC. The 530 dollars, entered as "Mathews rent," appears in the McSween—Tunstall account, Exhibit 11 to McSween's deposition in the Angel Report.

Corbet's listing of assets also identified six land warrants in the names of McSween, Brewer, himself, Florencio Gonzales, A. M. Clenny, and Dr. Spencer Gurney. If each took out 640 acres, the total would have been 3,840 acres. This figure is generally consonant with an entry in the McSween—Tunstall account, Exhibit 11 to McSween's deposition in the Angel Report, which notes 850 dollars "by U.S. lands," which doubtless represents the filing fee of 25 cents an acre. It also reflects McSween's statement in his deposition that Tunstall acquired four thousand acres. On the other hand, Sue McSween's attorney, Huston Chapman, wrote to John P. Tunstall on February 10, 1879: "I find that your son was owner of 2,300 acres of land entered under the Desert Land Law, all of which is in the names of other men." Nolan, *Life and Death of Tunstall*, p. 397.

When the filing occurred is puzzling. It is clear from subsequent letters that Tunstall took some action at the land office in Mesilla when he and McSween were there in February 1877. Yet the Desert Land Act did not become law until March 3, and he could not have filed before then. More likely, he filed under that law when he returned to Mesilla in June. What he did in February is a mystery. Possibly, he took some preliminary actions to perfect the Mathews claim under the Homestead Act, and then in June, after McSween had rounded up the surrogates, filed under the Desert Land Act. Corbet's letter of October 1879, cited above, makes clear that Corbet, on behalf of Tunstall, filed for 640 acres on the old Mathews place on the Peñasco, which leaves the other five surrogates as claimants for land on the Feliz.

9. Civil Cases 747 and 748, First Judicial District Court Records, Santa Fe County, NMSRCA, show that a sheriff's sale was held in Lincoln County on May 11, 1877, to satisfy a judgment against Mrs. Casey in favor of James L. Johnson et al., of Santa Fe. McSween entered the high bid: 64 yearlings at $4.10 a head and 145 other cattle at $5.00 a head, for a total of 209 head. With sheriff's fees and interest, this came to $950. The Tunstall—McSween account, Exhibit 11 to McSween's deposition in the Angel Report, bears an entry of $987 for "209 head of cattle." See also Tunstall's letters home of May 27 and June 4, 1877, Nolan, *Life and Death of Tunstall*, pp. 217, 221—22.

10. Nolan, *Life and Death of Tunstall*, pp. 213, 219.

11. Tunstall divulges his plans for the grain notes and Fort Stanton in several letters from April through June 1877, in Nolan, *Life and Death*

of Tunstall, pp. 219–20, 224, 225. For the Indian agency, see McSween to Schurz, February 13, 1878, and McSween to Lowrie, February 25, 1878, RG 75, Office of Indian Affairs, LR, NARS (M234, roll 576).

12. Nolan, *Life and Death of Tunstall*, p. 227.

13. A copy of the articles of copartnership between Dolan and Riley, March 14, 1877, is in the Fulton Collection, box 12, folder 3, UAL. See also *Daily New Mexican* (Santa Fe), April 18, 1877, for news item and advertisement. In his deposition in the Angel Report, Dolan testified to the Catron "endorsement" in the amount of six thousand dollars; and the First National Bank's letter books for June through December 1877 reveal Catron's growing interest in Dolan & Co. Archive 177, Special Collections, UNML. In addition, a letter from the bank to Dolan, November 12, 1877, ibid., states that Dolan & Co. executed two notes to Murphy, one for five thousand dollars due in June 1878 and the other for the same amount due a year later.

14. Sue [McSween] Barber, interview with J. Evetts Haley, White Oaks, N.M., August 16, 1927, HHC. See also same to Maurice G. Fulton, White Oaks, N.M., March 10, 1928, Fulton Collection, box 1, folder 4, UAL.

15. For the Pecos War, which is not well documented in original sources, see Andrew Boyle to Thomas B. Catron, Mesilla, June 15, 1877, *Mesilla Valley Independent*, June 23, 1877; Joseph Boyle (Andy's brother) to Dear Sister, Fort Worth, Texas, December 11, 1877, HHC; and Philip J. Rasch, "The Pecos War," *Panhandle-Plains Historical Review* 29 (1956), pp. 101–11.

16. Philip J. Rasch, "The Story of Jessie Evans," *Panhandle-Plains Historical Review* 33 (1960), pp. 108–21; and Grady E. McCright and James H. Powell, *Jessie Evans: Lincoln County Badman* (College Station, Tex.: Creative Publishing Co., 1983). Albert J. Fountain, Mesilla attorney and editor-publisher of the *Mesilla Valley Independent*, one of the best contemporary reporters of Lincoln County events, wrote that the Evans gang were "in the employ of certain persons who had contracts to supply the government with beef cattle, and that the cattle stolen from the citizens by the outlaws were turned into the government on these contracts." *Independent*, April 27, 1878.

17. For Bristol, see Bristol biographical notes, Mullin Collection, HHC, and [William G. Ritch], Biographical Sketch concerning Warren Bristol, January 29, 1882, Ritch Collection, HL. For Rynerson, see Darlis A. Miller, "William Logan Rynerson in New Mexico, 1862–1893," *New Mexico Historical Review* 48 (April 1973), pp. 101–31; William G. Ritch, Biographical Sketch of William Logan Rynerson,

n.d. [1882], Ritch Collection, HL; and Rynerson biographical notes, Mullin Collection, HHC.

As territorial district attorney, Rynerson prosecuted territorial cases. The United States district attorney for New Mexico prosecuted federal cases. Judge Bristol sat as both federal and territorial judge. For the judiciary, see Arie Poldevaart, "Black-Robed Justice in New Mexico, 1846–1912," *New Mexico Historical Review* 22 (January 1947), pp. 18–50; (April 1947), pp. 109–39; (July 1947), pp. 286–314; (October 1947), pp. 351–88; 23 (January 1948), pp. 40–57; (April 1948), pp. 129–45; (July 1948), pp. 225–39. Even though a single institution, the district court bequeathed to historians two sets of records. Territorial records are in NMSRCA, federal records at DFRC.

18. For Brady, see Donald R. Lavash, *Sheriff William Brady: Tragic Hero of the Lincoln County War* (Santa Fe: Sunstone Press, 1986). Brady's debt, almost two thousand dollars, is carried on various accounts associated with the estate of Emil Fritz, appearing as exhibits to McSween's deposition in the Angel Report.

19. Quoted in Widenmann biographical notes, Mullin Collection, HHC.

20. Nolan, *Life and Death of Tunstall*, pp. 209, 214.

21. Sue [McSween] Barber, interview with J. Evetts Haley, White Oaks, N.M., August 16, 1927, HHC.

22. Original warranty deeds, Murphy to McSween, February 9, 1877; and Dolan to McSween, September 26, 1877, Fulton Collection, box 12, folder 4, UAL. The Murphy transaction was for one dollar "and other good and sufficient reasons," probably debts long owing to McSween for legal services. The Dolan transaction was for 250 dollars. Property and improvements are briefly described in Petition of Sue E. McSween, executrix of the McSween estate, for sale of real estate, January 8, 1879, copied from Lincoln County probate court records, WPA files, folder 212, NMSRCA. There is a description and ground plan of the Tunstall store in the Mullin Collection, HHC. For the church and school, see Norman J. Bender, ed., *Missionaries, Outlaws, and Indians: Taylor F. Ealy at Lincoln and Zuni, 1878–1881* (Albuquerque: University of New Mexico Press, 1984), pp. 7–8; and Ruth R. Ealy, *Water in a Thirsty Land* (p.p., n.p., 1955), pp. 25–26. Then a child, Ruth Ealy accompanied her missionary parents to Lincoln in response to McSween's call.

23. William Wier, interview with J. Evetts Haley, Monument, N.M., June 22, 1937, Vandale Collection 2H482, Barker History Center, University of Texas, Austin. The other quotations are from Tunstall's letters home in Nolan, *Life and Death of Tunstall*, pp. 208, 209, 266.

24. "There is a ring here opening letters," Tunstall wrote home on May 21, 1877, "& I am sorry that I ever wrote you those that I allude to"—setting forth his plans. Nolan, *Life and Death of Tunstall*, p. 217. Other indications of mail tampering are in depositions of McSween and David P. Shield, Angel Report, and Taylor F. Ealy to Rush Clark, Lincoln, May 18, 1878, Adjutant General's Office LR (Main Series), 1871–80, file 1405 AGO 1878, NARS (M666, rolls 397 and 398). This immensely valuable file, military records relating to civil disturbances in Lincoln County, will be cited as file 1405 AGO 1878. In August 1877, McSween arranged with Roswell Postmaster Ash Upson, for $1.50 per week, to intercept his mail and bring it to Lincoln in a separate locked pouch. Photocopy of bill, Upson against McSween estate, June 15, 1879, Fulton Collection, box 12, folder 2, UAL.

25. The debts are itemized in First National Bank of Santa Fe to Dolan, November 12, 1877, in Bank Letter Book, Records of the First National Bank, Archive 177, Special Collections, UNML.

26. Patrón's deposition, Angel Report; Farmer's affidavit, Watkins Report; and undated statement by Widenmann on stationery of Lincoln County Bank, Mullin Collection, HHC.

27. The characterizations are from contemporary newspaper descriptions in the *New York Sun*, December 27, 1880, and *Las Vegas Gazette*, December 28, 1880; and also from Frank Coe, interview with J. Evetts Haley, San Patricio, N.M., March 20, 1927, HHC. For the Kid's accession to the Evans gang, see *Mesilla Valley Independent*, October 13, 1877; for his killing of F. P. Cahill at Fort Grant, ibid., September 1, 1877.

Several diligent researchers have tracked Billy the Kid through public records and stripped away much of the myth. For his years before Lincoln, see Philip J. Rasch, "New Light on the Legend of Billy the Kid," *New Mexico Folklore Record* 7 (1952–53), pp. 1–5; Rasch and Robert N. Mullin, "Dim Trails: The Pursuit of the McCarty Family," *New Mexico Folklore Record* 8 (1953–54), pp. 6–11; Rasch, "A Man Named Antrim," Los Angeles Westerners, *Brand Book* 6 (1956), pp. 48–54; and Jack De-Mattos, "The Search for Billy the Kid's Roots—Is Over!" *Real West* 23 (January 1980), pp. 26–28, 59–60.

28. *Mesilla Valley Independent*, September 22, 1877. Depositions of McSween and Widenmann, Angel Report. Tunstall to "My Much Beloved Parents," November 29, 1877, in Nolan, *Life and Death of Tunstall*, pp. 243–44. On the day of the theft, McSween offered a reward for recapture of the animals. Curiously, he claimed ownership of the two horses belonging to Brewer. To relieve Brewer's dependence on the enemy, he had picked up a note of Brewer's held by The House and seems,

therefore, to have regarded Brewer's property as his own. *Independent,* September 29, 1877.

29. Tunstall repeated the conversation in the letter of November 29, 1877, in Nolan, *Life and Death of Tunstall,* p. 246. For the posse, see also this letter; *Mesilla Valley Independent,* October 27, 1877; and *Daily New Mexican* (Santa Fe), October 27, 1877. Lincoln County, District Court Journal, 1875–79, October 1877 term, pp. 231–65, NMSRCA. Brewer was foreman of the grand jury.

30. Tunstall describes this episode in detail in his letter of November 29, 1877, in Nolan, *Life and Death of Tunstall,* pp. 248–49. Florencio Chavez, interview with J. Evetts Haley, Lincoln, N.M., August 15, 1927, HHC. Chavez was one of Brewer's men. James D. Shinkle, *Robert Casey and the Ranch on the Rio Hondo* (Roswell, N.M.: Hall-Poorbough Press, 1970), pp. 147–54.

31. Nolan, *Life and Death of Tunstall,* pp. 251–52.

32. This reconstruction rests on Tunstall's account in a letter home, in Nolan, *Life and Death of Tunstall,* pp. 253–56; depositions of McSween and Juan Patrón in Angel Report; "Lincoln" to Ed., November 20, 1877, in *Mesilla Valley Independent,* November 24, 1877; and same to Ed., December 3, 1877, ibid., December 13, 1877. The case against Tunstall and Brewer is best stated in "Cowboy" to Ed., Rio Pecos, April 8, 1878, *Weekly New Mexican* (Santa Fe), April 20, 1878; and the case against Dolan in McSween to Ed., *New Mexican,* Lincoln, April 27, 1878, which appeared in the *Cimarron News and Press,* and is reproduced in Maurice G. Fulton, *History of the Lincoln County War,* ed. Robert N. Mullin (Tucson: University of Arizona Press, 1968), pp. 189–92. The Kid's presence with the gang is documented in Francisco Trujillo, interview with Edith Crawford, San Patricio, N.M., May 10, 1937, WPA files, folder 212, NMSRCA. Trujillo and his brother encountered the escape party, and his brother lost his horse and arms to them. Later, he rode with the Kid in the Regulators, and so knew him well. Although eighty-five at the time of the interview, his recollections of many of the incidents of the Lincoln County War contain too many verifiable specifics to be discounted. His brother's loss of horse and arms, for example, is corroborated by the account in the *Independent* of December 13, cited above.

33. The McSween-Tunstall account, Exhibit 11 to McSween's deposition in the Angel Report, carries an entry of $15.03 to "2 suits for Boys."

34. First National Bank of Santa Fe to Dolan & Co., November 12, 19, 20, and 26, and December 3, 1877. Bank to Catron, December 3, 1877. Records of the First National Bank of Santa Fe, Archive 177, Spe-

cial Collections, UNML. Photocopy of mortgage deed, Dolan & Co. to Catron, January 19, 1878, Fulton Collection, box 12, folder 4, UAL.

35. McSween's bank account, Ledger Book 2, and Bank to McSween, December 7, 1877, Letter Book, both in Records of the First National Bank of Santa Fe, Archive 177, Special Collections, UNML. McSween also had an account in an East St. Louis bank. There is no way to know how much was in it. At a minimum, as detailed in the next chapter, it contained more than seven thousand dollars in Fritz insurance money, but that was not legally available for his personal use and could not be illegally tapped at this time without great risk.

CHAPTER 4

1. The principal source for the complex story of the Fritz estate is McSween's deposition in the Angel Report. Many of the legal documents in the case are annexed to this deposition as exhibits. Also of value are the depositions in the Angel Report of Dolan and David P. Shield, McSween's law partner and brother-in-law. McSween wrote an informative letter of explanation, January 10, 1878, which was printed in *Eco del Rio Grande* (Las Cruces), January 24, 1878.

2. McSween deposition, Angel Report.

3. Affidavit of Emilie Scholand, Mesilla, December 21, 1877, Lincoln County, District Court, Civil Case no. 141, *Fritz and Scholand v. McSween:* assumpsit, NMSRCA. Depositions of McSween and Dolan, Angel Report. McSween to Ed., Lincoln, January 10, 1878, *Eco del Rio Grande* (Las Cruces), January 24, 1878.

4. "J.H.T." to Ed., Lincoln, January 18, 1878; and Dolan to Ed., Las Cruces, January 29, 1878, in *Mesilla Valley Independent,* January 26 and February 2, 1878. Dolan's version is sustained by the territorial auditor's account book for January 8, 1878, and the territorial treasurer's ledger of receipts, sheriff's accounts, January 9, 1878, which show Brady's deposit of 1,968 dollars, the total territorial share of the 1877 tax assessment for Lincoln County. NMSRCA. On July 31, 1877, McSween wrote a check for $1,545.13 "in territorial warrants" to Sheriff Brady as tax collector, and, as Tunstall stated, it was subsequently endorsed by Riley. This check is Exhibit 1 to McSween's deposition in the Angel Report. It was entered against McSween's account at the First National Bank of Santa Fe on August 20, according to the McSween account, Ledger Book 2, Records of the First National Bank of Santa Fe, Archive 177, Special Collections, UNML.

An explanation of the history of this check remains speculation. The check could not, as Tunstall implied in his public letter, have represented McSween's tax bill, which was only $105.95, as disclosed by the 1877 tax rolls in the Lincoln County Records, NMSRCA. McSween's bank records, however, show that he was speculating in territorial warrants—that is, buying them on the market at discounted rates and spending them for purposes in which they had to be honored in full. His accounts also show that he paid other people's taxes, probably in exchange for debits against accounts at the Tunstall store. It is possible that the full value of the taxes went into the store's books, while the taxes were paid with territorial warrants at full value that had been purchased at discount. The check for $1,545.13 may well have represented his taxes and those of others to this amount. The largest taxpayer in the county was Robert D. Hunter, who had bought out John Chisum. His total tax bill for 1877 was 3,060 dollars, of which 1,224 dollars was the territorial share. McSween was Hunter's attorney in Lincoln County. Therefore, Hunter's territorial taxes may well have accounted for most of McSween's check to Brady.

Brady probably used The House as his bank, to hold his tax receipts as he collected them until the end of the year, when he took them to Santa Fe to be deposited with the territorial treasurer. And while Dolan and Riley did not steal the taxes, they may indeed have used them until Brady had to turn them in. Thus, McSween's check, endorsed by Riley, reportedly went to Nash and Underwood of Seven Rivers for beef to supply the Indians. Borrowing tax money is not generally viewed as an honorable practice, but compared with the other methods in vogue at the time and place, it was probably not widely frowned upon either.

5. *Mesilla Valley Independent*, February 9, 1878. Civil Case no. 141, document file, as cited in n. 3. Depositions of McSween and Dolan, Angel Report.

6. The legal documents are in Lincoln County, District Court, Civil Case no. 141, *Fritz and Scholand v. McSween*: assumpsit, NMSRCA. In addition, see Tunstall's account in Frederick W. Nolan, ed., *The Life and Death of John Henry Tunstall* (Albuquerque: University of New Mexico Press, 1965), p. 267; and depositions of McSween, Deputy Barrier, and Dolan employee James Longwill, Angel Report. Barrier gives the most detailed account and the only chronology that can be reconciled with the dates on the legal documents. Dolan denied having an appointment to meet Evans at Shedd's Ranch, but the other witnesses tell of Evans's lieutenant Frank Baker coming to their camp in the evening, asking for Dolan, and saying that he was to meet the Evans party at this time and place. The *Mesilla Valley Independent*, January 26, 1878, reports the Evans raid on the Mimbres River, near Silver City, and the wounding of Evans,

which occurred on January 19. Dolan said that he brought the attachment writ with him to Lincoln. But he left Mesilla before the writ was finally executed on February 7. More likely, the writ was carried from Mesilla by courier and turned over en route to Dolan. A rider bearing an envelope addressed to John H. Riley paused at the McSween–Tunstall camp on the second morning out of Mesilla, and he was later seen with the Dolan party.

7. So Bristol declared in his charge to the grand jury at the April term of district court in Lincoln. The charge is reproduced verbatim in a supplement to the *Mesilla Valley Independent*, April 20, 1878. James Longwill, a Dolan associate who was present at the hearing, also declared that Tunstall testified to the partnership in Mesilla. Longwill deposition, Angel Report. Both Shield and Barrier, who were also present, swore in Angel Report depositions that no such testimony was offered by either Tunstall or McSween. In his deposition for Angel, McSween explained that articles of partnership were to be signed in May 1878, under terms that had already been negotiated. In fact, bank records disclose that the finances of the two had become all but inseparable.

For the attachment, see deposition of Widenmann, Angel Report, and Brady to Rynerson, March 5, 1878, in *Mesilla Valley Independent*, March 30, 1878. The inventories of the contents of the Tunstall store and McSween home are in Lincoln County, District Court, Docket Book F, NMSRCA.

8. Depositions of McSween and Barrier, Angel Report.

9. Nolan, *Life and Death of Tunstall*, p. 259.

10. Depositions of James Longwill (a posseman in the store), Widenmann, and Bonney, Angel Report.

11. The McSween–Tunstall account, Exhibit 11 to McSween's deposition in the Angel Report, does not record that Tunstall reimbursed McSween for the Casey cattle. Some of the cattle ultimately impounded, moreover, bore a brand registered to McSween. Tunstall had no brand registered in Lincoln County. This conclusion is reached from a comparison of the brands in the attachment document (Lincoln County District Court Records, Docket Book F, NMSRCA) with the brands compiled by Governor Lew Wallace a year later (Wallace to Capt. Henry Carroll, March 12, 1879, Wallace Papers, IHS).

12. Principal sources for this event are the depositions of Widenmann, Jacob B. Mathews, John Middleton, William H. Bonney, Godfrey Gauss, and John Hurley, Angel Report; testimony of Widenmann and Jesse Evans before Judge Bristol, *Mesilla News*, July 6, 1878; and

Brady to Rynerson, March 5, 1878, in *Mesilla Valley Independent*, March 30, 1878. Mathews's posse consisted of himself, George Hindman, John Hurley, Andrew L. "Buckshot" Roberts, and Manuel Segovia, also known as "Indian." Evans's followers were Frank Baker, Tom Hill, George Davis, and Frank Rivers (alias John Long). At the ranch, besides Widenmann and Brewer, were John Middleton, William H. Bonney, Frederick T. Waite, cook Godfrey Gauss, William McCloskey, and "Dutch Martin" Martz.

13. On November 21, 1877, a federal grand jury at Mesilla indicted Evans, Baker, Hill, Davis, and Nicholas Provencia for larceny, and on November 24 the case was continued, with arrest warrants to issue. U.S. District Court, Third Judicial District, Record Book, 1871—79, pp. 659 and 663, RG 21, Records of the District Court of the United States, Territory of New Mexico, DFRC. In his deposition in the Angel Report, Widenmann tells of going to Murphy's ranch, and of Evans later admitting that he was at the ranch at the time. See also endorsement of Capt. George A. Purington, March 14, 1878, Angel Report.

14. Brady to Mathews, Lincoln, February 15, 1878, *Mesilla Valley Independent*, March 30, 1878. For the organization and movement of the expanded posse, see depositions of Mathews, John Hurley, Pantaleón Gallegos, and Samuel R. Perry, Angel Report. The Lincoln contingent of the posse consisted of Mathews, John Hurley, George Hindman, Pantaleón Gallegos, A. H. Mills, Thomas Moore, Ramón Montoya, E. H. Wakefield, Manuel Segovia, Andrew Roberts, James J. Dolan, Felipe Mes, and Pabo Pino y Pino. The Seven Rivers contingent consisted of William S. Morton, Charles Wolz, Charles Kruling, Charles Marshall, John Wallace Olinger, Robert W. Beckwith, Thomas Green, Thomas Cochran, George Kitt, and Samuel Perry. Evans was accompanied by Frank Baker, George Davis, and Tom Hill.

15. For Tunstall's decision on the evening of the seventeenth, see depositions of Widenmann, Middleton, Gauss, and Bonney, Angel Report. For the encounter with Longwill, see his deposition, Angel Report. McSween, in his deposition, says that Tunstall decided on February 14 to offer no resistance. If so, it was after Widenmann left to organize resistance.

16. The scene at the ranch cabin is reconstructed from the depositions in the Angel Report of Mathews, Gauss, Dolan, Gallegos, Kruling, and Perry. The subposse consisted of Morton, John Hurley, Pantaleón Gallegos, Manuel Segovia, George Hindman, John Wallace

Olinger, Robert W. Beckwith, Ramón Montoya, Thomas Green, Thomas Cochran, George Kitt, Charles Kruling, Charles Marshall, and Samuel Perry.

17. The experiences of the Tunstall party are reconstructed from the depositions of Widenmann, Middleton, and Bonney, Angel Report; from the undated Widenmann draft on stationery of the Lincoln County Bank, HHC; and from Widenmann's testimony before Judge Bristol as reported in the *Mesilla News*, July 6, 1878.

18. Depositions of Samuel Perry, Thomas Cochran, Robert Beckwith, John Wallace Olinger, Pantaleón Gallegos, John Hurley, and Charles Kruling, Angel Report.

19. In a hearing before Judge Bristol, reported in the *Mesilla News*, July 6, 1878.

20. Deposition of Howe, Angel Report.

CHAPTER 5

1. Both Reverend Ealy and his wife Mary wrote several accounts of their experiences in Lincoln. Each gives details missing from the others, but except for some chronological confusion they are internally consistent. Ealy also kept a diary and wrote letters to family members in the East. These are all in the Ealy Papers, Special Collections, UAL, and have been edited and annotated in published form in Norman J. Bender, ed., *Missionaries, Outlaws, and Indians: Taylor F. Ealy at Lincoln and Zuni, 1878–1881* (Albuquerque: University of New Mexico Press, 1984). See also Ruth R. Ealy (one of the two daughters), *Water in a Thirsty Land* (p.p., n.p., 1955).

2. Frank Coe, interview with J. Evetts Haley, San Patricio, N.M., August 27, 1927, HHC. The night before, McSween had sent a note to Newcomb asking him to recover the body. With Florencio Gonzales, Patricio Trujillo, Lazaro Gallegos, and Roman Barregon, Newcomb drove out to the scene. The body had to be packed by horseback to the road and loaded into Newcomb's wagon. Depositions of McSween, Newcomb, Gonzales, and Barregon, Angel Report. Dr. Appel's detailed description of the results of the autopsy is in his deposition in the Angel Report. For the coroner's report, see *Mesilla Valley Independent*, March 9, 1878. The coroner's jury consisted of George Barber, R. W. Gilbert, Benjamin Ellis, John Newcomb, Samuel Smith, and Frank Coe. It concluded that Tunstall met his death at the hands of Evans, Baker, Hill, Hindman, Dolan, Morton, "and others not identified by witnesses."

3. Ealy, "The Lincoln County War As I Saw It," n.d. (c. 1927), Ealy Papers, UAL. There are two drafts of this document, and a final

draft copied by Mary Ealy. All are slightly different. The quotation is from Ealy to Dear Father, Lincoln, February 25, 1878.

4. Depositions of McSween and Longwill, Angel Report. The usual version has the men gathering in response to news of Tunstall's death. But the timing hardly allows for these scattered people to learn of the killing and ride to Lincoln. Longwill, still in the Tunstall store next door, testified that the men collected before it was known that Tunstall had been shot. Longwill is also authority for Tunstall's absence on the sixteenth and for the speculation that he was riding the country lining up the men who filled the house on the eighteenth.

5. I deduce the wage offer from Purington to Angel, June 25, 1878, Angel Report. Captain Purington said that he went to town a day or so after Tunstall's death (February 20, according to my deductions) and visited the McSween house, where he found between thirty-five and fifty men, "a large majority of whom were men of reputed bad character." Most of these, McSween explained to Purington, were in his employ, some for as much as four dollars a day. McSween was bankrupt, so he could not pay them, which leaves Tunstall or, now, Tunstall's estate.

6. Rynerson's letter, Las Cruces, February 14, 1878, is Exhibit 19 to McSween's deposition in the Angel Report. The Riley code book is dealt with in McSween's second deposition in the Angel Report and "Stanton" [McSween] to Ed., Fort Stanton, April 1, 1878, *Cimarron News and Press*, April 11, 1878.

7. The affidavits of Brewer, Bonney, and Middleton, February 19, 1878, together with an explanatory affidavit of Justice Wilson, August 31, 1878, are Exhibits 10a and 13 appended to McSween's deposition in the Angel Report. For the larceny charge, see Exhibit 14, which is a certified copy of an entry of February 20, 1878, in Wilson's docket book, which says that the warrants based on the larceny charge were issued on February 19. Brady's request for military protection, February 18, 1878, is annexed to Purington to Angel, June 25, 1878, in the Angel Report. Although the Fort Stanton post returns do not record the dispatch of troops to Lincoln before February 20, Purington must have sent them at once in order for Wilson to have issued warrants based on use of the hay, as his docket book shows. Also Purington to Judge Bristol, February 21, 1878, RG 393, Post Records, Fort Stanton, vol. 18, NARS, states that Brady is under the protection of U.S. troops.

8. So Martínez confided to Lt. Millard F. Goodwin. Deposition of Goodwin, Angel Report.

9. Widenmann to Purington, Fort Stanton, February 20, 1878, Angel Report. In his deposition for the Angel Report, Widenmann testi-

fied that he went to the fort on the nineteenth and spent the night in the quarters of Lt. Samuel S. Pague, and that about 1:00 A.M. on the twentieth Captain Purington awoke him with a letter from someone in Lincoln saying that Evans was in town and asking troops for his arrest. On the strength of this, Widenmann officially requested military aid. Purington had already been authorized by the district commander, on request of U.S. Marshal John Sherman, to supply troops for this purpose, and in fact had provided Widenmann with the detachment that searched the Murphy ranch on February 3. Sherman to Hatch, Santa Fe, December 3, 1877; 1st end., Loud to Purington, December 10; 2d end., Purington to Loud, March 14, 1878, RG 393, LR, Hq. DNM, NARS (M1088, roll 30).

10. The events of February 20 are amply documented, but the chronology and sequence are badly confused in the sources. This reconstruction, which differs from the usual version, is based on the depositions of McSween, Widenmann (2), Martínez (2), Longwill, Bonney, Wilson, Florencio Gonzales, and Lt. M. F. Goodwin, with annexed documents; endorsement of Capt. George A. Purington, March 14, 1878; and Purington to Angel, June 25, 1878, all in Angel Report. Also Purington to AAAG, DNM, Fort Stanton, February 21, 1878, RG 393, LR, Hq. DNM, NARS (M1088, roll 32); Purington to Judge Bristol, February 21, 1878, RG 393, Post Records, Fort Stanton, LS, vol. 18, NARS; affidavit of George W. Peppin (a Brady deputy in the Tunstall store), April 15, 1878, in Lincoln County, District Court, Civil Case no. 141, document file, NMSRCA; McSween's "Stanton" letter, April 1, 1878, in *Cimarron News and Press*, April 11, 1878; McSween to John Partridge Tunstall, Lincoln, April 14, 1878, in Frederick Nolan, ed., *The Life and Death of John Henry Tunstall* (Albuquerque: University of New Mexico Press, 1965), p. 314; *Mesilla Valley Independent*, April 27 and 30, 1878 (the latter contains Brady to Rynerson, March 5, 1878); and *Weekly New Mexican* (Santa Fe), May 4, 1878.

The Widenmann–Martínez seizure of the Tunstall store is usually dated February 23, the date given by Longwill, one of the men in the store, in his Angel Report deposition. But District Attorney Rynerson knew about it by the twenty-fourth (Teleg., Rynerson to Axtell, February 24, 1878, encl. to Axtell to Hatch, Santa Fe, February 25, 1878, RG 393, LR, Hq. DNM, NARS [M1088, roll 32]), and Mesilla was a two- or three-day ride from Lincoln. He learned of it from Dolan, who left Lincoln on the twenty-first. Also, Bonney and Waite took part in the store raids, which means that these raids occurred *before* the attempt to arrest the possemen in the Dolan store, for, as noted, this attempt resulted in the detention of Bonney and Waite for at least twenty-four hours.

Those charged with riot, and thus forming part or all of the Martínez posse, were Martínez, Tunstall store clerk Sam Corbet, Lincoln's black handymen George Washington and George Robinson, Middleton, Bonney, Waite, Doc Scurlock, Sam Smith, Frank and George Coe, Frank McNab, Ignacio Gonzales, Jesús Rodríguez, Esequio Sanchez, Roman Barregon, and one Edwards. Lincoln County, District Court Journal, 1875–79, April 1878 term, pp. 264–91, NMSRCA.

11. Depositions of McSween and Barrier, Angel Report. The bond, with Rynerson's disapproving endorsement, is Exhibit 15 to McSween's deposition, Angel Report.

12. Depositions of McSween and Barrier, Angel Report. Typed copy of will from Book A, Journal and Record of Lincoln County Probate Court, in Fulton Collection, box 12, folder 2, UAL.

13. The core group included at least the following men, perhaps others: Dick Brewer, John Middleton, Billy Bonney, Fred Waite, Frank McNab, Doc Scurlock, Charles Bowdre, Henry Brown, Jim French, the cousins George and Frank Coe, John Scroggins, and Steve Stevens.

14. During the April term of district court, Albert J. Fountain, both deputy clerk of the court and editor of the *Mesilla Valley Independent*, addressed a long letter to his paper that is one of the most objective assessments of conditions in Lincoln County at the time. In it, he gave the Regulators' self-appraisal. Issue of April 27, 1878.

15. C. L. Sonnichsen, *I'll Die Before I'll Run: The Story of the Great Feuds of Texas* (New York: Devin-Adair, 1962), p. 15.

16. The standard authority on vigilantism is Richard Maxwell Brown, *Strain of Violence: Historical Studies of American Violence and Vigilantism* (New York: Oxford University Press, 1975), Pt. 3. See also Brown, "The American Vigilante Tradition," in Hugh Davis Graham and Ted Robert Gurr, eds., *The History of Violence in America: Historical and Comparative Perspectives* (New York: Frederick A. Praeger, 1969), chap. 5; and Joe B. Frantz, "The Frontier Tradition: An Invitation to Violence," in Graham and Gurr, *History of Violence in America*, chap. 4.

17. The details of the chase come from this letter, published in the *Mesilla Valley Independent*, April 13, 1878.

18. *Mesilla Valley Independent*, March 16, April 13 and 23, 1878. Morton's letter is printed in the April 13 issue. *Weekly New Mexican* (Santa Fe), May 4, 1878. Morton biographical notes, Mullin Collection, HHC. For reminiscent accounts, none very satisfactory, see Francisco Trujillo, interview with Edith Crawford, San Patricio, N.M., May 10,

1937, WPA files, folder 212, NMSRCA; Frank Coe, interview with J. Evetts Haley, San Patricio, N.M., August 14, 1927, HHC; and Florencio Chavez, interview with J. Evetts Haley, Lincoln, N.M., August 15, 1927, HHC.

19. On February 24, 1878, almost certainly in response to Dolan's appearance in Mesilla, Rynerson wired Axtell. He told of the "bogus charge" against Brady and the seizure of the Tunstall store and urged him to get the aid of U.S. troops. Axtell did so in a letter of February 25 to Col. Edward Hatch, commander of the District of New Mexico. On February 28, Sheriff Brady, at Fort Stanton, composed a message to Catron which was taken to Mesilla and telegraphed to Santa Fe. It described McSween's army and its defiance of the law, portrayed Brady as powerless to keep the peace, and asked Catron to see Axtell and get an order for the Fort Stanton troops to protect him in his duties. Catron took this communication to Axtell, who enclosed it with a telegram to President Hayes, March 4, asking for military assistance. On March 5, telegraphic orders from the secretary of war started down the chain of command. These and other military documents bearing on the issue are in two sources: RG 393, LR, Hq. DNM, NARS (M1088, roll 32); and RG 94, file 1405 AGO 1878, NARS.

20. The proclamation is Exhibit 16 to McSween's deposition in the Angel Report. James H. Farmer had been elected justice of the peace in the 1876 election, but he had resigned, and on February 14, 1877, the county commission had appointed Wilson, who had held the office in the past, pending another election. Axtell's proclamation declared this appointment illegal and all actions of Wilson void. Actually, the appointment was in accord with the 1876 act of the territorial legislature creating county commissions, but this act, in turn, contravened the New Mexico organic act, which required justices to be elected. Since the organic act took precedence, Axtell was technically correct; but since he himself had sponsored the law setting up county commissions, his action was hardly beyond reproach. Moreover, Bristol's court was clearly not the only legal source of writs and processes and Brady not the only authority to execute them. Lincoln County contained other precincts with lawfully endowed justices and constables. Also bearing on Axtell's Lincoln visit are: Montague R. Leverson to President Hayes, March 16, 1878; and deposition of David P. Shield, both in Angel Report. Widenmann's version is in a letter to Ed., Lincoln, March 30, 1878, *Cimarron News and Press*, April 11, 1878. Axtell's account is in his response to Angel's "interrogatories," Angel Report.

21. Ealy diary, March 10, 1878, Ealy Papers, Special Collections, UAL.

22. Francisco Trujillo, interview with Edith Crawford, San Patricio, N.M., May 10, 1937, WPA files, folder 212, NMSRCA. At first reading, Trujillo's account seems the wild fancy of a confused old man. Further study, however—especially after the phonetically rendered names of the principals are translated—shows most of his account either verifiable or plausible when compared with other sources. According to Trujillo, the group split during the ride back to Lincoln, with the Hispanics going to San Patricio because the Anglos did not want them to share in the killing of Brady, who had a Hispanic wife.

There is contemporary corroboration for this possibility, albeit highly partisan. In its issue of March 18, 1878, the *Mesilla Valley Independent* editorialized that when people lost confidence in the courts, they took the law into their own hands. This was a terrible alternative, but "mob law is better than no law." The anti-McSween *Mesilla News*, June 8, 1878, blamed this editorial for Brady's murder. "Two prominent men" seized upon it, said the *News*, to incite the Regulators. "First the persuasive talents of one influential individual [McSween] was used upon McNab and the 'Regulators' for an hour or so; then the cunning appliances of a wealthy individual [Chisum] were 'put where they would do the most good' with McNab and the 'Regulators,' and each of them used the article in the 'Independent' to clinch the villainous scheme."

23. Affidavits that Lt. Col. Nathan A. M. Dudley caused to be sworn by various Lincoln citizens in November 1878 aimed specifically at destroying Sue's reputation, so must be used with caution. However, they do tend to show what people believed about her. The strongest evidence for my generalizations appears in these affidavits and in the testimony of some of the witnesses in the Dudley court of inquiry, especially the Bacas. The affidavits are Exhibits 6C through 12, Records Relating to the Dudley Inquiry (CQ 1284), RG 153, Judge Advocate General's Office, NARS (hereafter cited as Dudley Court Record). There is a microfilm copy in Special Collections, UAL, a copy of which I have used, courtesy of Donald R. Lavash.

24. The basic facts are set forth in *Mesilla Valley Independent*, April 13 and 27 and May 4, 1878, and *Weekly New Mexican* (Santa Fe), May 4, 1878. Reminiscent accounts are Robert Brady (William's young son), interview with Edith L. Crawford, Carrizozo, N.M., c. 1937; Gorgonio Wilson (son of Justice Wilson), interview with Edith L. Crawford, Roswell, N.M., 1938; and Carlota Baca Brent (daughter of Saturnino

Baca), interview with Francis E. Totty, December 6, 1937, all in WPA files, folder 212, NMSRCA; Juan Peppin (son of George Peppin), interview with Maurice G. Fulton, Artesia, N.M., c. 1930, Mullin Collection, HHC. The conventional account has the Kid running out to steal Brady's rifle. More plausibly, he risked this dash for the arrest warrant. Frank Coe said that the Kid jumped the wall "and ran to get the papers from Brady." Interview with J. Evetts Haley, San Patricio, N.M., March 20, 1927, HHC. Billy probably failed in this mission, for Deputy Peppin served the warrant on McSween that afternoon. Also in Brady's pocket was the writ of attachment on McSween's property issued by Judge Bristol. The original writ (Lincoln County, District Court, Civil Case no. 141, NMSRCA) bears a notation that it was retrieved from the body of Sheriff Brady.

25. Ealy and his wife Mary wrote several accounts of these experiences in the 1920s, Ealy Papers, Special Collections, UAL; and Ealy affidavit, June 18, 1878, Watkins Report, NARS. The Ealys lived for a week after their arrival with the Shields in the east wing of the McSween house. After McSween fled, however, and in Sue's continued absence, the Ealys occupied the McSween quarters in the west wing. Frank Coe said Corbet put French in the cellar under the kitchen of the Tunstall store, next door, and spread a carpet over the trap door. Interview with J. Evetts Haley, San Patricio, N.M., March 20, 1927, HHC.

26. Many witnesses gave self-serving accounts of the events of April 1. The clearest bearing on the exchange at the Ellis store was Sgt. Houston Lusk, deposition in Angel Report.

27. There were nine witnesses to this argument. McSween and his friends all related Purington's "damn the constitution" expletive, while Purington, Peppin, and all the anti-McSween people denied it. To me, the weight of credibility on this score seems to be with the McSween side. See depositions of McSween, Widenmann, Shield, Peppin, John Galvin, Calvin Simpson, Sgt. Houston Lusk, and Pvt. Berry Robinson, and Purington to Angel, June 25, 1878, Angel Report. Leverson to President Hayes, April 2, 1878, in Nolan, *Life and Death of Tunstall*, pp. 310–12.

28. Frank Coe, interview with J. Evetts Haley, San Patricio, N.M., March 20, 1927, HHC.

29. Ealy draft, "The Lincoln County War as I Saw It," c. 1927, Ealy Papers, Special Collections, UAL. The most direct testimony bearing on the Blazer's Mills fight is by David M. Easton, an eyewitness, before the Dudley court of inquiry on June 7, 1879, Dudley Court Record, NARS. His account agrees with one in the *Mesilla Valley Indepen-*

dent, April 13, 1878, and generally with the recollection of Frank Coe, interview with J. Evetts Haley, San Patricio, N.M., March 20 and August 14, 1927, HHC; and a comment by Coe, c. 1927, on the version given in Walter Noble Burns's *Saga of Billy the Kid*, Mullin Collection, HHC. Dr. Blazer's son, thirteen at the time and a witness, steadfastly maintained that firing broke out without any preliminary conversation involving Coe, and that the Kid counted the shots from Roberts's rifle and after the sixth rushed to the doorway and fired the shot that downed Roberts. Blazer said that the Kid gave this version in words and pantomime at Blazer's Mills on the way to Lincoln after his trial for Brady's murder in Mesilla in 1881. See A. N. Blazer to Maurice G. Fulton, Mescalero, N.M., April 24, 1931, and August 27, 1937, Fulton Collection, box 1, folder 7, UAL; and Paul A. Blazer (Dr. Blazer's grandson), "The Fight at Blazer's Mill: A Chapter in the Lincoln County War," *Arizona and the West* 6 (Autumn 1964), pp. 203–11. It should be noted in this connection that Easton stated that Roberts told him before dying that it was Bowdre who had shot him, and that Dr. Blazer was the foreman of the grand jury that heard testimony and indicted Bowdre for the murder of Roberts. Besides those named in the text, participating Regulators were Doc Scurlock, Frank McNab, John Scroggins, "Dirty Steve" Stevens, Fred Waite, and Henry Brown. There is some question whether Frank Coe was a member of the group or just happened to be there. See *Mesilla Valley Independent*, June 14, 1879. Ignacio Gonzales and Sam Smith arrived with the Regulators, but did not stop.

    30. *Mesilla Valley Independent*, April 13, 1878. The accusation had enough substance for the commanding officer at Fort Stanton to send a military escort to meet the judge and his party.

    31. Ealy, "The Lincoln County War As I Saw It," c. 1927. Ealy to Dear Brother, March 17, 1878. Ealy Papers, Special Collections, UAL. Ealy affidavit, June 18, 1878, Watkins Report, NARS.

    32. Ealy to Sheldon Jackson, March 19, 1878, in Bender, *Missionaries, Outlaws and Indians*, p. 27.

    33. Diary, March 11, 1878, Ealy Papers, Special Collections, UAL.

    34. William Wier, interview with J. Evetts Haley, Monument, N.M., June 22, 1937, Vandale Collection 2H482, Barker History Center, University of Texas.

CHAPTER 6

    1. Much about Dudley personally and professionally is revealed by his military personnel file in the National Archives: 6674 ACP 1876, RG

94, Appointments, Commissions, and Promotions [ACP] Files. See also Philip J. Rasch, "The Trials of Lieutenant-Colonel Dudley," English Westerners, *Brand Book* 7 (January 1965), pp. 17; and Rasch, "The Men at Fort Stanton," English Westerners, *Brand Book* 3 (April 1961), pp. 27.

2. Loud (AAAG, DNM) to CO Fort Stanton, Santa Fe, March 24, 1878, encl. to Pope to AAG, Military Division of the Missouri, Fort Leavenworth, April 24, 1878, file 1405 AGO 1878, NARS.

3. Dudley to Judge Bristol, Fort Stanton, April 18, 1878, Exhibit 77–11, Dudley Court Record, NARS. The date on the original was probably April 8 and was miscopied for the court record as April 18, which does not fit with the known chronology.

4. *Mesilla Valley Independent*, March 16 and 23, 1878. Grady E. McCright and James H. Powell, *Jessie Evans: Lincoln County Badman* (College Station, Tex.: Creative Publishing Co., 1983), pp. 109–13.

5. Dudley to AAAG, DNM, Fort Stanton, May 4, 1878, with enclosures, especially McSween to Dudley and Widenmann to Dudley, Fort Stanton, April 6; John Sherman for Widenmann to Dudley, Fort Stanton, April 8; and Bristol to Dudley, Fort Stanton, April 8. File 1405 AGO 1878, NARS. The original warrant issued by Bristol, April 8, is in the Fulton Collection, box 12, folder 2, UAL. On the back is Bristol's appointment of Copeland to serve the warrant, with Copeland's certification, same date, that he had served it.

6. Lincoln County, District Court Journal, 1875–79, April 1878 term, April 824, 1878, pp. 164–91, gives a chronological account of the proceedings, NMSRCA. In addition to the journal, case files exist for Criminal Case 259, *Territory v. Jesse Evans, George Davis, Frank Rivers, and Manuel Segovia:* murder; and Civil Case 141, *Fritz and Scholand v. McSween:* assumpsit. The original indictment by the grand jury in Criminal Case 257, *Territory v. Fred Waite,* for the murder of Hindman, is in the Fulton Collection, box 12, folder 2, UAL. Judge Bristol's charge to the grand jury is reproduced verbatim in a supplement to the *Mesilla Valley Independent*, April 20, 1878; and two reports of the grand jury are printed in ibid., May 4, 1878. For commentary beyond what is revealed by the official record, see ibid., April 27 and May 4, 1878; and *Weekly New Mexican* (Santa Fe), May 4, 1878.

7. McSween and B. H. Ellis to Secretary of War, April 26, 1878, file 1405 AGO 1878, NARS. This is the copy transmitted to the secretary of war. Copies also went to the president, secretary of the interior, territorial governor, and the press, and so may be consulted elsewhere. The *Mesilla Valley Independent*, May 4, 1878, contains a copy, together with a "card to the public," April 23, in which Dolan and Riley give

notice of closing the store. Murphy went to Fort Stanton on April 23 and asked for military protection. Murphy to Dudley, April 23, 1878, Exhibit 77–12, Dudley Court Record, NARS.

8. *Mesilla Valley Independent*, May 4, 1878. The *Independent* is especially authoritative for this period because its editor, Albert J. Fountain, was deputy clerk of the court and sat through the court proceedings in Lincoln. His dispatches show him to be a close observer as well as comparatively nonpartisan. No friend of Murphy, Dolan, and Riley, and a bitter, public critic of Jesse Evans, Fountain could still condemn the excesses of the Regulators even while appreciating their motives. Dudley reported that no one was more mortified at the failure of the court to restore peace than Judge Bristol. Dudley to AAAG, DNM, Fort Stanton, May 4, 1878, file 1405 AGO 1878, NARS.

9. Copy of Record of Proceedings, Lincoln County Commission, April 10, 1878, Mullin Collection, HHC.

10. A revealing chronicle of Copeland's activities during the last week of April, featuring excitement, confusion, and heavy drinking, is in the report of a soldier detailed to aid him: Cpl. Thomas Dole to CO Fort Stanton, May 1, 1878, File 1405 AGO 1878, NARS. See also "J" to Ed., Lincoln, May 3, 1878, *Weekly New Mexican* (Santa Fe), May 18, 1878; and *Mesilla News*, May 18, 1878. Copeland told Colonel Dudley that District Attorney Rynerson had not left warrants with him when court adjourned, but Rynerson vigorously denied this. Dudley to AAAG, DNM, May 25, 1878, Exhibit 77–21, Dudley Court Record, NARS.

11. Mary Ealy to Maurice G. Fulton, n.d., c. 1928, Fulton Collection, box 1, folder 8, UAL.

12. A photocopy of McNab's surety bond for his appointment as deputy constable, April 27, 1878, is in the Mullin Collection, Research Files, HHC. That he obtained his commission at San Patricio is speculation, but Wilson had not yet been reelected to his old post from which Axtell had dismissed him, and the inference seems reasonable. The justice at San Patricio, Gregorio Trujillo, proved to be a consistently reliable McSween supporter.

13. The group included at least the following men and possibly a few more: Peppin, Mathews, Johnson, John Hurley, Robert and John Beckwith, John Long, Robert and Wallace Olinger, Lewis Paxton, Milo Pearce, Buck Powell, Joseph Nash, Samuel Perry, Thomas Cochran, Thomas Green, Richard Lloyd, Charles Kruling, Reuben Kelly, Charles Martin, John Galvin, _____ Perez, and "Indian" (Manuel Segovia).

14. Frank Coe, interview with J. Evetts Haley, San Patricio,

N.M., August 14, 1927, HHC, gives a detailed account of this event. See also "Outsider" to Ed., Fort Stanton, May 1, 1878, *Mesilla Valley Independent*, May 11, 1878.

15. George Coe, interview with J. Evetts Haley, Glencoe, N.M., March 20, 1927, describes the shot in detail.

16. For newspaper accounts of the Battle of Lincoln, see *Weekly New Mexican* (Santa Fe), May 11, 1878; "El Gato" to Ed., Fort Stanton, May 10, 1878, ibid., June 1, 1878; "Van" to Ed., Lincoln, May 3, 1878, *Mesilla News*, May 18, 1878; and "Outsider" to Ed., Fort Stanton, May 1, 1878, *Mesilla Valley Independent*, May 11, 1878. "Outsider," whose account is the most reliable and objective, was probably Edgar A. Walz, Catron's brother-in-law, who had been sent to manage Catron's property after the foreclosure on Dolan. Military sources: Dudley to AAAG, DNM, Fort Stanton, May 4, 11, and 15, with enclosures (including Lieutenant Smith's informative report of May 1) in file 1405 AGO 1878, NARS. Frank and George Coe left detailed and graphic reminiscences in interviews with J. Evetts Haley, HHC. Also, George Coe gives an account in his *Frontier Fighter, The Autobiography of George W. Coe*, as related to Nan Hillary Harrison (Boston and New York: Houghton Mifflin Co., 1934).

17. Those arrested and held at Fort Stanton with McSween were Rob Widenmann, Isaac and William Ellis, Ignacio Gonzales, Sam Corbet, George Washington, Doc Scurlock, and John Scroggins.

18. Dudley to AAAG, DNM, Fort Stanton, May 4, 1878, with enclosures, file 1405 AGO 1878, NARS. Dudley to Easton, May 1, 1878, RG 393, Post Records, Fort Stanton, LS, vol. 19, pp. 15–16, NARS. These documents set forth events from the military perspective in great detail. McSween's arrest is described in the deposition of Lt. Millard F. Goodwin, the detachment commander, in the Angel Report, which erroneously dates it May 6. Other military documents show it to have been May 2.

19. Dudley to AAAG, DNM, Fort Stanton, May 25, 1878, file 1405 AGO 1878, NARS. "S" to Ed., Silver City, May 31, 1878, *Grant County Herald* (Silver City), June 8, 1878.

20. Ealy to Dear Uncle, Lincoln, April 5, 1878, encl. to Clark to Secretary of War, Washington, May 28, 1878, file 1405 AGO 1878, NARS. Leverson to Hayes, Lincoln, March 16, 1878, Angel Report. Portions are in Frederick Nolan, ed., *The Life and Death of John Henry Tunstall* (Albuquerque: University of New Mexico Press, 1965), pp. 295–96. Leverson to Hayes, April 1, and Leverson to Schurz, same date; Leverson to Hayes, April 2, in ibid., pp. 306–14. See also Philip J. Rasch, "The Loquacious Mr. Leverson," New York Westerners, *Brand*

Book 11 (1964), pp. 92—93. McSween to Thornton, Lincoln, February 25, 1878. Widenmann to Thornton, Lincoln, February 26, 1878. Leverson to Thornton, March 16 and 21, 1878. Thornton to Marquis of Salisbury, Washington, April 2, 1878, and John P. Tunstall to Marquis of Salisbury, London, April 29, 1878. All in Nolan, *Life and Death of Tunstall*, pp. 266, 289—95, 298—99, 301—04.

21. Nolan, *Life and Death of Tunstall*, chap. 9. Nolan, "A Sidelight on the Tunstall Murder," *New Mexico Historical Review*, 31 (July 1956), pp. 206—22. Lee Scott Theisen, ed., "Frank Warner Angel's Notes on New Mexico Territory, 1878," *Arizona and the West* 18 (Winter 1976), pp. 333—38. Philip J. Rasch, "Frank Warner Angel, Special Agent," Potomac Westerners, *Corral Dust* 7 (April 1972), p. 13.

22. A biographical sketch is Philip J. Rasch, Joseph E. Buckbee, and Karl K. Klein, "Man of Many Parts," English Westerners, *Brand Book* 5 (January 1963), pp. 9—12.

23. For press accounts, see *Mesilla News*, June 1, 1878; *Cimarron News and Press*, June 6, 1878; and *Weekly New Mexican* (Santa Fe), June 8, 1878. Francisco Trujillo, who was present, said Bonney and Chavez killed "Indian." Interview with Edith Crawford, San Patricio, N.M., May 10, 1937, WPA files, folder 212, NMSRCA. "Indian" is variously named in the sources and identified both as part Navajo and part Comanche. Most likely, his name was Manuel Segovia. Sheriff Copeland denied giving Scurlock and his men orders to seize the horses, and Colonel Dudley interpreted this to mean that Scurlock was not a deputy, which is not what Copeland said. Sources also designate Chavez as a deputy. It seems likely that Copeland had deputized Scurlock and Chavez, even though he did not instruct them to take the horses. Another cover for the expedition was a probate court order to impound a horse belonging to the estate of Billy Morton, former boss of the Dolan cow camp killed by the Regulators in March. *Weekly New Mexican* (Santa Fe), June 1, 1878.

24. Dudley to AAAG, DNM, Fort Stanton, May 25, 1878, enclosing Riley to Dudley, May 17 and 19, and Copeland to Thornton, May 24. Dudley to AAAG, DNM, Fort Stanton, May 30, 1878, enclosing Godfroy to Dudley, South Fork, May 27; Riley to Godfroy, Beckwith's Ranch, May 22; and Dudley to Godfroy, Fort Stanton, May 29. All in file 1405 AGO 1878, NARS. Dudley to Godfroy, Fort Stanton, May 25 and 28, 1878, Records of the Bureau of Indian Affairs, Records of the Mescalero Agency, 1874—91, box 6, DFRC.

25. Dudley to AAAG, DNM, Fort Stanton, May 25, 1878, file 1405 AGO 1878, NARS.

26. Larry D. Ball, *The United States Marshals of New Mexico and Arizona Territories, 1846–1912* (Albuquerque: University of New Mexico Press, 1978), pp. 3–5, 12–13.

27. In the territories, the county sheriff usually also bore commission as deputy U.S. marshal. Thus, Sheriff Brady requested military posses in his capacity as a federal officer. Col. Edward Hatch, commanding the District of New Mexico, ruled that the proper and only civil officer to give military aid was the sheriff in execution of the decrees of the district judge, who was both territorial and federal judge. Loud (AAAG, DNM) to CO Fort Stanton, Santa Fe, March 24, 1878, encl. to Pope to AAG, Military Division of the Missouri, Fort Leavenworth, April 24, 1878, file 1405 AGO 1878, NARS. These orders prevailed even though Sheriff Copeland never received appointment as deputy U.S. marshal.

28. Dudley to AAAG, DNM, Fort Stanton, May 4, 1878, file 1405 AGO 1878, NARS.

29. Capt. Henry Carroll to Post Adjutant, Fort Stanton, July 1, 1878, encl. to Dudley to AAAG, DNM, Fort Stanton, July 6, 1878, file 1405 AGO 1878, NARS.

CHAPTER 7

1. The proclamation, with Axtell's notice to Copeland, May 28, 1878, is printed in the *Weekly New Mexican* (Santa Fe), June 1, 1878. Dolan's letters to the *New Mexican*, May 16 and 29, are in the issues of May 25 and June 1, 1878. For Peppin's appointment, see Executive Record Book no. 2, May 31, 1878, TANM, roll 21, frame 502, NMSRCA. Axtell's reference to Rynerson as the source of Peppin's support is in his answers to Angel's "interrogatories," Angel Report.

2. Catron to Axtell, May 30, 1878, and Axtell to Hatch, same date; Hatch to AAG, DM, June 1, 1878; Loud to CO Fort Stanton, June 1; endorsement by Brig. Gen. John Pope, June 7, 1878, all in file 1405 AGO 1878, NARS.

3. The warrants were transmitted to Peppin by U.S. Marshal John Sherman, June 14, 1878 (Exhibit 77–33, Dudley Court Record, NARS), ordering the arrest of Charles Bowdre, Doc Scurlock, Henry Brown, Henry Antrim [Bonney, alias Kid], John Middleton, Stephen Stevens, John Scroggins, Frank and George Coe, Fred Waite, and even the dead Brewer, and their appearance before the U.S. district court in Mesilla. On June 22, none of the warrants having been served, the U.S. grand jury in Mesilla indicted those named in the warrants, and Judge Bristol, sitting as federal judge, issued alias warrants (that is, second warrants

where the first had failed). U.S. District Court, Third Judicial District, Record Book 1871—79, Criminal Case 411, June 22, 1878, p. 687, RG 21, Records of the District Court of the United States, Territory of New Mexico, DFRC.

4. *Mesilla News*, June 15, 1878. "Scrope" to Ed., Fort Stanton, June 18, 1878, and same to same, Lincoln, June 22, 1878, both in ibid., June 29, 1878. "Scrope" was probably Dolan himself. Andrew Boyle to Ira Bond, Lincoln, August 2, 1878, *Grant County Herald* (Silver City), August 24, 1878 (repeated from *Mesilla News*). Peppin to Dudley, Fort Stanton, June 18, 1878 (noon); Goodwin to Post Adjutant, Fort Stanton, June 19, 1878; Dudley to AAAG, DNM, Fort Stanton, June 22, 1878, all in file 1405 AGO 1878, NARS. Special Order 44, Hq. Fort Stanton, June 16 [*sic.*, June 18], 1878; Dudley to Axtell, Fort Stanton, June 20, 1878, Exhibits 77—34 and 77—28, Dudley Court Record, NARS. See also Philip J. Rasch, "John Kinney: King of the Rustlers," English Westerners, *Brand Book* 4 (October 1951), pp. 10—12; and Robert N. Mullin, "Here Lies John Kinney," *Journal of Arizona History* 14 (Autumn 1973), pp. 223—42.

5. Widenmann to John P. Tunstall, Lincoln, June 11, 1878, in Frederick Nolan, ed., *The Life and Death of John Henry Tunstall* (Albuquerque: University of New Mexico Press, 1965), pp. 343—44.

6. *Mesilla News*, July 6, 1878.

7. A. M. Gildea to Maurice Fulton, Del Rio, Texas, June 5, 1929; and same to same, Pearce, Arizona, August 9, 1929, in Fulton Collection, box 2, folder 2, UAL.

8. Testimony of Saturnino Baca, Dudley Court Record, NARS.

9. *Weekly New Mexican* (Santa Fe), July 6, 1878. *Mesilla News*, July 6, 1878. "Julius" (probably Dolan) to Ed., Lincoln, June 27, 1878, ibid. Andrew Boyle to Ed., Lincoln, August 2, 1878, *Grant County Herald* (Silver City), August 24, 1878 (repeated from *Mesilla News*). Dudley to AAAG, DNM, Fort Stanton, June 29, 1878, with enclosure, affidavit of George W. Peppin, June 27, 1878; and Capt. Henry Carroll to Post Adjutant, July 1, 1878, file 1405 AGO 1878, NARS. Special Order 48, Fort Stanton, June 27, 1878; Dudley to Carroll, Fort Stanton, June 27, 1878 (midnight); Special Order 49, Fort Stanton, June 28, 1878, Exhibits 77—43, 77—44, and 78—2, Dudley Court Record, NARS. Fort Stanton Post Returns, June 1878, NARS (M617, roll 1218). Francisco Trujillo, interview with Edith Crawford, May 10, 1937, WPA files, folder 212, NMSRCA.

10. The original warrant, June 29, 1878, in Wilson's virtually illegible handwriting, is in the Fulton Collection, box 12, folder 2, UAL.

There is no direct evidence of a special election returning Wilson to the post, but the warrant and subsequent events show him plainly to be functioning as justice without anyone's objection. Also the "Scrope" letter of June 22 to the *Mesilla News*, which appeared in the issue of June 29 and was probably written by Dolan, mentions "the election of Juan Bautista Wilson to be justice of the peace."

11. Judge Advocate General W. M. Dunn to Secretary of War McCrary, Washington, D.C., June 8, 1878, file 1405 AGO 1878, NARS.

12. Loud to CO Fort Stanton, Santa Fe, June 25, 1878; SO 49, Fort Stanton, June 28, 1878, Exhibits 77–45 and 78–2, Dudley Court Record, NARS. Larry D. Ball, *The United States Marshals of New Mexico and Arizona Territories, 1846–1912* (Albuquerque: University of New Mexico Press, 1978), pp. 91–92.

13. *Mesilla News*, July 13, 1878. Andrew Boyle to Ed., Lincoln, August 2, 1878, *Grant County Herald* (Silver City), August 24, 1878 (repeated from *Mesilla News*). George Coe, interview with J. Evetts Haley, Glencoe, N.M., March 20, 1927, HHC. Dudley to AAAG, DNM, Fort Stanton, July 6, 1878, with enclosures, file 1405 AGO 1878, NARS.

14. Letter from Lincoln, July 7, 1878, in *Mesilla News*, July 13, 1878.

15. The most detailed account of this exchange is the testimony of José María de Aguayo, who was present, but see also testimony of Baca and Mrs. Baca, Dudley Court Record, NARS. Also affidavit of Baca, November 6, 1878, ibid.

16. *Weekly New Mexican* (Santa Fe), July 27, 1878. George Coe, interviews with J. Evetts Haley, Glencoe, N.M., March 20, 1927, and Ruidoso, N.M., June 12, 1939, HHC. Robert Beckwith to Josie Beckwith, Lincoln, July 11, 1878, Mullin Collection, HHC.

17. *Weekly New Mexican* (Santa Fe), July 27, 1878, quoting *Las Vegas Gazette*. Dudley to AAAG, DNM, July 13, 1878, file 1405 AGO 1878, NARS.

18. Dudley to AAAG, DNM, Fort Stanton, July 6, 1878. Petition to Dudley, July 10, 1878, and Dudley to Capt. Thomas Blair, same date, encl. to Dudley to AAAG, DNM, Fort Stanton, July 13, 1878. All in file 1405 AGO 1878, NARS. Capt. Thomas Blair to Dudley, Fort Stanton, July 12, 1878, Fulton Collection, box 11, folder 7, UAL. The last is the original of Blair's lengthy report of his investigation of the posse's excesses at San Patricio. Testimony of Juan Patrón, Dudley Court Record, NARS. Patrón was at Stanton when the women arrived and served as interpreter for them as well as for Captain Blair when he went to San Patricio.

19. Dudley to AAAG, DNM, Fort Stanton, July 13, 1878. Affidavit of J. G. Scurlock, sworn by Juan Patrón, July 15, 1878, encl. to Appel to Post Adjutant, Fort Stanton, July 15, 1878, encl. to Dudley to AAAG, DNM, July 18, 1878. File 1405 AGO 1878, NARS.

20. Dudley to AAAG, DNM, Fort Stanton, July 13, 1878, file 1405 AGO 1878, NARS.

21. McSween to Baca, Lincoln, July 15, 1878; Baca to CO Fort Stanton, Lincoln, July 15, 1878, Exhibits 47 and 47A, Dudley Court Record, NARS. Testimony of Assistant Surgeon Daniel Appel, ibid. Appel to Post Adjutant, Fort Stanton, July 15, 1878, encl. to Dudley to AAAG, DNM, Fort Stanton, July 18, 1878, file 1405 AGO 1878, NARS.

22. Appel to Post Adjutant, Fort Stanton, July 15, 1878, encl. to Dudley to AAAG, DNM, Fort Stanton, July 18, 1878, file 1405 AGO 1878, NARS. W. R. "Jake" Owens, interview with J. Evetts Haley, Carlsbad, N.M., March 2, 1933, HHC.

23. Walter Noble Burns to Sue [McSween] Barber, February 18, 1926, and Sue Barber to Maurice Fulton, White Oaks, N.M., October 12, 1928, Fulton Collection, box 1, folder 4, UAL. Mary Ealy to Fulton, December 7, 1927, ibid., box 1, folder 8.

24. U.S. District Court, Third Judicial District, Record Book, 1871—79, p. 696 (June 28, 1878), RG 21, Records of the District Court of the United States, Territory of New Mexico, DFRC. *Mesilla News*, July 6, 1878. U.S. Marshal John Sherman and Deputy Widenmann had arrested Evans on the federal charge at Fort Stanton in April. Sherman had taken him to Mesilla in mid-June to stand trial. After his acquittal, he still faced the territorial charge of murdering Tunstall. On July 2, he appeared before Judge Bristol on a writ of habeas corpus. Widenmann was the principal witness, and the hearing turned into a persecution of him by Judge Bristol, who then released Evans on bail pending trial.

25. R. M. Beckwith to "Dear Sister," Lincoln, July 11, 1878, Beckwith biographical notes, Mullin Collection, HHC.

CHAPTER 8

1. Testimony of David Easton, George Peppin, José María de Aguayo, Saturnino Baca, and John Long, Dudley Court Record, NARS. Easton watched the scene from the Dolan store, across the street from the hotel.

2. Sources for the events of July 15—19, 1878, are voluminous and contradictory. The richest is the Dudley Court Record, NARS. The

court of inquiry was held in the spring of 1879, less than a year later. Though most of the witnesses gave highly partisan testimony, a careful comparison of their accounts permits a sound reconstruction. The best synthesis is Philip J. Rasch, "Five Days of Battle," Denver Westerners, *Brand Book* 11 (1955), pp. 295–323.

3. Peppin, Long, and others of the posse consistently numbered it at between twenty-five and thirty. From various contemporary sources (chiefly in the Dudley Court Record, NARS), however, at least forty are identifiable by name: Robert Beckwith, John Beckwith, Andrew Boyle, Roscoe L. Bryant, John Chambers, José Chavez y Baca, Thomas Cochran, John Collins, Charles Crawford, James J. Dolan, "Dummy," Jesse Evans, Pantaleón Gallegos, John Galvin, Charles Hart, John Hurley, John Irvin, William H. Johnson, John Jones, James Jones, John Kinney, John Long, Jacob B. Mathews, James McDaniels, "Mexican Eduardo," Lucio Montoya, Joseph H. Nash, Robert Olinger, John Wallace Olinger, W. R. "Jake" Owens, L. R. Parker, Milo L. Pearce, George W. Peppin, Samuel Perry, William B. "Buck" Powell, James B. Reese, George A. Rose (Roxie), John Thornton, Marion Turner, and Buck Waters.

Of the McSween forces, those at the Ellis store included John Middleton, Charles Bowdre, Josiah G. Scurlock, and Stephen Stevens. Those at the Montaño store and Patrón house were the Hispanics under Martín Chavez of Picacho. At the McSween house were McSween, William H. Bonney, Thomas O'Folliard (a recently arrived Texas youth who had formed a worshipful friendship with Bonney), James French, George Coe, Henry Brown, Joseph Smith, Thomas Cullens, Harvey Morris (a tubercular Kansan reading law in McSween's office), José Chavez y Chavez, Florencio Chavez, Yginio Salazar, Ignacio Gonzales, Vicente Romero, Francisco Zamora, and José María Sanchez. Also in the McSween house were Sue McSween; her sister, Mrs. Shield; and her five children (David Shield was in Las Vegas), and Susan Gates, the teacher who had come with the Ealys.

4. Peppin to Dudley, Lincoln, July 16, 1878. Dudley to Peppin, same date. Exhibits 48 and 49, Dudley Court Record, NARS. Dudley to AAAG, DNM, Fort Stanton, July 16, 1878, file 1405 AGO 1878, NARS.

5. The report of the board, July 17, 1878, was an enclosure to Dudley to AAAG, DNM, Fort Stanton, July 18, 1878, which also contained much informative material, file 1405 AGO 1878, NARS. See also testimony of Capt. George A. Purington and Asst. Surgeon Daniel Appel, Dudley Court Record, NARS. The board consisted of Purington, Appel, and Capt. Thomas Blair.

6. Pink Simms to Maurice Fulton, Great Falls, Montana, April 18, 1932, Fulton Collection, box 4, folder 5, UAL.

7. Dudley to AAAG, DNM, Fort Stanton, July 18, 1878, file 1405 AGO 1878, NARS. Affidavit of John Long, Fort Stanton, July 24, 1878, Mullin Collection, HHC. This original copy was found by Mullin in a Lincoln trash heap in 1914. Testimony of Saturnino Baca, Dudley Court Record, NARS. From his front door, Baca saw Crawford shot. Affidavits of John Long, November 9, 1878, and George Peppin, November 6, 1878, Exhibits 6C and 8, ibid. Crawford bore the nickname "Lallycooler," a reference to a winning poker hand.

8. Taylor F. Ealy, "The Lincoln County War as I Saw It," n.d., c. 1927, Ealy Collection, UAL. Mary Ealy to Maurice Fulton, n.d., c. 1928, Fulton Collection, box 1, folder 8, UAL.

9. Affidavit of John Long, July 24, 1878, Mullin Collection, HHC. Sue McSween testified that the men in the McSween house had agreed on the evening of the seventeenth to fire no more at the posse— as well they might in view of the Robinson and Crawford incidents— and that they did not fire at all on the eighteenth. She said some firing came from the Wortley Hotel. Testimony in Dudley Court Record, NARS.

10. Testimony of José María de Aguayo, Dudley Court Record, NARS.

11. Testimony of Baca and Asst. Surgeon Daniel Appel, Dudley Court Record, NARS. Notes of Dr. D. M. Appel, Fort Stanton, July 20, 1878, Exhibit B6, ibid.

12. Testimony of Capt. George A. Purington, Dudley Court Record, NARS.

13. Dudley to AAAG, DNM, Fort Stanton, July 20, 1878, enclosing document dated July 18 and signed by Dudley, Purington, Appel, Capt. Thomas Blair, Lt. M. F. Goodwin, and Lt. S. S. Pague, file 1405 AGO 1878. See also testimony of Dudley, Purington, Appel, and Goodwin, Dudley Court Record, NARS.

14. Two witnesses in the Dudley Court, Alexander Rudder and Samuel Beard, testified to overhearing a conversation between Dudley and Dolan at Fort Stanton on July 18, in which Dolan said he had to have army help and Dudley promised to come down next day and give help. Over the years, several fanciful tales based on this allegation found their way into the memories of participants. Dudley denied the conversation, and his officers supported him. Dolan testified that he spent the afternoon of the eighteenth at the home of the post butcher, Charles McVeagh, three-fourths of a mile east of the fort, and did not go to the

fort at all. McVeagh confirmed this. In his summation, Dudley's counsel convincingly refuted the stories of Rudder and Beard, and in fact their testimony is flawed with inconsistencies and obscurities. Rudder was known as "Crazy Alex." Dudley Court Record, NARS.

15. Testimony of Lt. M. F. Goodwin (Dudley's adjutant on July 19), Dudley Court Record, NARS. Fort Stanton Post Returns, July 1878, NARS (M617, roll 1218).

16. Dudley to AAAG, DNM, Fort Stanton, July 20, 1878, file 1405 AGO 1878, NARS. Affidavit of Deputy John Long, Fort Stanton, July 21, 1878, Mullin Collection, HHC. Testimony of Peppin, Purington, Appel, Goodwin, George Washington, José María de Aguayo, and Pvt. James Bush; notes by Appel, July 20, 1878; affidavits of Peppin and Long, November 6 and 9, 1878, all in Dudley Court Record, NARS.

17. Testimony of Sue McSween, William H. Bonney, and George Peppin, Dudley Court Record, NARS. McSween to Dudley, July 19, 1878, encl. to Dudley to AAAG, DNM, Fort Stanton, July 20, 1878, file 1405 AGO 1878, NARS.

18. Testimony of Goodwin, Dudley Court Record, NARS. Goodwin gave the message from memory, since no copy had been retained.

19. Testimony of Purington, Appel, Goodwin, George Washington, José María de Aguayo, and Pvt. James Bush; notes by Appel, July 20, 1878, Dudley Court Record, NARS.

20. Testimony of Peppin, Dudley, Ellis, Purington, Goodwin, Sgt. Harlin Lusk, Sgt. Andrew Keefe, and Pvt. James Bush, Dudley Court Record, NARS. Dudley to AAAG, DNM, Fort Stanton, July 20, 1878, file 1405 AGO 1878, NARS.

21. Testimony of Purington, Goodwin, Appel, Peppin, Lusk, Washington, John B. Wilson, Theresa Phillipowski, Josefita Montaño, Martín Chavez, and Sgt. O. D. Kelsey (who had charge of the howitzer), Dudley Court Record, NARS. Dudley to AAAG, DNM, Fort Stanton, July 20, 1878, file 1405 AGO 1878, NARS.

22. Testimony of Ellis, Washington, Chavez, Lusk, Bush, Peppin, Kelsey, Purington, Appel, and Samuel Corbet, Dudley Court Record, NARS. Sergeant Lusk and Private Bush testified, none too coherently, that Dudley sent Bush to alert Peppin to the withdrawal of these McSween men from the Ellis store; then Dudley criticized him for not coming soon enough to catch them. In his summation at the close of the court of inquiry, however, Dudley's counsel effectively discredited this testimony.

23. Pink Simms to Maurice Fulton, Great Falls, Mont., April 18, 1932, Fulton Collection, box 4, folder 5, UAL.

24. Fifteen witnesses, including Dudley and Wilson, gave their version of the conversation between them, Dudley Court Record, NARS. About half related the double ironing threat, and half denied that it occurred at all. Denial, however, is easier than invention, and the language is wholly consistent with Dudley's character. See also affidavit of Wilson, c. March 1879, Wallace Papers, IHS.

25. Testimony of Peppin, Dudley Court Record, NARS. McSween partisans testified that the posse fell in immediately behind the troops and followed them to the McSween house. Peppin partisans testified that thirty to forty-five minutes elapsed after the troops passed the Wortley before the possemen went into position. Given the timing of the posse's movements in relation to Peppin's movements, the latter construction seems most probable.

26. Testimony of Peppin, David M. Easton, Andrew Boyle, Robert Olinger, Joseph Nash, Milo Pearce, and Marion Turner, Dudley Court Record, NARS.

27. Testimony of Peppin, Isaac Ellis, and John Long, Dudley Court Record, NARS.

28. Testimony of Peppin and Sue McSween, Dudley Court Record, NARS.

29. A parade of witnesses, including Dudley and Sue, gave contradictory and partisan accounts of this conversation, Dudley Court Record, NARS. The disagreement, however, was less of substance than tone. Sue and her friends accused Dudley of rudeness and anger. Dudley and his friends protested dignity and courtesy in the face of great provocation.

30. Testimony of Long, Boyle, Nash, and William H. Bonney, Dudley Court Record, NARS.

31. Testimony of Long, Boyle, and Powell, Dudley Court Record, NARS. George Coe, interview with J. Evetts Haley, Glencoe, N.M., March 20, 1927, HHC.

32. Testimony of Boyle, Long, and Nash, Dudley Court Record, NARS.

33. Testimony of Peppin, Washington, Phillipowski, Chavez, Corbet, Lusk, Kelsey, Keefe, Goodwin, Purington, Sebrian Bates, and Francisco Romero y Valencia, Dudley Court Record, NARS. Sergeant Keefe, who had charge of the Gatling gun, denied that it was ever aimed at the hills north of the river, but he was contradicted by all the other witnesses named. Peppin's bullets, rather than the threat of the artillery, probably drove off these men. Martín Chavez, the only one of this group to testify, did not even see the artillery.

217

34. Testimony of David Easton and Sue McSween, Dudley Court Record, NARS. *Weekly New Mexican* (Santa Fe), August 10, 1878. Most contemporary accounts refer to two deaths in the McSween house before the breakout, of whom Cullens was one. Bowers is usually named as the other, but is identified in subsequent events. To confuse matters further, Bowers is sometimes said to have been an alias for Cullens.

35. The quotation is from Sue [McSween] Barber, interview with J. Evetts Haley, White Oaks, N.M., August 16, 1927, HHC. Sue's testimony in the Dudley Court Record, NARS, is vague, sometimes incoherent, and mainly an emotional diatribe against Colonel Dudley. Her correspondence with Maurice Fulton, Fulton Collection, UAL, is moderately useful, but contains little detail bearing on the events of July 19, 1878.

36. Testimony of Ealy, Sgt. George Murison, and Cpl. Frederick Berghold, Dudley Court Record, NARS. Notes of Dr. D. M. Appel, Fort Stanton, July 20, 1878, Exhibit B6, ibid.

37. Testimony of Peppin, Dudley Court Record, NARS. Affidavit of John Long, November 9, 1878, Exhibit 63, ibid.

38. Testimony of Purington, Dudley Court Record, NARS. Notes of Appel, July 20, 1878, Exhibit B6, ibid.

39. The following account is reconstructed chiefly from these sources: testimony of William H. Bonney, José Chavez y Chavez, Joseph Nash, and Andrew Boyle, Dudley Court Record, NARS; and affidavit of Yginio Salazar, Lincoln, July 20, 1878, encl. to Dudley to AAAG, DNM, Fort Stanton, July 23, 1878, file 1405 AGO 1878, NARS.

40. Notes of Dr. D. M. Appel, July 20, 1878; and Proceedings of Coroner's Jury, July 20, 1878, Exhibits B6 and 78, Dudley Court Record, NARS. Sam Corbet to J. P. Tunstall, Lincoln, September 13, 1878, Mullin Collection, HHC.

41. George Coe, interview with J. Evetts Haley, Glencoe, N.M., March 20, 1927, HHC.

42. Yginio Salazar, interview with J. Evetts Haley, Lincoln, N.M., August 17, 1927, HHC. In another interview, Salazar said that it was Andy Boyle who kicked him. Salazar biographical notes, Mullin Collection, HHC. Notes of Dr. D.M. Appel, July 20, 1878, Exhibit B6, Dudley Court Record, NARS.

43. Testimony of Peppin, Dudley, David M. Easton, and Sebrian Bates, Dudley Court Record, NARS. Affidavit of John Long, July 24, 1878, Mullin Collection, HHC. Dudley fulsomely characterized Beckwith as "one of the most upright, energetic, and industrious men of the

community, who I believe lost his life in the conscientious discharge of loyal duty." Dudley to AAAG, DNM, Fort Stanton, July 20, 1878, file 1405 AGO 1878, NARS.

44. Testimony of Sam Corbet, Peppin, Appel, Dudley, Easton, Sue McSween, and M. L. Pearce, Dudley Court Record, NARS.

45. For allegations of military help to Peppin, see testimony of Sue McSween, George Washington, Sebrian Bates, William Bonney, and José Chavez y Chavez. For denials, see testimony of Dudley, Purington, Goodwin, Appel, Sgt. Andrew Keefe, Sgt. Harlin Lusk, Pvt. James Bush, and Sgt. George Murison. Dudley Court Record, NARS. Several witnesses testified to possemen in military gear; the most convincing was Milo Pearce. Authorized forays: twice Dudley sent details to summon Peppin; twice he sent patrols to notify citizens of his intentions, one through town and another to the foothills; twice he sent soldiers to Ellis's store, once for water from a nearby spring and again to buy chickens for Dudley's supper; and finally, late in the afternoon, he authorized troops to move the Ealys' possessions from the Tunstall store to the Patrón house.

46. Testimony of Peppin, Appel, Dudley, Samuel Corbet, David Easton, Sue McSween, and M. L. Pearce, Dudley Court Record, NARS. Corbet, the store's clerk, and Easton, custodian of the Catron interests in the Dolan store, tried to get Peppin to stop the looting, but he said he was powerless. It is clear that the store had been ransacked and looting was about to take place. But Milo Pearce, a Seven Rivers stockman and posse member, intervened. No one, except possibly Jesse Evans, seems to have stolen anything at this time. Both Corbet and Easton admitted this under cross-examination. Easton further testified that the store was broken into again on the night of July 20 and wagons parked in front and loaded with merchandise. He described the offenders as mostly Hispanics acting with the resigned acquiescence of Sue McSween, who explained that she would rather these people had the goods than Peppin's "murderers." With the help of Easton and Corbet, Sue persuaded many of them to return what they had taken, but much of the store's contents disappeared.

47. Testimony of Sebrian Bates, Dudley Court Record, NARS.

CHAPTER 9

1. These letters are in the French biographical notes, Mullin Collection, HHC. For Dudley, see Dudley to AAAG, DNM, Fort Stanton, August 24 and 31, September 7, 1878, file 1405 AGO 1878, NARS.

2. Capt. Thomas Blair to Post Adjutant, Fort Stanton, August 1,

1878, encl. to Dudley to AAAG, DNM, Fort Stanton, August 3, 1878; same to same, August 22, 1878; Loud to Dudley, Santa Fe, August 15, 1878, file 1405 AGO 1878, NARS.

3. For McSween's charges, see McSween to Schurz, February 13, 1878, and McSween to Lowrie, February 25, 1878, RG 75, Office of Indian Affairs, LR, NARS (M234, roll 576). The investigation revealed that Godfroy had been "lending" flour and other supplies to The House to meet temporary shortages. Apparently, the loans were repaid in kind, but such casual handling of government stores got Godfroy dismissed. Watkins Report, NARS.

4. Godfroy to Post Adjutant, Fort Stanton, August 3, 1878, encl. to Dudley to AAAG, DNM, same date, file 1405 AGO 1878, NARS.

5. The best sources for this affair are military records: Dudley to AAAG, DNM, Fort Stanton, August 3, 6, 7, 8, and 10, 1878, with enclosures, file 1405 AGO 1878, NARS. A rich source, enclosure to Dudley's of August 10, is a lengthy report of an investigation by Capt. Thomas Blair, which includes the accounts of Agent Godfroy, Dr. Blazer, and Interpreter José Carillo. See also *Mesilla Valley Independent*, August 15, 1878; and *Cimarron News and Press*, September 19, 1878. The Coes gave especially good reminiscent accounts: George Coe, interview with J. Evetts Haley, Glencoe, N.M., March 20, 1927; and Frank Coe, same, San Patricio, N.M., August 14, 1927, both HHC.

6. For the whereabouts of the Kid and other prominent Regulators, see Dudley to AAAG, DNM, August 31, September 7 and 28, 1878, with enclosures, file 1405 AGO 1878, NARS; diary of Sallie Chisum, Chaves County Historical Society, Roswell, N.M., excerpts provided by Harwood P. Hinton; George Coe, interview with J. Evetts Haley, Glencoe, N.M., March 20, 1927, HHC; and Henry F. Hoyt, *A Frontier Doctor* (Boston: Houghton Mifflin Co., 1929), pp. 91–94. These sources generally support the sequence traced in the usually unreliable Pat F. Garrett, *The Authentic Life of Billy the Kid* (Santa Fe: New Mexican, 1882), chap. 13. There have been many editions of this work, ghosted by Ash Upson. I have used the University of Oklahoma Press edition of 1954, which went into a twelfth printing in 1980.

7. A biography is Leon C. Metz, *John Selman, Gunfighter* (New York, 1966; 2d ed., Norman: University of Oklahoma Press, 1980). Much about the origins of the Wrestlers is contained in a statement Billy Bonney gave to Governor Lew Wallace on March 29, 1879, Wallace papers, IHS.

8. Corbet to Lee Keyser [clerk at Dowlin's Fort Stanton store], Lincoln, August 22, 1878, encl. to Dudley to AAAG, DNM, August 24, 1878, File 1405 AGO 1878, NARS. Corbet to J. P. Tunstall, September

23, 1878, Mullin Collection, HHC. Godfrey Gauss to J. P. Tunstall, August 22, 1878, in Frederick Nolan, ed., *The Life and Death of John Henry Tunstall* (Albuquerque: University of New Mexico Press, 1965), pp. 385–86.

9. Frank Coe, interview with J. Evetts Haley, San Patricio, N.M., August 14, 1927, HHC. Dudley to AAAG, DNM, September 28 and 29, October 3, 1878, file 1405 AGO 1878, NARS. Sam Corbet to J. P. Tunstall, Lincoln, October 1, 1878, Mullin Collection, HHC. The men killed were Desiderio and Cleto Chavez y Sanchez, Lorenzo Lucero, and Gregorio Sanchez. Those indicted for the murders, though never brought to trial, were John Goss alias John Gunter (both aliases for John Selman), Gus Gildea, Reese Gobles, "Rustling Bob," Charles Snow, Robert Speakes, James Irwin, William Dwyer, and one Collier (possibly John Collins). Lincoln County, District Court, Criminal Cases 272, 273, 275, 276: *Territory v. John Goss et al.*: murder. Case Files. District Court Journal, April 25, 1879 (pp. 323–25), May 1, 1879 (pp. 361–62, 371). NMSRCA.

10. Lyon to Post Adjutant, Fort Stanton, October 1, 1878, file 1405 AGO 1878, NARS.

11. Daniel Dow, Robert Stewart, and August Cline to CO Fort Stanton, Hondo, October 1, 1878, encl. to Dudley to AAAG, DNM, Fort Stanton, October 3, 1878; M. A. Upson to Dudley, Picacho, October 3, 1878, encl. to Dudley to AAAG, DNM, October 5, 1878, file 1405 AGO 1878, NARS. E. T. Stone and J. C. Lea to CO Fort Stanton, October 10, 1878, RG 393, Post Records, Fort Stanton, LR, box 2, NARS.

12. Dudley to AAAG, DNM, September 29, 1878 (2), file 1405 AGO 1878, NARS.

13. Dudley to Attorney General Charles Devens, Fort Stanton, August 15, 1878, RG 393, Post Records, Fort Stanton, LS, vol. 19, pp. 107–08, NARS.

14. Petition of Probate Judge Florencio Gonzales, County Commissioner Saturnino Baca, Justice of the Peace of Precinct 4 George Kimball, and County Treasurer José Montaño, Santa Fe, [August 20, 1878], encl. to Axtell to Hayes, same date, file 1405 AGO 1878, NARS.

CHAPTER 10

1. Angel Report, passim. The "scratch of a pen" reference is in Axtell's response to the interrogatories. See also Lee Scott Thiesen, ed., "Frank Warner Angel's Notes on New Mexico Territory, 1878," *Arizona and the West* 18 (Winter 1976), pp. 333–70.

2. Schurz to Hayes, August 31, 1878, Hayes Memorial Library,

Fremont, Ohio, copy in Fulton Collection, box 12, folder 4, UAL.

3. There are two standard biographies of Lew Wallace: Irving McKee, *"Ben-Hur" Wallace: The Life of General Lew Wallace* (Berkeley and Los Angeles: University of California Press, 1947); and Robert E. and Katherine M. Morsberger, *Lew Wallace: Militant Romantic* (New York: McGraw Hill, 1980). While both are good, neither is adequate in its treatment of the New Mexico years. For the New Mexico governorship, see Calvin P. Horn, *New Mexico's Troubled Years: The Story of Early Territorial Governors* (Albuquerque: Horn and Wallace, 1963), pp. 193–97; and Oakah L. Jones, "Lew Wallace: Hoosier Governor of Territorial New Mexico, 1878–81," *New Mexico Historical Review* 60 (April 1985) pp. 129–58. There is also some useful material in Wallace, *Lew Wallace: An Autobiography*, vol. 2 (New York and London: Harper and Bros., 1906).

4. Schurz to Wallace, Washington, D.C., September 4, 1878. Wallace to "Dear Sue" [his wife], Santa Fe, October 8, 1878. Both in Wallace Papers, IHS.

5. Quoted in Morsberger, *Lew Wallace*, p. 264.

6. Teleg., Wallace to Schurz, Santa Fe, October 5, 1878, enclosing Dudley to Hatch, September 29; Bristol to Sherman, October 4; and Sherman to Wallace, October 4. Wallace Papers, IHS.

7. Printed copies, in English and Spanish, are in the Wallace Papers, IHS.

8. Teleg., Wallace to Schurz, Santa Fe, October 14, 1878, Wallace Papers, IHS.

9. Wallace to Hatch, Santa Fe, October 26, 1878; Loud to CO Fort Stanton, Santa Fe, October 27, 1878, Wallace Papers, IHS. Secretary of War George W. McCrary to Gen. W. T. Sherman, Washington, October 8, 1878; disseminated as General Order 74, Hq. of the Army, Adjutant General's Office, same date, file 1405 AGO 1878, NARS.

10. Wallace to Schurz, Santa Fe, October 22, 1878, Wallace Papers, IHS.

11. Wallace's proclamation, November 13, 1878, in both English and Spanish, is in Records of Territorial Governors: Lew Wallace, TANM, roll 99, frames 133–37, NMSRCA. See also Wallace to Schurz, Santa Fe, November 13, 1878, Wallace Papers, IHS. Schurz to Wallace, Washington, D.C., December 9, 1878, Wallace Papers, says he knows of no move in the Senate to defeat confirmation. Dudley to AAAG, DNM, Fort Stanton, October 26 and November 2, 1878, Dudley Court Record, NARS, reported an absence of any offenses.

12. *Mesilla Valley Independent*, November 23, 1878. *Mesilla News*, November 23, 1878. *Weekly New Mexican* (Santa Fe), December 7, 1878. Dudley to AAAG, DNM, Fort Stanton, November 16 and 30, Decem-

ber 17, 1878, Dudley Court Record, NARS. Same to same, December 7 and 9, 1878, file 1405 AGO 1878, NARS.

13. Wallace to Schurz, Santa Fe, October 1 and December 21, 1878, Wallace Papers, IHS. Chapman to Wallace, Lincoln, November 25 and 29, 1878, Dudley Court Record, NARS. *Mesilla News,* November 23, 1878. *Mesilla Valley Independent,* same date.

14. Wallace, *Autobiography,* vol. 2, pp. 935–36, paints a graphic picture of the setting in which he wrote the eighth and last book of *Ben-Hur.*

15. Dudley to AAAG, DNM, Fort Stanton, November 30, December 8 and 24, 1878, Exhibits 23, 79–6, and 79–17, Dudley Court Record, NARS. Same to same, December 7, 1878, file 1405 AGO 1878, NARS. Same to same, January 26, 1879, RG 393, LR, Hq. DNM, NARS (M1088, roll 36).

16. Hatch to AAG, DM, Santa Fe, December 17, 1878; Wallace to Hatch, Santa Fe, February 14, 1879; Hatch to AAG, DM, February 17, 1879; endorsement of Brig. Gen. John Pope, February 24, 1879; endorsement of Gen. W. T. Sherman, March 6; endorsement of chief clerk of War Department, March 12, file 1405 AGO 1878, NARS. Wallace advised Wilson that U.S. Marshal John Sherman refused to appoint a deputy marshal in Lincoln. Wallace to Wilson, Santa Fe, February 6, 1879, Wallace Papers, IHS.

CHAPTER 11

1. Dudley to AAAG, DNM, Fort Stanton, July 20, 1878, file 1405 AGO 1878, NARS.

2. Chapman to Wallace, Las Vegas, October 24, 1878, Wallace Papers, IHS.

3. Wallace to Hatch, Santa Fe, October 28, 1878, endorsed to Dudley October 30, Exhibit 14, Dudley Court Record, NARS.

4. Dudley to AAAG, DNM, Fort Stanton, November 7 and 9, 1878, enclosing statement of Dr. D. M. Appel, November 9; affidavits of John Long, November 9; Saturnino Baca, November 6; George W. Peppin, November 6; John Priest, November 6; Francisco Gómez, November 6; Lt. G. W. Smith, November 7; and Lt. S. S. Pague, November 7. Dudley to Wallace, Fort Stanton, November 9, 1878. Exhibits 6–13, Dudley Court Record, NARS. Wallace to Hatch, November 14, 1878; Loud to Dudley, November 15, 1878, Exhibit 63, ibid.

5. Testimony of Wallace, Dudley Court Record, NARS. Sue E. [McSween] Barber, interview with J. Evetts Haley, White Oaks, N.M., August 16, 1927, HHC.

6. Dudley to Wallace, Fort Stanton, November 30, 1878, in *New*

Mexican (Santa Fe), December 14, 1878. Annexed as Exhibit 2, Dudley Court Record, NARS.

7. Chapman to Wallace, Lincoln, November 25 and 29, 1878, Exhibits 24 and 25, Dudley Court Record, NARS. Wallace to Hatch, Santa Fe, December 7, 1878, with endorsements by Hatch, n.d.; Brig. Gen. John Pope, December 18; Lt. Gen. Philip H. Sheridan, December 21; Gen. William T. Sherman, December 26; and chief clerk of the War Department, January 3, 1879. File 1405 AGO 1878, NARS.

8. Loud to CO Fort Stanton, Santa Fe, October 27, 1878. Wallace to Hatch, Santa Fe, December 14, 1878; Hatch to AAG, DM, Santa Fe, December 17, 1878. File 1405 AGO 1878, NARS. For Chapman's advice to shoot army officers, see Chapman to Wallace, Lincoln, November 25, 1878, Exhibit 25, Dudley Court Record, NARS.

9. Dudley to AAAG, DNM, November 30, December 6, 9, and 17, 1878, file 1405 AGO 1878, NARS.

10. General Order 62, Fort Stanton, December 20, 1878, Exhibit 45, Dudley Court Record, NARS. *Weekly New Mexican* (Santa Fe), January 4, 1879.

11. The proceedings of the military board, including depositions by Chapman and other principals, is Exhibit 28, Dudley Court Record, NARS. See also Dudley to AAAG, DNM, Fort Stanton, December 15 and 17, 1878, Exhibits 79 and 79–13; and Special Order 158, Fort Stanton, December 16, 1878, ibid.

12. Dudley to AAAG, DNM, Fort Stanton, January 26, 1879, RG 393, LR, DNM, NARS (M1088, roll 36). Chapman biographical notes, Mullin Collection, HHC.

13. Statement of Peppin and French, in proceedings of a board of officers convened at Fort Stanton by virtue of SO 154, Fort Stanton, December 14, 1878, Exhibit 28; Dudley to AAAG, DNM, December 15 and 17, 1878, Exhibits 79-9 and 79-13; SO 158, Fort Stanton, December 16, 1878, Exhibit 79-10; Affidavit of W. H. Hudgens, Fort Stanton, December 16, 1878, Exhibit 79-11, Dudley Court Record, NARS. Dudley to AAAG, DNM, Fort Stanton, December 14, 1878, RG 393, Post Records, Fort Stanton, N.M., LS, Vol. 20, pp. 59–60, NARS.

14. Dudley to AAAG, DNM, Fort Stanton, December 15, 1878, Exhibit 79-9, Dudley Court Record, NARS.

15. Dudley to AAAG, DNM, Fort Stanton, February 1, 1879, enclosing Thomas Gardner to the Governor of New Mexico, Roswell, January 29, 1879, RG 393, LR, Hq. DNM, NARS (M1088, roll 36). Garst to Carroll, Fort Stanton, December 22, 1878, RG 393, Post Records, Fort Stanton, N.M., LS, vol. 20, pp. 84–85, NARS.

16. Carroll to Post Adjutant Fort Stanton, March 10, 1879, RG 393, Post Records, Fort Stanton, LR, box 3, NARS, is a lengthy and detailed report of this operation. See also Carroll to Post Adjutant Fort Stanton, Roswell, February 25, 1879, ibid. In Sue E. McSween to Dudley, Lincoln, February 11, 1879; and Dudley to Sue E. McSween, Fort Stanton, February 13, 1879, Exhibits 79–32 and 79–33, Dudley Court Record, NARS, Sue informs Dudley of locating the cattle, and Dudley says he will help recover them. See also Dudley to AAAG, DNM, Fort Stanton, February 15, 1879, Exhibit 79–35, ibid. The recovery expenses ($842.45) and other information relating to the Tunstall cattle are detailed in Statement of Sue E. McSween, October 30, 1880, copied from records of Lincoln County probate court by Edith L. Crawford, January 24, 1938, WPA files, folder 212, NMSRCA. Captain Carroll told Governor Wallace about the cigar in the mouth of the skull: Wallace to Schurz, March 21, 1879, Wallace Papers, IHS. For the killing from the Jones perspective, see Eve Ball, *Ma'am Jones of the Pecos* (Tucson: University of Arizona Press, 1969), chap. 19. For a time under arrest by Bowers, Marion Turner protested to Governor Wallace that he was "being insulted by an officer of the U.S. army who has me in Charge and Sitizens of n.m. and Texas being charged upon and Shot at by the military I Deem it necessary to inform you of this imposicion and Pray for releif." Turner to Wallace, February 16, 1879, Wallace Papers, IHS.

17. Teleg., Dudley to AAAG, DNM, Fort Stanton, through Mesilla, December 29, 1878, Exhibit 79–19; Teleg., Loud to CO Fort Stanton, Santa Fe, January 6, 1879, Exhibit 79–20; SO 6, Fort Stanton, January 10, 1879, Exhibit 79–22; Circular, signed Lt. M. F. Goodwin, Fort Stanton, February 17, 1879, Exhibit 79–23, Dudley Court Record, NARS. Dudley to Carroll, Fort Stanton, January 10, 1879; Dudley to AAAG, DNM, Fort Stanton, February 18, 1879, with enclosures, RG 393, LR, DNM, NARS (M1088, roll 36).

18. Lt. S. S. Pague to David M. Easton, Fort Stanton, November 3, 1878, RG 393, Post Records, Fort Stanton, N.M., LS, vol. 19, p. 214. Adjutant Pague wrote that Dudley was anxious to see Easton's friend Campbell and asked that he come to the fort at once, by noon if possible. See also Dudley to AAAG, DNM, Fort Stanton, February 18, 1878, RG 393, LR, DNM, NARS (M1088, roll 36).

19. Corbet to John Middleton, Lincoln, February 3, 1880, Fulton Collection, box 11, folder 8, UAL.

20. Dudley to AAAG, DNM, Fort Stanton, February 19, 1879, file 1405 AGO 1878, NARS. Dudley was shown the letter and told of the reply.

21. Edgar A. Walz, "Retrospection," October 1931, MS. in Museum of New Mexico Historical Library, Santa Fe. Some accounts place Charlie Bowdre in the group rather than Joe Bowers. The most detailed and authoritative evidence is a newspaper account summarizing the testimony of participants and witnesses in Judge Bristol's court in Mesilla in July 1879. *Mesilla Valley Independent*, July 5, 1879. See also ibid., March 9 and 22, 1879; *Mesilla News*, March 1, 1879; *Las Vegas Gazette*, same date; *Las Cruces Thirty-Four*, March 6 and 19 and April 9, 1879; and Dudley to AAAG, DNM, Fort Stanton, February 19, 1879, with enclosures, file 1405 AGO 1878, NARS. For a synthesis of the evidence, see Philip J. Rasch, "The Murder of Huston I. Chapman," Los Angeles Westerners, *Brand Book* 8 (1959) pp. 69–82.

22. Dudley to AAAG, DNM, Fort Stanton, February 21, 1879, Exhibit 79–43, Dudley Court Record, NARS. Three parties to the agreement told Dudley its terms.

23. Some accounts say Chapman's body was drenched with whiskey and set afire. I think it more likely, as the witnesses before Judge Bristol agreed, that the pistol shot ignited his clothing.

24. All the dialogue in the above account is from the court testimony summarized in the *Mesilla Valley Independent*, July 5, 1879.

25. Kimball to CO Fort Stanton, February 18, 1879; Lt. Byron Dawson to Post Adjutant Fort Stanton, February 19, 1879, both encl. to Dudley to AAAG, DNM, Fort Stanton, February 19, 1879, file 1405 AGO 1878, NARS.

26. Dudley to AAAG, DNM, Fort Stanton, February 19, 20, 21, and 24, 1879, with enclosures, file 1405 AGO 1878, NARS. Testimony of Dr. W. B. Lyon, Lee Keyser, B. J. Baca, and Lt. M. F. Goodwin, Dudley Court Record, NARS.

27. *Mesilla Valley Independent*, July 5, 1879.

28. *Mesilla Valley Independent*, March 1 and 22, July 5, 1879. *Las Cruces Thirty-Four*, April 9, 1879.

29. The fifty-dollar loan is described in a note in Wallace's handwriting, undated but probably March 1879, Wallace Papers, IHS. The note says that a clerk at the post trader's store told of crediting the sum to Dolan and debiting it in Dudley's account and that Lt. S. S. Pague witnessed Dolan paying the money to Campbell. For Scase, see testimony of Dolan, Sgt. David Kellehie, Sgt. George Davis, and Sgt. Ezra Shanks, Dudley Court Record, NARS.

30. Wilson's action was reported in Goodwin to CO Fort Stanton, Lincoln, February 20, 1879, and John B. Wilson to Dudley, Lincoln, same date, Exhibits 53 and 74, Dudley Court Inquiry, NARS.

31. Walz, "Retrospection."

CHAPTER 12

1. *Weekly New Mexican* (Santa Fe), February 8, 1879.

2. J. H. Watts to Wallace, Fort Stanton, February 24, 1879, Wallace Papers, IHS.

3. Wallace to John B. Wilson, Santa Fe, January 18, 1879, Wallace Papers, IHS.

4. Wallace to Schurz, Santa Fe, February 27, 1879, Wallace Papers, IHS. Wallace to Hatch, Santa Fe, February 27, 1879, file 1405 AGO 1878, NARS. Hatch to AAG, DM, Santa Fe, March 2, 1879, RG 393, LS, Hq. DNM, NARS (M1072, roll 6).

5. Hatch to AAG, DM, Santa Fe, March 2, 1879, RG 393, LS, Hq. DNM, NARS (M1072, roll 6). While serving as district commander, Hatch was also colonel of the Ninth Cavalry and Dudley lieutenant colonel. For the Dudley-Hatch quarrel, and other details of Dudley's contentious career, see Philip J. Rasch, "The Trials of Lieutenant-Colonel Dudley," English Westerners, *Brand Book* 7 (January 1965), pp. 1–7.

6. Wallace to Hatch, Lincoln, March 7, 1879. Special Field Order no. 2, Hq. DNM, March 8, 1879. Wallace to Hatch, Lincoln, March 9, 1879. Wallace Papers, IHS. For the public meeting of March 8, see testimony of Dr. Spencer H. Gurney and William M. Roberts, Dudley Court Record, NARS.

7. Dudley to Hatch, Fort Stanton, March 9, 1879. Teleg., Dudley to Adjutant General, Fort Stanton, through Mesilla, March 10, 1879. Same to same, through Hq. DM, March 12, 1879. Dudley Court Record, NARS. Dudley to Sherman, Fort Stanton, March 18, 1879, file 1405 AGO 1878, NARS. See also Wallace to Schurz, March 21, 1879, Wallace Papers, IHS.

8. Wallace to Hatch, Lincoln, March 9, 1879, Wallace Papers, IHS. For Carroll, see his personnel file in RG 94, 3754 ACP 1874, NARS.

9. Wallace to Carroll, Lincoln, March 11 and 12, 1879, Wallace Papers, IHS. A number of fragmentary notes in this collection record names and other information obtained from these sources, including Justice Wilson.

10. Wallace to Hatch, Lincoln, March 5, 1879. Wallace to Carroll, Lincoln, March 10, 1879. Carroll to Wallace, March 11, 1879. Dolan to Wallace, Fort Stanton, March 14, 1879. Wallace to Schurz, Lincoln, March 21, 1879. Wallace Papers, IHS. Carroll to AAAG, DNM, Fort Stanton, March 15, 1879, RG 393, LR, Hq. DNM, NARS (M1088, roll 36). Hatch to Goodwin, Fort Stanton, March 6, 1879, Exhibit 79–57, Dudley Court Record, NARS. Anon. letter from Fort Stanton, March 13, 1879, in *Las Cruces Thirty-Four*, March 19, 1879.

11. Wallace to Schurz, March 31, 1879, Wallace Papers, IHS. "Rio Bonito" to Ed., Fort Stanton, April 8, 1879, *Mesilla Valley Independent*, April 12, 1879.

12. Wallace to Hatch, Lincoln, March 6, 1879, Wallace Papers, IHS.

13. Wallace to J. B. Wilson, Fort Stanton, March 8, 1879, Wallace Papers, IHS.

14. This opening letter in the famous exchange between Wallace and Bonney does not seem to be in the Wallace Papers, which contains all that followed. It is given in full in Philip J. Rasch, "The Governor Meets the Kid," English Westerners, *Brand Book* 8 (April 1966), p. 9. Rasch cites a photocopy in the possession of the Old Lincoln County Commission, now the Lincoln State Monument, in Lincoln, N.M.

15. The exchange of correspondence is in the Wallace Papers, IHS. Wallace's account of the meeting is in the *Indianapolis World*, June 8, 1902. For a synthesis, see Rasch, "The Governor Meets the Kid." For the escape of Campbell and Evans, see *Mesilla Valley Independent*, April 5, 1879, and Carroll to COs Forts Bayard, Craig, and Bliss, Fort Stanton, March 19, 1879, RG 393, Post Records, Fort Stanton, N.M., LS, vol. 20, p. 241.

16. Notes by Wallace of meeting with Kid, March 29, 1879, Wallace Papers, IHS.

17. Wallace to Schurz, Lincoln, March 31, 1879, Wallace Papers, IHS.

18. Wallace to Schurz, Lincoln, March 21 and 31, 1879. Bristol to Wallace, Mesilla, March 16, 1879. Wallace Papers, IHS. *Mesilla Valley Independent*, March 22, 1879.

19. Wallace to Hatch, Lincoln, March 9, 1879. Wallace to Purington, Lincoln, March 21, 1879 (three messages). Purington to Wallace, Fort Stanton, same date (three replies). Wallace to Schurz, Lincoln, March 31, 1879. Hatch to Purington, El Paso, March 18, 1879. Loud to Purington, Santa Fe, March 19, 1879. RG 393, LS, Hq. DNM, NARS (M1072, roll 6).

20. Campaign Records, Lincoln County Rifles, 1879, TANM, Roll 87, Frames 185–202. Patrón to Wallace, Santa Fe, January 10, 1880 (Patrón's final report), Records of the Territorial Governors: Lew Wallace, ibid., roll 99, frames 20–21. Both in NMSRCA. The Wallace Papers contain numerous exchanges between Patrón and Wallace during the governor's stay in Lincoln. For Scurlock, see Patrón to Wallace, Fort Sumner, April 12, 1879. See also J. B. Wilson to Wallace, May 18, 1879. Both in Wallace Papers, IHS, and *Weekly New Mexican* (Santa Fe),

May 17, 1879. During the Civil War, Texans called their undisciplined home guard units "Heel Flies."

21. Wallace to Schurz, Lincoln, March 31, 1879. Wallace to Hayes, through Schurz, same date. Wallace Papers, IHS.

22. Wallace to Schurz, Lincoln, April 4, 1879. Wallace to Bristol, same date. Wallace Papers, IHS.

CHAPTER 13

1. Wallace to Schurz, Lincoln, April 18, 1879, Wallace Papers, IHS.

2. Wallace to Schurz, Lincoln, March 31, 1879. Wallace to Waldo, Lincoln, April 3, 1879. Leonard to Wallace, April 9, 1879. Wallace to Leonard, same date. Leonard to Wallace, May 20, 1879, recounts the origins of their association. All in Wallace Papers, IHS.

3. Leonard to Wallace, Lincoln, May 20, 1879, Wallace Papers, IHS.

4. Taylor to Wallace, April 15, 1879, Wallace Papers, IHS.

5. Leonard to Wallace, Lincoln, May 20, 1879. Taylor to Wallace, Lincoln, April 25, 1879. Wallace Papers, IHS.

6. Leonard to Wallace, Lincoln, May 20, 1879. Anon. to Kimball, Lincoln County, May 18, 1879. Both in Wallace Papers, IHS.

7. Lincoln County, District Court Journal, April 1879 term, pp. 319–20 (April 22, 1879). Criminal Case no. 279, True Bill of Grand Jury, April 28, 1879, *Territory v. Jesse Evans*: accessory to murder. NMSRCA.

8. Leonard to Wallace, Lincoln, April 20, 1879, Wallace Papers, IHS.

9. Lincoln County, District Court Journal, pp. 316–18 (April 21, 1879), NMSRCA.

10. Lincoln County, District Court Journal, April 1879 term, pp. 296–387 (April 13–May 1, 1879), NMSRCA. Photostats of the indictments of Dolan and Campbell for the Chapman slaying, and Turner and Jones for the McSween slaying, the originals of which seem to have vanished, are in the Fulton Collection, box 12, folder 2, UAL. *Mesilla Valley Independent*, April 26, 1879. *Weekly New Mexican* (Santa Fe), May 17, 1879. Leonard to Wallace, May 20, 1879, Wallace Papers, IHS.

11. *Mesilla Valley Independent*, May 10, 1879. *Weekly New Mexican* (Santa Fe), May 17, 1879. Purington to AAAG, DNM, Fort Stanton, May 3, 1879, file 1405 AGO 1878, NARS. Leonard to Wallace, Lincoln, May 29, 1879, Wallace Papers, IHS.

12. Taylor to Hayes, Fort Stanton, June 3, 1879, Hayes Memorial

Library, copy in Fulton Collection, box 11, folder 8, UAL. Leonard to Wallace, Lincoln, May 23, June 6 and 13, 1879; Wilson to Wallace, Lincoln, April 21, 1879; Wallace to Schurz, Santa Fe, July 23, 1880, Wallace Papers, IHS.

13. Leonard to Wallace, Las Vegas, February 24, 1879, Wallace Papers, IHS.

14. Leonard to Secretary of War, Las Vegas, March 4, 1879, file 1405 AGO 1878, NARS. At the opening of the Dudley court, Dudley stated that Leonard had drawn up the charges as a paid attorney for Sue McSween.

15. For Leonard's impressions, see his letters to Wallace of May 20 and 23, June 6 and 13, 1879, Wallace Papers, IHS.

16. See testimony of Wallace and summation of Waldo, Dudley Court Record, NARS.

17. Judge Advocate D. G. Swain to AAG, DM, September 29, 1879; endorsement of Brig. Gen. John Pope, October 15, 1879. Pope to Adjutant General, Fort Leavenworth, October 15, 1879, enclosing charges and specifications; endorsement of Judge Advocate General W. M. Dunn, October 22, 1879; endorsement of chief clerk of War Department, December 27, 1879; endorsement of Gen. W. T. Sherman, December 30, 1879. Dudley to Adjutant General, Fort Union, October 8, 1879. All in file 1405 AGO 1878, NARS.

18. Socorro County, District Court Journal, Criminal Case no. 92, *Territory v. Dolan and Mathews*: accessory to murder; and Criminal Case no. 98, *Territory v. Dolan*: murder, pp. 272–73 (November 1, 1879), and p. 289 (November 5, 1879). Ibid., Criminal Case no. 102, *Territory v. Peppin*: arson, pp. 290–91 (November 5, 1879). NMSRCA.

19. Lincoln County, District Court, April 1879 term, Criminal Case no. 298, *Territory v. John Kinney, N. A. M. Dudley, and George Peppin*: arson. Document file. District Court Journal, pp. 344, 353–56. Doña Ana County, District Court, November 1879 term, Criminal Case no. 533. Document file. District Court Journal, pp. 104, 142, 177–80. All in NMSRCA. Dudley to Attorney General Charles Devens, through Hq. of the army, Fort Union, N.M., September 16, 1879. Devens to Secretary of War, October 1, 1879. Dudley to Adjutant General, Fort Union, N.M., November 4 and December 4, 1879. Teleg., U.S. Attorney Sidney M. Barnes to Attorney General Devens, Mesilla, November 30, 1879. Same to same, Santa Fe, December 4, 1879. All in file 1405 AGO 1878, NARS. *Mesilla News*, December 6, 1879. *Weekly New Mexican* (Santa Fe), December 6, 1879.

20. The reward was offered on December 13, 1880, and is re-

corded in Executive Record Book no. 2, 1867–82, pp. 507–08, TANM, roll 21, frame 581, NMSRCA.

21. The missives are all in the Wallace Papers, IHS.

22. Executive Record Book no. 2, 1867–82, TANM, roll 21, frame 581. Doña Ana County, District Court, Criminal Case files 531 and 532, *Territory v. William Bonney alias Kid alias William Antrim*: murder. Doña Ana County, District Court Journal, pp. 194, 249, 268–69, 384, 385–90, 391, 406–07, 411. NMSRCA.

23. *Mesilla Valley Independent*, May 10, 1879.

24. Wallace to Schurz, Santa Fe, June 11, 1879, Wallace Papers, IHS.

25. Hatch's superior, Brig. Gen. John Pope, wanted Maj. James F. Wade relieved from recruiting duty and sent to New Mexico. Wade belonged to Hatch's regiment, the Ninth Cavalry, and the substitution could have been easily arranged. Pope endorsement, March 8, 1879, on Wallace to Hatch, February 27, 1879, file 1405 AGO 1878, NARS.

26. Wallace to Susan Wallace, Santa Fe, December 4, 1879, Wallace Papers, IHS.

CHAPTER 14

1. John P. Wilson, "Lincoln: A New Mexico Epic" (unpublished report, Santa Fe: Museum of New Mexico, State Monuments Division, May 1986), pp. 201–38.

2. Maurice G. Fulton, *History of the Lincoln County War*, ed. Robert N. Mullin (Tucson: University of Arizona Press, 1968), chap. 52. Dolan biographical notes, Mullin Collection, HHC. Wilson, "Lincoln: A New Mexico Epic," pp. 201–02.

3. Dolan biographical notes, Mullin Collection, HHC. Frank Coe, interview with J. Evetts Haley, San Patricio, N.M., March 20, 1927, HHC.

4. Fulton, *History of the Lincoln County War*, chap. 53. Riley biographical notes, Mullin Collection, HHC.

5. *Illustrated History of New Mexico* (Chicago: Lewis Publishing Co., 1895), pp. 574–77.

6. Wilbur Coe, *Ranch on the Ruidoso: The Story of a Pioneer Family in New Mexico, 1871–1968* (New York: Alfred A. Knopf, 1968).

7. Patrón biographical notes, Mullin Collection, HHC. Philip J. Rasch, "The Murder of Juan Patron," Potomac Westerners, *Corral Dust* 5 (July 1960), pp. 20–21. J. J. Clancey to Maurice G. Fulton, Anton Chico, N.M., November 26, 1932, Fulton Collection, box 1, folder 4, UAL.

8. Baca biographical notes, Mullin Collection, HHC.

9. *Lincoln County Leader*, July 28, 1888, quoted in Darlis A. Miller, "The Women of Lincoln County, 1860–1890," in Joan M. Jensen and Darlis A. Miller, eds., *New Mexico Women: Intercultural Perspectives* (Albuquerque: University of New Mexico Press, 1986), p. 189.

10. Ibid., pp. 188–91. Fulton, *History of the Lincoln County War*, chap. 55. Sue's letters are in the Fulton Collection, UAL.

11. *Weekly New Mexican* (Santa Fe), October 26, 1878.

12. Frank Coe, interview with J. Evetts Haley, San Patricio, N.M., March 20, 1927, HHC.

13. For these events, see Leon C. Metz, *Pat Garrett: The Story of a Western Lawman* (Norman: University of Oklahoma Press, 1973), chaps. 3–9; and Philip J. Rasch, "The Hunting of Billy, the Kid," English Westerners, *Brand Book* 2 (January 1969), pp. 1–10. Garrett gives his version in *The Authentic Life of Billy, the Kid* (Santa Fe: New Mexican, 1882), chaps. 22 and 23.

14. Billy the Kid in legend is surveyed in Stephen Tatum, *Inventing Billy the Kid: Visions of the Outlaw in America, 1881–1981* (Albuquerque: University of New Mexico Press, 1982); and Jon Tuska, *Billy the Kid: A Bio-Bibliography* (Westport, Conn.: Greenwood Press, 1983).

15. All these men have biographical sketches in Bill O'Neal, *Encyclopedia of Western Gunfighters* (Norman: University of Oklahoma Press, 1979). Several are the subject of biographical notes, Mullin Collection, HHC. For Scurlock, see Philip J. Rasch, Joseph E. Buckbee, and Karl K. Klein, "Man of Many Parts," English Westerners, *Brand Book* 5 (January 1963), pp. 9–12. For O'Folliard, see Philip J. Rasch, "The Short Life of Tom O'Folliard," Potomac Westerners, *Corral Dust* 6 (May 1961), pp. 9–11, 14. Doc Scurlock's wife was the daughter of Fernando Herrera, the marksman who shot Charlie Crawford from the Montaño store on July 17, 1878.

16. Harwood P. Hinton, "John Simpson Chisum," *New Mexico Historical Review* 32 (January 1957), pp. 53–65.

17. Beckwith biographical notes, Mullin Collection, HHC. Philip J. Rasch and Lee Myers, "The Tragedy of the Beckwiths," English Westerners, *Brand Book* 5 (July 1963), pp. 1–6.

18. Beckwith, Jones, and Olinger biographical notes, Mullin Collection, HHC. Rasch and Myers, "The Tragedy of the Beckwiths." Rasch, "The Olingers, Known Yet Forgotten," Potomac Westerners, *Corral Dust* 8 (February 1963), pp. 1, 4.

19. Grady E. McCright and James H. Powell, *Jessie Evans: Lincoln County Badman* (College Station, Texas: Creative Publishing Co., 1983), chaps. 13–15.

20. Robert N. Mullin, "Here Lies John Kinney," *Journal of Arizona History* 14 (Autumn 1973), pp. 223–42. Jack DeMattos, "John Kinney," *Real West* 27 (February 1984), pp. 20–25.

21. Leon C. Metz, *John Selman, Gunfighter*, 2d ed. (Norman: University of Oklahoma Press, 1980), chaps. 12–19.

22. Widenmann to Mrs. R. H. Kempf [his sister], February 3, 1927, Mullin Collection, HHC.

23. Bruce T. Ellis, ed., "Lincoln County Postscript: Notes on Robert A. Widenmann By His Daughter, Elsie Widenman," *New Mexico Historical Review* 50 (July 1975), pp. 213–30.

24. Norman J. Bender, ed., *Missionaries, Outlaws, and Indians: Taylor F. Ealy in Lincoln and Zuni, 1878–1881* (Albuquerque: University of New Mexico Press, 1984), Pt. 2.

25. See Dudley's personnel file, RG 94, 6674 ACP 1876, NARS. See also *Army and Navy Journal*, May 7, 1910; and *Army and Navy Register*, May 7, 1910.

26. Hatch to Wallace, Santa Fe, April 9, 1879, Wallace Papers, IHS.

CHAPTER 15

1. Richard Maxwell Brown, *Strain of Violence: Historical Studies of American Violence and Vigilantism* (New York: Oxford University Press, 1975), pp. 112–13. See also, William G. Carleton, "Cultural Roots of American Law Enforcement," *Current History* 53 (July 1967), pp. 3–4.

2. Brown, *Strain of Violence*, pp. 103–05. Ray A. Billington, *America's Frontier Heritage* (Albuquerque: University of New Mexico Press, 1974), chap. 5.

3. Richard Maxwell Brown is the acknowledged authority on vigilante movements. See *Strain of Violence*, Pt. 3; and "The American Vigilante Tradition," in Hugh Davis Graham and Ted Robert Gurr, eds., *The History of Violence in America: Historical and Comparative Perspectives* (New York: Frederick A. Praeger, 1969), pp. 154–225.

4. These conclusions are based on extensive reading of the records of the Third Judicial District Court, NMSRCA, and Mesilla, Cimarron, Las Vegas, and Santa Fe newspapers. Meaningful statistics for Lincoln are hampered by the absence of a Lincoln newspaper.

5. An able study of ethnic conflict is Robert J. Rosenbaum, *Mexicano Resistance in the Southwest: "The Sacred Right of Self-Preservation"* (Austin: University of Texas Press, 1981). Rosenbaum sketches the cultural dissimilarities between Anglos and Hispanics in Lincoln County, especially the fundamental differences in attitudes toward land and water. Against the backdrop of the Horrell and Tularosa conflicts, which were heavily

ethnic, he assumes or at least implies ethnic conflict in the Lincoln County War. I find only light overtones of such conflict.

6. Helena Huntington Smith, *War on Powder River* (Lincoln: University of Nebraska Press, 1967), p. 282.

7. Jim B. Pearson, *The Maxwell Land Grant* (Norman: University of Oklahoma Press, 1961).

8. Earl R. Forrest, *Arizona's Dark and Bloody Ground* (Caldwell, Ida.: Caxton Printers, 1953). Clara T. Woody and Milton L. Schwartz, "War in Pleasant Valley: The Outbreak of the Graham–Tewksbury Feud," *Journal of Arizona History* 18 (Spring 1977), pp. 43–68.

9. Harwood P. Hinton, to me and other historians of conflict in the Southwest.

10. C. L. Sonnichsen, *I'll Die Before I'll Run: The Story of the Great Feuds of Texas* (New York: Devin-Adair, 1962), pp. 8–9. See also William C. Holden, "Law and Lawlessness on the Texas Frontier, 1875–1890," *Southwestern Historical Quarterly* 44 (October 1940), pp. 188–203.

11. Brown, *Strain of Violence*, p. 268.

12. *Daily New Mexican* (Santa Fe), May 15, 1877. Dolan and Jaramillo biographical notes, Mullin Collection, HHC.

13. The thesis of the social bandit was propounded as an English phenomenon in Eric J. Hobsbawm, *Social Bandits and Primitive Rebels* (Glencoe, Ill.: The Free Press, 1959). For application to the American West, see Richard White, "Outlaw Gangs of the Middle Border: American Social Bandits," *Western Historical Quarterly* 12 (October 1981), pp. 387–408.

14. Among the better expressions of this viewpoint are Eric Mottram, "'The Persuasive Lips': Men and Guns in America, the West," *Journal of American Studies* 10 (April 1976), pp. 53–84; and Joe B. Frantz, "The Frontier Tradition: An Invitation to Violence," in Graham and Gurr, *History of Violence in America*, pp. 127–53. Earlier commentaries: James Truslow Adams, "Our Lawless Heritage," *Atlantic Monthly* 142 (December 1928), pp. 732–40; R. W. Monday, "Analysis of Frontier Social Instability," *Southwestern Social Science Quarterly* 24 (September 1943), pp. 167–77; and Mabel A. Elliott, "Crime and the Frontier Mores," *American Sociological Review* 9 (April 1944), pp. 185–92.

15. See especially W. Eugene Hollon, *Frontier Violence: Another Look* (New York: Oxford University Press, 1974); Frank R. Prassel, *The Western Peace Officer: A Legacy of Law and Order* (Norman: University of Oklahoma Press, 1972); Robert R. Dykstra, *The Cattle Towns* (New York: Alfred A. Knopf, 1968); and Roger D. McGrath, *Gunfighters, Highwaymen, and Vigilantes: Violence on the Frontier* (Berkeley and Los Angeles: University of California Press, 1984), chap. 13.

16. The historiography of frontier violence is presented in McGrath, *Gunfighters, Highwaymen, and Vigilantes*, appendix: "Scholarly Assessments of Frontier Violence," and Richard Maxwell Brown, "Historiography of Violence in the American West," in Michael P. Malone, ed., *Historians and the American West* (Lincoln: University of Nebraska Press, 1983), chap. 11.

Sources

THE LINCOLN COUNTY WAR generated an enormous body of contemporary documentation. Practically all of it, however, reflects the passions of the time and thus challenges the historian's power to discount the partisanship and self-interest without sacrificing the genuine.

For the months before June 1878, first in importance is the voluminous report of Frank Warner Angel, special agent of the Departments of Justice and the Interior. The Angel Report contains forty-three depositions sworn by active participants on both sides, together with copies of many documents critical to reconstructing the origins and early progress of the war. For the killing of Tunstall, it is indispensable. Angel himself had obvious biases, and he was not skilled in taking depositions. But his report is full of firsthand material recorded within months and even weeks of the events treated. Submitted in October 1878, the report is entitled "Report on the Death of John H. Tunstall." It is file 44–4–8–3 in RG 60, Records of the Department of Justice, NARS. A complete copy is in the Victor Westphall Collection, NMSRCA.

Perhaps the least appreciated and most valuable body of source material lies in the records of the U.S. Army. After Colonel Dudley took command of Fort Stanton, he was ordered to submit weekly reports on civil disorders in Lincoln County. This he did conscientiously, pouring forth long descriptions of people and events and appending a variety of documents that came to him from civilian sources. These and other documents relating to the Lincoln County War found their way into a special file in the Adjutant General's Office in Washington, D.C. Its designation is RG 94, AGO, LR (Main Series), 1871–80, file 1405 AGO 1878, NARS, available on microfilm as M666, rolls 397 and 398.

Other important military records include: RG 393, LR, Hq.

DNM, on microfilm as M1088; the same, LS, M1072; and LR and LS of the post of Fort Stanton, RG 393, NARS (not on microfilm). The monthly Fort Stanton post returns, NARS, recording troop and other statistics as well as events of the month, are available on microfilm.

The Dudley Court Record deserves special notice. The inquiry into Colonel Dudley's conduct in Lincoln on July 19, 1878, produced several thousand pages of testimony by participants and copies of official documents, many of which did not find their way into other files. In all, sixty-four people testified. Unfortunately, the court limited the inquiry to events leading to and during the intervention of July 19, which deprived history of much of value that the witnesses could have related. Some evidence bearing on earlier events crept in, but not much. Even so, the Dudley Court Record is one of the richest sources of the Lincoln County War, and it is crucial to reconstructing the Five-Day Battle. Its citation is RG 153, Judge Advocate General's Office, Records Relating to the Dudley Inquiry (CQ 1284), NARS.

Less bountiful are the Interior Department records. The territorial governor reported to the Secretary of the Interior. Pertinent are RG 48, Interior Department Territorial Records: New Mexico (on microfilm as M364); RG 48, Interior Department Appointment Papers (on microfilm as M750); RG 75, Office of Indian Affairs, LR (on microfilm as M234); and RG 75, Office of Indian Affairs, Records of the New Mexico Superintendency, 1849–80 (on microfilm as T21), all NARS. Affairs at the Mescalero Apache Indian Agency were intertwined with the Lincoln County War. Investigating the charges of fraud brought by McSween against Agent Frederick C. Godfroy, Inspector E. C. Watkins took affidavits from thirty-five witnesses, many of whom also supplied testimony for the Angel Report and the Dudley Court. Although centering on relations between Dolan & Co. and the Indian agency, the evidence also illuminates important aspects of the Lincoln County War. The citation is Report of Inspector E. C. Watkins, Report no. 1981, June 27, 1878, RG 75, Records of the BIA, Inspectors' Reports, 1873–80, NARS. Another important agency source is Special Case 108, Reduction of the Mescalero Reservation, RG 75, NARS, which contains important material documenting fraudulent practices of L. G. Murphy & Co. Finally, a few items of value are in the letter files of the agency at DFRC.

For Governor Lew Wallace, his personal papers at the Indiana Historical Society in Indianapolis are unusually rich in documenting his role in the concluding stages of the war. Wallace, of course, was a professional writer, and his letters are informative, graphic, and quotable. His reports to the Secretary of the Interior are in his papers as well as in the official records. The papers relating to the New Mexico governorship are consolidated on two rolls of microfilm.

A storehouse of original documentation is the NMSRCA, which contains the Territorial Archives of New Mexico, a scattering of county records, and the records of the Third Judicial District Court in Mesilla. Court records consist of docket books recording the sequence of actions in individual cases, journals chronologically recording courtroom actions, and case files containing various documents relating to individual cases, such as indictments and arrest warrants. Court records are frustrating to use, both because most of the key case files have not survived and because of appalling verbosity that yields the most minimal information. Even so, they are indispensable. The territorial district court also functioned as federal district court. Records of federal cases are housed at the DFRC.

NMSRCA also contains copies of the WPA interviews conducted in the 1930s with surviving participants in the war and copies of important historical documents collected and authored by Territorial Secretary William G. Ritch. The original Ritch Collection is in the Huntington Library, San Marino, California.

Another valuable body of sources, little used in the past, consists of financial records. McSween, Murphy, Dolan, and other participants had accounts in the First National Bank of Santa Fe, whose records are preserved as Archive 177, Special Collections, UNML. These records consist of ledger books containing individual bank accounts, cash books recording transactions of the bank, and letter books preserving copies of correspondence to customers. Other financial records of value are the Lincoln County tax rolls and territorial auditor's accounts in the NMSRCA. McSween's deposition in the Angel Report appends a series of significant financial records.

The territorial newspapers, for all their rhetorical excess, are necessary sources. They published letters from the scene, usually by anonymous correspondents, and when shorn of bias they help in establishing the chronology and course of major events. The most helpful are the *Mesilla Valley Independent* and the *Mesilla News*, although the latter's rabid partisanship has to be discounted. Albert J. Fountain edited the *Independent* and, as a lawyer and sometime officer of the district court, brought firsthand knowledge to his dispatches. Also of value are Cimarron *News and Press*, *Las Vegas Gazette*, Santa Fe *New Mexican*, Silver City *Grant County Herald*, and Las Cruces *Thirty-Four*.

Serious researchers in this field must acknowledge a large debt to the studies and acquisitive habits of several longtime students. Maurice

Garland Fulton was an English professor at New Mexico Military Institute in Roswell, who devoted decades to collecting and studying Lincoln County material, and who interviewed and corresponded with many of the participants. Fulton's collection is now at the University of Arizona Library, which also houses papers of the Blazer family, owners of Blazer's Mills, the ledger books for 1871 and 1872 of Lawrence G. Murphy, and some papers of Reverend Taylor F. Ealy and his wife. Many of the Ealy papers are set forth in Norman J. Bender, ed., *Missionaries, Outlaws, and Indians: Taylor F. Ealy at Lincoln and Zuñi, 1878 – 1881* (Albuquerque: University of New Mexico Press, 1984).

Robert N. Mullin, an oil executive whose hobby was the Lincoln County War, also amassed a huge body of material. Mullin was not careful about noting his sources, and much of what he recorded must therefore be viewed with skepticism. No researcher, however, can afford to ignore the Mullin Collection. It is housed in the J. Evetts Haley History Center, Midland, Texas.

Evetts Haley himself, premier historian of Texas cows and cowmen, interviewed participants in the Lincoln County War in the 1920s and 1930s. The transcripts are in the Haley Center and, more carefully organized and recorded than Fulton's, are more useful.

Another who devoted much of his lifetime to the subject is Philip J. Rasch. He wrote many articles on various facets and donated his extensive collection to the Lincoln State Monument in Lincoln, New Mexico.

Albuquerque lawyer William A. Keleher spent several decades researching and writing about New Mexico history. His collection has yet to find its way into a public depository where researchers may consult it. Almost certainly, it contains rich materials.

The reminiscent accounts assembled by Fulton, Haley, and the WPA interviewers are all of interest, but have to be carefully used. Virtually all were transcribed in the 1920s and 1930s, by which time the subjects suffered from bad memory and were influenced by the romanticization that had suffused the literature. They are good more for local color and characterization of people than for chronology and events, but consulted in conjunction with contemporary sources they are quite valuable.

In large part because of the involvement of Billy the Kid, the Lincoln County War has inspired a huge literature. The standard works, cited by nearly all authorities, are William A. Keleher, *Violence in Lincoln County, 1869 – 1881: A New Mexico Item* (Albuquerque: University of New Mexico Press, 1957; 2d ed., with introduction by C. L. Sonnichsen,

1982), and Maurice Garland Fulton, *History of the Lincoln County War*, edited by Robert N. Mullin (Tucson: University of Arizona Press, 1968). While of great value, both are deficient in organization, synthesis, and documentation. More reliable is a series of articles by Philip J. Rasch, appearing mostly in publications of various corrals of the Westerners, some of which are cited in the footnotes. Possessing hardly more than a shadow of redeeming value is Walter Noble Burns's enormously successful *Saga of Billy the Kid* (New York: Doubleday, Page and Co., 1926).

In general, the published reminiscences of participants are full of misinformation and useful chiefly for local color and personality portraits. Among these are George W. Coe, *Frontier Fighter, The Autobiography of George W. Coe*, as related to Nan Hillary Harrison (Boston and New York: Houghton Mifflin Company, 1934; 2d ed., Albuquerque: University of New Mexico Press, 1951; Lakeside Classics ed., edited by Doyce B. Nunis, Jr., Chicago: R. R. Donnelly and Co., 1984); Pat F. Garrett, *Authentic Life of Billy the Kid* (Santa Fe: New Mexican Printing Co., 1882; edited by Maurice Garland Fulton, New York: Macmillan, 1927; edited by Jeff C. Dykes, Norman: University of Oklahoma Press, 1954); Miguel A. Otero, *My Life on the Frontier, 1864–1882* (New York: Press of the Pioneers, 1935); Miguel A. Otero, *The Real Billy the Kid: With New Light on the Lincoln County War* (New York: Rufus Rockwell Wilson, 1936); and George W. Curry, *An Autobiography* (Albuquerque: University of New Mexico Press, 1958). Lily Klasner, *My Girlhood among Outlaws*, edited by Eve Ball (Tucson: University of Arizona Press, 1972) is especially good for characterizations.

A cross between narrative and documentary history is Frederick W. Nolan, ed., *The Life and Death of John Henry Tunstall* (Albuquerque: University of New Mexico Press, 1965). It contains long excerpts from Tunstall's letters to his family in London, with commentary by Nolan. The origins of the Lincoln County War cannot be understood without constant resort to this work.

For the historian, the Lincoln County War offers a formidable challenge. Virtually all of the primary material, both contemporary and reminiscent, is tainted with partisanship. Much of the secondary literature reflects this partisanship and is also more or less encumbered by the mythology of Billy the Kid. Yet for the diligent researcher the story is there, waiting to be extracted, piece by piece, from the overburden of passion and prejudice. Few historical episodes of similar scope have bequeathed to posterity such a rich trove of the ores from which history is refined.

PUBLISHED MATERIAL

Adams, James Truslow. "Our Lawless Heritage." *Atlantic Monthly* 142 (December 1928), pp. 732–40.

Adams, Ramon F. *A Fitting Death for Billy the Kid*. Norman: University of Oklahoma Press, 1960.

Ball, Eve. *Ma'am Jones of the Pecos*. Tucson: University of Arizona Press, 1969.

Ball, Larry D. *The United States Marshals of New Mexico and Arizona Territories, 1846–1912*. Albuquerque: University of New Mexico Press, 1978.

Bender, Norman J., ed. *Missionaries, Outlaws, and Indians: Taylor F. Ealy at Lincoln and Zuni, 1878–1881*. Albuquerque: University of New Mexico Press, 1984.

Billington, Ray Allen. *America's Frontier Heritage*. Albuquerque: University of New Mexico Press, 1973.

Blazer, Paul A. "The Fight at Blazer's Mill: A Chapter in the Lincoln County War." *Arizona and the West* 6 (Autumn 1964), pp. 203–11.

Brown, Richard Maxwell. "The American Vigilante Tradition." In Hugh Davis Graham and Ted Robert Gurr, eds., *The History of Violence in America: Historical and Comparative Perspectives*. New York: Frederick A. Praeger, 1969.

Brown, Richard Maxwell. *Strain of Violence: Historical Studies of American Violence and Vigilantism*. New York: Oxford University Press, 1975.

Burns, Walter Noble. *The Saga of Billy the Kid*. New York: Doubleday, Page and Co., 1926.

Carleton, William G. "Cultural Roots of American Law Enforcement." *Current History* 53 (July 1967), pp. 1–7, 49.

Cawelti, John G. "Cowboys, Indians, Outlaws." *The American West* 1 (Spring 1964), pp. 28–35, 77–79.

Cawelti, John G. "The Gunfighter and Society." *The American West* 5 (March 1968), pp. 30–35, 76–78.

Coe, George. *Frontier Fighter, The Autobiography of George W. Coe*, as related to Nan Hillary Harrison. Boston and New York: Houghton Mifflin Co., 1934. 2d ed., Albuquerque: University of New Mexico Press, 1951. Lakeside Classics ed., edited by Doyce B. Nunis, Jr., Chicago: R. R. Donnelly and Co., 1984.

Coe, Wilbur. *Ranch on the Ruidoso: The Story of a Pioneer Family in New Mexico, 1871–1968*. New York: Alfred A. Knopf, 1968.

DeMattos, Jack. "John Kinney." *Real West* 27 (February 1984), pp. 20–25.

DeMattos, Jack. "The Search for Billy the Kid's Roots—Is Over!" *Real West* 23 (January 1980), pp. 26–28, 59–60.

Dykes, J. C. *Billy the Kid, the Bibliography of a Legend.* Albuquerque: University of New Mexico Press, 1952.

Dykstra, Robert R. *The Cattle Towns.* New York: Alfred A. Knopf, 1968.

Ealy, Mary R. "Reminiscences of Old Lincoln." *New Mexico Magazine* 32 (March 1954), pp. 17, 42–43.

Ealy, Ruth R. "A Medical Missionary." *New Mexico Magazine* 32 (March 1954), pp. 16, 38–39.

Ealy, Ruth R. *Water in a Thirsty Land.* p.p., n.p., 1955.

Elliott, Mabel A. "Crime and the Frontier Mores." *American Sociological Review* 9 (April 1944), pp. 185–92.

Ellis, Bruce T., ed. "Lincoln County Postscript: Notes on Robert A. Widenmann By His Daughter, Elsie Widenman." *New Mexico Historical Review* 50 (July 1975), pp. 213–30.

Forrest, Earl R. *Arizona's Dark and Bloody Ground.* Caldwell, Ida.: Caxton Printers, 1953.

Frantz, Joe B. "The Frontier Tradition: An Invitation to Violence." In Hugh Davis Graham and Ted Robert Gurr, eds., *The History of Violence in America: Historical and Comparative Perspectives.* New York: Frederick A. Praeger, 1969.

Fulton, Maurice G. *History of the Lincoln County War.* Edited by Robert N. Mullin. Tucson: University of Arizona Press, 1968.

Ganoe, John T. "The Desert Land Act in Operation, 1877–1891." *Agricultural History* 11 (January 1937), pp. 142–57.

Garrett, Pat F. *The Authentic Life of Billy the Kid.* Santa Fe: New Mexican, 1882. Edited by Maurice G. Fulton, New York: Macmillan, 1927. Edited by Jeff C. Dykes, Norman: University of Oklahoma Press, 1954. Edited by Jarvis P. Garrett, Albuquerque: Horn and Wallace, 1964.

Gastil, Raymond D. *Cultural Regions of the United States.* Seattle: University of Washington Press, 1975.

Graham, Hugh Davis, and Ted Robert Gurr, eds. *The History of Violence in America: Historical and Comparative Perspectives.* New York: Frederick A. Praeger, 1969.

Haley, J. Evetts. *Charles Goodnight: Cowman and Plainsman.* Norman: University of Oklahoma Press, 1949.

Hinton, Harwood P. "John Simpson Chisum, 1877–84." *New Mexico Historical Review* 31 (July 1956), pp. 177–205; (October 1956), pp. 310–37; and 32 (January 1957), pp. 53–65.

Hobsbawm, Eric J. *Social Bandits and Primitive Rebels.* Glencoe, Ill.: The Free Press, 1959.

Holden, William C. "Law and Lawlessness on the Texas Frontier, 1875–1890." *Southwestern Historical Quarterly* 44 (October 1940), pp. 188–203.

Hollon, W. Eugene. *Frontier Violence: Another Look.* New York: Oxford University Press, 1974.

Horn, Calvin P. *New Mexico's Troubled Years: The Story of Early Territorial Governors.* Albuquerque: Horn and Wallace, 1963.

Hoyt, Henry F. *A Frontier Doctor.* Boston: Houghton Mifflin Co., 1929.

Illustrated History of New Mexico. Chicago: Lewis Publishing Co., 1895.

Jensen, Joan M., and Darlis A. Miller, eds. *New Mexico Women: Intercultural Perspectives.* Albuquerque: University of New Mexico Press, 1986.

Jones, Okah L. "Lew Wallace: Hoosier Governor of Territorial New Mexico, 1878–1881." *New Mexico Historical Review* 60 (April 1965), pp. 129–58.

Keleher, William A. *The Fabulous Frontier: Twelve New Mexico Items.* Albuquerque: University of New Mexico Press, 1962.

Keleher, William A. *Violence in Lincoln County, 1869–1881.* Albuquerque: University of New Mexico Press, 1957. 2d ed., with introduction by C. L. Sonnichsen, 1982.

Klasner, Lily Casey. *My Girlhood among Outlaws.* Edited by Eve Ball. Tucson: University of Arizona Press, 1972.

Lamar, Howard R. *The Far Southwest, 1846–1912: A Territorial History.* New Haven: Yale University Press, 1966. 2d ed., New York: W. W. Norton, 1970.

Larson, Robert W. *New Mexico's Quest for Statehood, 1846–1912.* Albuquerque: University of New Mexico Press, 1969.

Larson, Robert W. "Territorial Politics and Cultural Impact." *New Mexico Historical Review* 60 (July 1985), pp. 249–69.

Lavash, Donald R. *Sheriff William Brady: Tragic Hero of the Lincoln County War.* Santa Fe: Sunstone Press, 1986.

Malone, Michael P. ed. *Historians and the American West.* Lincoln: University of Nebraska Press, 1983.

McCright, Grady E., and James H. Powell. *Jessie Evans: Lincoln County Badman.* College Station, Tex.: Creative Publishing Co., 1983.

McGrath, Roger D. *Gunfighters, Highwaymen, and Vigilantes: Violence on the Frontier.* Berkeley: University of California Press, 1984.

McKee, Irving. *"Ben-Hur" Wallace: The Life of General Lew Wallace.* Berkeley and Los Angeles: University of California Press, 1947.

Mehren, Lawrence L. "A History of the Mescalero Apache Reservation, 1869–1881." Master's thesis, University of Arizona, 1969.

Metz, Leon C. *John Selman, Gunfighter*. New York, 1966. 2d ed., Norman: University of Oklahoma Press, 1980.

Metz, Leon C. *Pat Garrett: The Story of a Western Lawman*. Norman: University of Oklahoma Press, 1973.

Miller, Darlis A. "William Logan Rynerson in New Mexico, 1862–1893." *New Mexico Historical Review* 48 (April 1973), pp. 101–32.

Monday, R. W. "Analysis of Frontier Social Instability." *Southwestern Social Science Quarterly* 24 (September 1943), pp. 167–77.

Morsberger, Robert E. and Katherine M. *Lew Wallace: Militant Romantic*. New York: McGraw-Hill, 1980.

Mottram, Eric. "'The Persuasive Lips': Men and Guns in America, the West." *Journal of American Studies* 10 (April 1976), pp. 53–84.

Mullin, Robert N. *A Chronology of the Lincoln County War*. Santa Fe: Press of the Territorian, 1966.

Mullin, Robert N. "Here Lies John Kinney." *Journal of Arizona History* 14 (Autumn 1973), pp. 223–42.

Nolan, Frederick W., ed. *The Life and Death of John Henry Tunstall*. Albuquerque: University of New Mexico Press, 1965.

Nolan, Frederick W. "A Sidelight on the Tunstall Murder." *New Mexico Historical Review* 31 (July 1956), pp. 206–22.

O'Neal, Bill. *Encyclopedia of Western Gunfighters*. Norman: University of Oklahoma Press, 1979.

Pearson, Jim B. *The Maxwell Land Grant*. Norman: University of Oklahoma Press, 1961.

Poldevaart, Arie. "Black-Robed Justice in New Mexico, 1846–1912." *New Mexico Historical Review* 22 (January 1947), pp. 18–50; (April 1947), pp. 109–39; (July 1947), pp. 286–314; (October 1947), pp. 351–88; 23 (January 1948), pp. 40–57; (April 1948), pp. 129–45; (July 1948), pp. 225–39.

Prassel, Frank R. *The Western Peace Officer: A Legacy of Law and Order*. Norman: University of Oklahoma Press, 1972.

Rasch, Philip J. "A. Ham Mills—Sheriff of Lincoln County." English Westerners, *Brand Book* 4 (April 1962), pp. 11–12.

Rasch, Philip J. "A Man Named Antrim." Los Angeles Westerners, *Brand Book* 6 (1956), 48–54.

Rasch, Philip J. "Exit Axtell: Enter Wallace." *New Mexico Historical Review* 32 (July 1957), pp. 231–45.

Rasch, Philip J. "Five Days of Battle." Denver Westerners, *Brand Book* 11 (1955), pp. 295–323.

Rasch, Philip J. "Frank Warner Angel, Special Agent." Potomac Westerners, *Corral Dust* 7 (April 1972), p. 13.

Rasch, Philip J. "Frederick C. Godfroy, Indian Agent." Potomac Westerners, *Corral Dust* 8 (Summer 1963), pp. 17, 19, 24.

Rasch, Philip J. "George Washington of Lincoln County." Potomac Westerners, *Corral Dust* 6 (December 1961), pp. 45–46.

Rasch, Philip J. "John Kinney: King of the Rustlers." English Westerners, *Brand Book* 4 (October 1951), pp. 10–12.

Rasch, Philip J. "New Light on the Legend of Billy the Kid." *New Mexico Folklore Record* 7 (1952–53), pp. 15.

Rasch, Philip J. "Prelude to War: The Murder of J. H. Tunstall." Los Angeles Westerners, *Brand Book* 7 (1957), pp. 78–96.

Rasch, Philip J. "The Governor Meets the Kid." English Westerners, *Brand Book* 8 (April 1966), pp. 5–12.

Rasch, Philip J. "The Horrell War." *New Mexico Historical Review* 31 (July 1956), pp. 223–31.

Rasch, Philip J. "The Hunting of Billy the Kid." English Westerners, *Brand Book* 2 (January 1969), pp. 1–10.

Rasch, Philip J. "The Loquacious Mr. Leverson." New York Westerners, *Brand Book* 11 (1964), pp. 92–93.

Rasch, Philip J. "The Men at Fort Stanton." English Westerners, *Brand Book* 3 (April 1961), pp. 2–7.

Rasch, Philip J. "The Murder of Huston I. Chapman." Los Angeles Westerners, *Brand Book* 8 (1959), pp. 69–82.

Rasch, Philip J. "The Murder of Juan Patron." Potomac Westerners, *Corral Dust* 5 (July 1960), pp. 20–21.

Rasch, Philip J. "The Olingers, Known Yet Forgotten." Potomac Westerners, *Corral Dust* 8 (February 1963), pp. 1, 4.

Rasch, Philip J. "The Pecos War." *Panhandle-Plains Historical Review* 29 (1956), pp. 101–11.

Rasch, Philip J. "The Rise of the House of Murphy." Denver Westerners, *Brand Book* 12 (1956), pp. 53–84.

Rasch, Philip J. "The Short Life of Tom O'Folliard." Potomac Westerners, *Corral Dust* 6 (May 1961), pp. 9–11, 14.

Rasch, Philip J. "The Story of Jessie Evans." *Panhandle-Plains Historical Review* 33 (1960), pp. 108–21.

Rasch, Philip J. "The Trials of Lieutenant Colonel Dudley." English Westerners, *Brand Book* 7 (January 1965), pp. 1–7.

Rasch, Philip J. "The Tularosa Ditch War." *New Mexico Historical Review* 43 (July 1968), pp. 229–35.

Rasch, Philip J. "War in Lincoln County." English Westerners, *Brand Book* 6 (July 1964), pp. 2–4.

Rasch, Philip J., Joseph E. Buckbee, and Karl K. Klein. "Man of Many Parts [Doc Scurlock]." English Westerners, *Brand Book* 5 (January 1963), pp. 9–12.

Rasch, Philip J., and Lee Myers. "The Tragedy of the Beckwiths." English Westerners, *Brand Book* 5 (July 1963), pp. 1–6.

Rasch, Philip J., and Robert N. Mullin. "Dim Trails: The Pursuit of the McCarty Family." *New Mexico Folklore Record* 8 (1953–54), pp. 6–11.

Roberts, Gary L. "The West's Gunmen." *The American West* 8 (January and March 1971), pp. 10–15, 64, and 18–23, 61–62.

Rosa, Joseph G. *The Gunfighter: Man or Myth?* Norman: University of Oklahoma Press, 1968.

Rosenbaum, Robert J. *Mexicano Resistance in the Southwest: "The Sacred Right of Self-Preservation".* Austin: University of Texas Press, 1981.

Shinkle, James D. *Robert Casey and the Ranch on the Rio Hondo.* Roswell, N.M.: Hall-Poorbough Press, 1970.

Smith, Helena Huntington. *War on Powder River.* Lincoln: University of Nebraska Press, 1967.

Sonnichsen, C. L. *I'll Die Before I'll Run: The Story of the Great Feuds of Texas.* New York: Devin-Adair, 1962.

Sonnichsen, C. L. *Tularosa: Last of the Frontier West.* 2d. ed., Albuquerque: University of New Mexico Press, 1980.

Sonnichsen, C. L., and William V. Morrison. *Alias Billy the Kid.* Albuquerque: University of New Mexico Press, 1955.

Steckmesser, Kent. *The Western Hero in History and Legend.* Norman: University of Oklahoma Press, 1965.

Tatum, Stephen. *Inventing Billy the Kid: Visions of the Outlaw in America, 1881–1981.* Albuquerque: University of New Mexico Press, 1982.

Theisen, Lee Scott, ed. "Frank Warner Angel's Notes on New Mexico Territory, 1878." *Arizona and the West* 18 (Winter 1976), pp. 333–70.

Theisen, Lee Scott, ed. "The Fight in Lincoln, N.M.: The Testimony of Two Negro Participants." *Arizona and the West* 12 (Summer 1970), pp. 173–98.

Tuska, Jon. *Billy the Kid: A Bio-Bibliography.* Westport, Conn.: Greenwood Press, 1983.

Wallace, Lew. *Lew Wallace: An Autobiography.* 2 vols. New York and London: Harper and Bros., 1906.

Westphall, Victor. *The Public Domain in New Mexico, 1854–1891.* Albuquerque: University of New Mexico Press, 1965.

Westphall, Victor. *Thomas Benton Catron and His Era.* Tucson: University of Arizona Press, 1973.

White, Richard. "Outlaw Gangs of the Middle Border: American Social Bandits." *Western Historical Quarterly* 12 (October 1981), pp. 387–408.

Wilson, John P. "Lincoln: A New Mexico Epic." Unpublished report, Santa Fe: Museum of New Mexico, State Monuments Division, May 1986.

Woody, Clara T., and Milton L. Schwartz. "War in Pleasant Valley: The Outbreak of the Graham–Tewksbury Feud." *Journal of Arizona History* 18 (Spring 1977), pp. 43–68.

Index